MANAGEMENT IN WESTERN EUROPE

Also by Peter Lawrence

Management in the USA
French Management (with Jean-Louis Barsoux)
Issues in European Business

MANAGEMENT IN WESTERN EUROPE

Peter Lawrence and Vincent Edwards

St. Martin's Press
New York

St. Martin's Press, Scholarly and Reference Division, 175 Fifth Avenue, New York, N.Y. 10010

First published in the United States of America in 2000

This book is printed on paper suitable for recycling and made from fully managed and sustained forest sources.

Printed in Great Britain

ISBN 0–312–22944–5

Library of Congress Cataloging-in-Publication Data
Lawrence, Peter A.
Management in Western Europe / Peter Lawrence and Vincent Edwards.
p.   cm.
Includes bibliographical references and index.
ISBN 0–312–22944–5
1. Management—Europe, Western.   I. Title.   II. Edwards, Vincent, 1947–

HD70.E8 L39   1999
658'.0094 21—dc21   99–045121

To my friends:
John Blake and Jed Fish

Contents

Acknowledgements

In writing the chapters on the individual countries I have drawn on 'hands-on' research over the last quarter of the twentieth century. This research was primarily in the form of company visits and interviews with working managers. So my greatest debt is to those many companies and to the hundreds of managers who gave up their time to talk to me about their work, spread around the western world from Uppsala to Barcelona, from Berlin to Lubbock, Texas.

I am also much indebted to several of my past and present Ph.D. students, and would particularly like to thank Jean-Louis Barsoux, Simon Mowatt, and Karen Pemberton, Christine Communal and also Andrew Geddes and Dwight Tanner. It has been a pleasure to work with all of them.

In several of the chapters I have drawn on two late 1990s surveys of management opinion and values. Both are on-going in the sense that we are continually enlarging the national samples and adding new countries to the list. The first of these is being done with my friend Barbara Senior at Nene University College Northampton, and Nene College have also funded this study. In the second case, it is a Loughborough University initiative where the research instrument was devised by John Whittaker and myself, among our colleagues John Calvert has added new countries, and Heidi Winklehofer and later John Calvert have been responsible for the data analysis.

The research in Denmark which has fuelled Chapter 10 was done with my friend Jette Schramm of the Copenhagen Business School. She did the planning and set it all up, so that all I had to do was get on planes to Denmark (I would have liked this experience more often).

Finally, I would like to thank my two secretaries at Loughborough University Business School, Freda Clarke and Janis Andrews, for their friendly support and tireless grappling with my dodgy handwriting!

PETER LAWRENCE
January 1999

Note on authorship

This book, and the companion volume *Management in Eastern Europe*, is our joint work. That is to say we have pooled our knowledge and ideas and in some cases engaged in jointly executed research projects. But we have divided the writing unequally between the two books, and Peter Lawrence has written all of the present work apart from the chapter on Turkey (and that is to whom the pronoun I in the text refers!).

VINCENT EDWARDS and PETER LAWRENCE

CHAPTER 1

Traffic lights and rainbows

There is a town in the eastern part of the Netherlands called Almelo. It is a smallish but pleasant and decent place, yet it lacks somehow the energy and ambience of London, Rio de Janeiro, and New York City, an idea that is caught in the Dutch joke about Almelo:

> *Het licht slaagt op rot*
> *Het licht slaagt op groen*
> *In Almelo vallt altijd iets te doen*

Translating the spirit rather than the letter of the Dutch:

> The (traffic) light goes to red
> The light goes to green
> In Almelo there's always something to be seen!

The answer to the beguilingly simple question 'Would you expect management to be the same or different in the different countries of the world?' has something of the quality of the Almelo traffic lights: the answer changes, red to green and maybe back to red, on an epochal basis, **and** the determinants of these changes are part of the excitement of the story.

In the beginning . . .

For management as a subject the beginning may be reasonably dated from the 1890s when the first business schools were being founded in the USA (and in France) and the scientific management literature began to appear. From this time until something like the 1970s the usual presumption was that management style and certainly management practice was pretty much the same around the world (implicitly the industrialized world). Since this view proved so durable it is only fair to consider some of the arguments that underpinned it.

First of all there was the effect of the scientific management movement to which we have just alluded which posited a universal (monetary) incentive for employees in manufacturing industry world-wide together with recommendations for functional specialization at lower organizational levels. This movement was in turn superseded by the classical management school with its emphasis on universal principles of management. It is worth pausing to note that the famous publication of Henri Fayol, French mining engineer turned chief executive, is entitled *L'Administration générale et industrielle* (Fayol, 1916) and *general* is what it is. That is to say, Fayol did not distinguish between the organizational needs of civil administration and manufacturing industry, regarding his exhortatory generalizations as equally applicable to both. And Fayol found disciples on both sides of the Atlantic who continued to preach the importance of universal principles of management well into the post Second World War period.

Second, and perhaps more down to earth was the consideration that, after all, companies everywhere aim to make a profit, and this simple fact will probably lead them all to do the same sort of things in the same ways (conform to a universal standard of management practice). This view carries the rider that any companies that depart from accepted wisdom by deviating from standard management practice might well fail in a business sense, and quit the field of battle thereby enhancing the norm.

Third, there was a tighter suffix to this 'here to make a profit' argument, which was that part of the effort to be profitable would be in the form of measures to promote efficiency and achieve cost reduction; again the thinking presumed a limited number of ways in which efficiency and cost reduction could be achieved, such that these strivings again became a force for homogeneity of management practice.

Fourth, there was the matter of American influence. That is to say the USA variously pioneered management education, made the largest contribution to management literature, by general consensus offered the world a standard and model of professional management, and dominated the world economy after 1945. The implication was that management world-wide would be in America's image and likeness, and any differences from country to country might be 'explained away' as failures of these countries to achieve American standards so far. These ideas are explored in more detail in the next chapter which seeks to 'unpack' the nature of American management both for it's *sui generis* interest and to provide an extra European standard of comparison for the other countries discussed in this book.

Finally, it was the case that twentieth-century history impacted on our understanding of the universality or otherwise of management in the sense that the authoritarian regimes of the 1920s–1940s plus period, and especially those of (fascist) Italy and (Nazi) Germany made much play with the theme of national character and destiny, this idea finding its apotheosis in the notion of the Germans as *Herrenvolk* or master race. Since these authoritarian regimes were all pretty unlovable, and the tension between them and other more democratic countries led to major conflict in the form of the Second World War, the idea that 'national character' or cultural differences between countries might be real and might serve to explain other phenomena, was discredited by association. It took a long time for this 'fascist effect' to wear off, to the point where academics and others could feel comfortable rather than ethically vulnerable in discussions of national differences.

End of a golden age?

In the later chapter on management in France we use the phrase *les trentes glorieuses*, the thirty glorious years of economic growth and increasing disposal income that followed the Second World War (1939–45), or perhaps more properly in the French case we should date the start from the Liberation of Paris from the occupying German forces on 20 August 1944. But although the expression is French, the phenomenon was world-wide or at least 'Western-world-wide' where this whole group of countries enjoyed growing prosperity against a background of vastly increased world trade.

There were, of course, differences in the economic performance of individual countries. France, for example, had a higher growth rate than West Germany in the 1950s and 1960s although Germany was credited with the *Wirtschaftswunder* (economic miracle). But nobody was much interested in these differences, indeed everything seemed to be getting so much better for everybody that nobody really cared. It was recognized that the USA was richer than anywhere else but that was pretty much it.

Then in the 1970s it all seemed to peter out. The watershed was the 1973 Yom Kippur war between Israel and several of its Arab neighbours that led to retaliatory rises in the price of crude oil by the middle eastern Arab oil pro-ducing states, provoking what became known as the First Oil Shock (the Second Oil Shock occurred in 1979 with the Fall of the Shah of Persia which was fol-lowed by a more anti-Western stance on the part of that country together with raised oil prices). These oil shocks caused widespread economic dislocation in the West. In the short-term there was petrol rationing and in many continental European countries a Sunday driving ban to conserve petrol stocks; in the longer term the raised oil prices put up living costs and raised manufacturers' costs in many branches of industry. *Les trentes glorieuses* had ended, inflation became a universal Western problem, unemployment rates started to rise, and the term 'stagflation' was coined to signify the unlikely mix of inflation and economic stagnation.

This ended the comfortable post-war expectation that the economy would always be in expanding mode and living standards would always rise. With the realization came a renewed interest in the determinants of economic well-being, and a new sensitivity to the differences between countries. While the Western countries had all seemed 'much of a muchness' during the good times, differences between them became glaring in the bad times that followed the First Oil Shock. Take for example the little matter of inflation. No doubt the First Oil Shock precipitated inflation but if one takes, say, the change in consumer price index over the twelve months to May 1978 as a percentage some remarkable differences emerge, viz:

Switzerland	1.6
West Germany	2.7
Japan	3.5
USA	6.6
UK	7.7
Italy	12.2
Iceland	42.8
Turkey	52.3

Not trifling differences.

Unemployment rates turned out to be similarly variable, as these proportions of the working population unemployed in 1977 show:

Switzerland	0.4
Japan	2.0
West Germany	4.0
France	4.9
UK	5.8
USA	6.9
Iceland	9.7

Indeed as soon as one dug beneath the surface it became clear that there were really quite marked differences in the wealthiness of 'the rich Western countries' as these GDP per capita figures in US$ for 1975 make clear:

Switzerland	8056
USA	7060
West Germany	6610
France	5766
Japan	4460
UK	3840

None of this had emerged, or become obvious, prior to the 1970s. But now these differences in country performance, and their causes, were studied avidly.

This was particularly the case with Britain, which developed an economic inferiority complex in the wake of the First Oil Shock. In this climate a debate began about the causes of 'the wealth of nations', a debate which has never ended.

A consequence of this new interest in the differential economic performance of countries was that attention turned, among other things, to differences in national culture, to the extent to which these cultures were functional for or favourable to economic activity. The expression 'the status of industry' was coined by the business press in Britain to indicate that the nation suffered from the fact that other occupations – the civil service and the free professions and the City – were more attractive to both the educational and social elite than were jobs in industrial management, to the detriment of the nation's economic performance (that is, the status of industry was low, lower than in competitor countries such as Germany or Sweden).

But the new inter-country awareness was not simply a British phenomenon. From the 1970s onwards there has been a lively interest world-wide in country-based differences in management style, practice, and values; in levels of management education and training, in government policies that might impact on the quality and achievements of management, indeed in a variety of institutions and systems that relate to a country's economic life. This interest, and the research and analysis that it has generated, has never really come to an end, though the collective interest has shifted from country to country, region to region, over the last three decades of the twentieth century.

Where do the differences come from?

From the 1970s onwards a growing literature documents differences between countries in regard to management style, practice, and values. But this in turn raises the question: Where do the differences come from? There is a miscellany of answers and non-answers to this question.

To begin confronting this ever interesting question one genre of research, the cross-cultural approach, does not usually offer an answer at all, being content to document interesting differences rather than striving to explain them. The cross-cultural approach thrives on survey methods, with samples of managers or other organizational members drawn from several countries. One strand of this survey research is exemplified for instance by Theodore Weinshall's research at the international business school INSEAD outside Paris (Weinshall, 1977). In a longitudinal series of studies Weinshall took advantage of the fact that INSEAD has cohorts of managers from different countries on the same courses, and surveyed them on aspects of their work in the companies that sent them to

INSEAD for advanced training – on the way their working time was spent, on patterns and means of communication, and so on.

A variation on this theme is cross-cultural research in which groups of managers are presented with propositions about management work, and are invited to respond, typically on a five-point scale from strongly agree to strongly disagree. One of the most interesting studies on these lines is the work of André Laurent in the 1980s, like that of Weinshall before him also conducted at INSEAD. In response to disarmingly simple propositions such as:

It would be better if conflict could be abolished altogether

or:

Managers should have precise answers to questions subordinates may put about work

Laurent was able to demonstrate vast differences between samples of managers from various European countries and from the USA. The same approach has also been used by Barbara Senior and by the present writer, and again has shown substantial differences between Britain and Italy and Britain and Germany (Lawrence, 1998) and has also highlighted Britain versus the USA differences (Lawrence, Senior, Smith, 1998).

The most famous of the cross-cultural studies, that by Geert Hofstede, uses survey material, but does so indirectly. That is to say Hofstede's raw material comes from IBM employee questionnaire data on some forty countries, but the data is not presented directly. Instead Hofstede has conceptualized four dimensions – power distance, or the willingness to accept differences in power; individualism versus collectivism; masculine values versus feminine ones; and the variable desire to avoid uncertainty – and used the questionnaire data to fix the various countries, in league order, on the four dimensions (Hofstede, 1980; Lawrence, 1986). So for instance employees in the different countries are asked if they expected to change employers in the next two years or so; responding negatively to this question helped to fix the country concerned at the strong end of the uncertainty avoidance dimension, in other words showed the national culture to be one with a low tolerance for uncertainty such that individuals would not relish the threat of adjusting to a new and unknown employer (Hofstede, 1980).

Now in all these cross-cultural studies the emphasis is on showing that some difference exists rather than on explaining why. This is not to criticize this genre, much of the output of which is quite fascinating, but rather to note that the data it generates has no context. So to return for instance to Laurent's famous question concerning conflict in organizations it emerges that the Italian managers in his sample are ten times more worried about organizational conflict than the Swedish managers. But to know *why* this is the case one has to look into Swedish and Italian society.

For those, however, who do embark on explanation, on trying to establish why as well as what, there are a variety of resources that tend to shade into each other. Most obvious is appeal to a country's history to explain some feature of the managerial or corporate present. So if, for example, one asks why the idea of leadership is seen as important in British management, and why it is conceived primarily in terms of personal qualities, then an answer might invoke Britain's glorious past, having won nearly every war the country engaged in from the end of the Hundred Years' War, having built up the world's largest empire, having been the world's first industrial power, with leaders and leadership having played a key role in these outcomes.

Or if that trick seems too easy, consider the question: Why until after the 1980s did Britain have managers that compared unfavourably with those of most other industrial countries with regard to higher educational qualifications? To explain this odd phenomenon one might again appeal to historical relativities, and argue that industrialization in Britain has a conventional start date in the 1760s, a century before there is universal primary education, a century and a half before there is compulsory secondary education, before the nineteenth-century explosion of scientific knowledge, before formal training courses for engineers have been developed – by anyone. All this produces a disjunction between industry and management on the one hand, and education, science, training, and the direction of the state on the other. This in turn gives us a sharp contrast between Britain and Germany, where the historical relativities in the latter country are the reverse of those in Britain, with the result that German management is better educated, specialist and *Technik*-driven, while Britain for long remained the home of the gifted amateur and improvising generalist.

An alternative is to explain phenomena of management behaviour or values by showing them to be consistent with broader, country-wide beliefs and behaviours. So why, for instance, do Swiss managers not blow their own trumpets, push their credentials, and put themselves forward for promotion? Well, would be the answer, Swiss society in general deplores affectation, flamboyant self-promotion, vanity and overweening ambition: as with clerks, so with executives.

Or again why are American managers highly mobile, in the sense of job moves between employing organizations? Two interacting answers might be cited. First, the USA puts a high value on success and achievement; after all it comes top out of forty countries on Hofstede's individualism (economic individualism, achievement) scale (Hofstede, 1980). At the same time the USA is a very mobile society, and people in any occupational group will be more ready than their European counterparts to make geographical and domiciliary moves to better themselves, or even to avoid unemployment.

A variation is to explain corporate or management phenomena with reference to other structures or institutions in a country. Why, for example, are military (old-boy) networks important for promotion and more generally for getting things done in Israel? Answer, because the military, and military service, pervades the life of the nation. The state of Israel was born in war in 1947–48 and has been in many wars in its fifty-year history (time of writing 1998). It has the highest military spend as a proportion of GDP in the world. Military service is a universal obligation; men serve three years and women two years (women are not excused by being married, only by pregnancy). And at least for men there is a recurring obligation to serve a month or more a year, up to the age of fifty-five. Not to perform military service would constitute a considerable social handicap – if you try to get out of it with flat feet you will be condemned as a wimp and a traitor (Lawrence, 1990). An Israeli who has not done military service is unlikely to be embarking on a career in management, while service with an elite unit, such as the paratroops, is a definite plus.

Patterns

Probably the key development in the 1990s has been the move to find patterns of difference that will facilitate generalizations across countries. There are basically two ways, again sometimes intermingling, in which this patterning is done.

The first possibility is that one picks a small number of key variables or linked pairs of opposites, which will then be used to 'map' societies or national cultures, or organizational culture, or management styles and management values. Some of this has been inspired by Hofstede's ground-breaking work from an earlier period (Hofstede, 1980) where any of his forty countries can be 'plotted' in terms of the four variables given earlier in this chapter which will clearly go some way to indicating the nature of any country's organizational culture and likely management behaviours. Or again others (Trompenaars, 1993; Hampden Turner and Trompenaars, 1993) have drawn on 1950s sociology to generate some pairs of linked opposites – universal versus particular, emotional versus rational, inherited status versus achieved status, and so on – and then moved to classify the business cultures of different countries in these terms. Other researchers have taken inspiration from anthropology, noting that different societies have different understandings of time – long term versus short term, time as a sequence versus time as flux (do one thing after another versus do several things together). Differences in the way communication is rendered meaningful have also been identified, with Edward and Mildred Hall (1990) noting that in some cases (cultures) the context of a communication provides much of the meaning (high context cultures, for example Japan) while in others the words uttered bear the whole burden of transmitting meaning (low context cultures, for example the USA).

The second broad approach to the patterning enterprise is to group countries into regions and then to ascribe at least some degree of homogeneity to all the countries in the group. This method proceeds primarily in terms of groups of contiguous countries, often with a shared language or religion, for instance Latin American countries, Arab speaking Moslem countries in the Middle East, or more generally 'Anglo' countries – ones speaking English, often having started life as British colonies (Ronen and Shenker, 1985). Or again Gatley and Lessem (1995) have proposed the existence of management cultures on an east, west, north, south basis, viz:

Western: action oriented
Northern: thought oriented
Southern: family oriented
Eastern: group oriented

Clearly what we have called here patterning is both helpful and legitimate. It is legitimate in the sense that it permits some generalization, which is an economical way to advance our understanding. And it is helpful in that many of the variables are clever and insightful, and go beyond common sense.

At the same time the approach does entail certain dangers:

- Any attempt to classify in terms of a few variables will be an exercise in simplification, so there is a risk of distortion or misrepresentation.
- The variables that one chooses may well be abstract/intangible, so indicators have to be chosen (for example, how do you decide what constitutes individualism in a particular culture) and the choice of these indicators may be arbitrary or ill-judged.
- The grouping of contiguous countries tends to ignore the effect of their separate histories and different sets of national institutions, the importance of which we have tried to illustrate in the preceding section.

The light turns to red?

If we try to bring this record of developments in the understanding of management and business cultures up to the beginning of the twenty-first century then there is a suggestion that, to use the Almelo metaphor again, the traffic lights are turning to red. Not in the sense that anyone wishes to pretend that management's internal dynamics make it the same everywhere, nor is there any inclination to deny cultural difference. But in the last decade or more of the twentieth century the emphasis has rather shifted to commonalities, to the presence of the same trends in a variety of countries, to globalizing forces.

This is how it goes, with probably three main planks to the argument. First, much of the very real growth in world trade in the thirty years after the Second

World War was quite literally a growth *in trade*; a rise in the volume of imports and exports, in a largely stable, free trade world under American leadership. But the internationalism of the 1980s and 1990s has been more than this, it has been a growth in international activity – in the establishment of manufacturing, sales and servicing subsidiaries in other countries, in cross-border merger and acquisition activity, in cross-border strategic alliances, in cross-border financing, in off-shore manufacturing, and even off-shore service and processing activity facilitated by developments in information technology and telecommunications. As Lester Thurow says, it is now possible to design anything anywhere, make it anywhere, and sell it anywhere (Thurow, 1996); he exaggerates of course (part of his charm) but the claim is largely true. In short there is more genuinely international activity in business.

The second plank in the argument is changes in the perception of the role of the state. Now we probably need to wait until we are further into the next century to get this development into the rear view mirror and to understand why, but at least we can already see these changes occurring. In brief, the state in Western countries has come to feel it should do less not more, borrow less not more, worry about its debts, and generally tell its citizens to go somewhere else for the satisfaction of their needs. This orientation, a very sharp contrast with that of the 1950s, 1960s, and 1970s, has a number of clear consequences:

- privatization,
- deregulation,
- government spending cuts and debt reduction programmes,
- citizens required to fund things previously provided by the state – health care, education, pensions, and so on,
- an increasing emphasis on competition, cost reduction, and efficiency everywhere,
- the rise of a 'value for money' ethic on the part of all customers, whether they are governments, employers, or private individuals,
- a situation where there is less difference between business and non-business organizations, less difference in organizational culture and operating principle; hence non-business organizations such as schools, hospitals, charities, and even the civil service itself are now more like profit-making business organizations than they were twenty years ago.

All this is leading to a greater homogeneity of business context, and for that matter of organizational culture, across different countries than was the case in the third quarter of the twentieth century.

The third plank in the argument is speculative at this stage. It is to say that the rise in competition, internationalization, and homogeneity of business context may lead to more commonalities of management style, practice, and values.

The road ahead

We have wanted to explore the issues raised in the previous pages both for their own interest and to show the considerations that have shaped the way we have gone about writing this book.

First of all we are concerned to highlight difference. Clearly there always have been commonalities in the management task and there always will be, but this is not where we want to put the emphasis. Instead our concern is with the differences that appear to exist between the various countries discussed in this book. At the same time, most of the differences we point to are not black and white differences, but differences of relative emphasis.

Second, while the foreground will be occupied by accounts of what business and management is like in the various countries, we will also try to explain where possible, to say why as well as what, though this will necessarily be an incomplete exercise.

A consequence of this desire to explain, or at least to place differences into a national-societal context, means that we will not in the first instance rely on cross-cultural studies of the kind where data or responses to value-driven propositions are obtained by survey means. This is because such studies tend to generate data/responses that are by definition out of context.

Thus the main findings of such surveys may be more of a challenge to our understanding than an extension of our understanding. Again we should add that there is nothing absolute about our inclination not to depend heavily on such survey studies – they will be used where they help to illuminate the nature of business or management in particular countries, or where they provide some further insight. Not only are we not hostile to this mode of inquiry, but both the authors have engaged in cross-cultural studies of this kind in the late 1990s.

Third, what we are relying on primarily in the characterization of business management in the countries discussed in this book is 'first hand' knowledge deriving from working or living in the countries concerned, having done research there, either ourselves or via the medium of doctoral-students or research assistants under our direction. At a practical level this has meant visits to companies, interviews with managers, and interviews with people in a position to offer an informed testimony (management educators, business consultants, business journalists, and so on) and in some of the countries observational studies where managers at work were observed by the researchers for a day or two. All this proceeds on the assumption that you are more likely to come to understand what people mean by what they say if you ask them person to person rather than sift questionnaire responses.

Fourth, this 'hands on' approach to the research has dictated our choice of countries. That is to say we have not felt confident about including any country of which we had no first hand knowledge, where we would have to depend on secondary sources and survey data, however valuable these might be. So for example, there is a chapter on Sweden since one of the authors lived there for a few months, did original research there, and can read Swedish a bit, but there is not unfortunately a chapter on Norway where neither of us have this first hand acquaintance.

Fifth, because we want to explain differences or at least put them in a wider context of national values and social institutions, we have had to recognize that these values also vary infinitely. This in turn has meant that we have treated each country on its merits, giving attention to whatever seemed most interesting and distinctive in each country. We have not adopted a standard formula of having for each country a section on management training, a section on industrial relations, a section on the legal format of companies, and so on. To do this, we feel, is to allow the formula to drive the output when it should be the other way round. It is also boring. That is to say, it will tend to suppress insights that do not fit the formula.

Finally, although this is a book about inter-country difference we are alive to the issue raised at the end of the last section that a more internationalized and homogenized business environment may impact on the dynamics of management recruitment, behaviour, and advancement. This issue is raised explicitly in the case of France, a country which until the very recent past has had a distinctive form of capitalism with high state involvement. Or again the issue is raised more subtly in the case of Germany, where the 'traditional' features of German management are tracked back to the smaller companies often in private ownership that are less exposed to the homogenizing trends outlined in the previous section.

Yet this idea that business is increasingly coming to predominate management and may thereby de-culturize it must be treated with caution at this stage. It is clearly an observable trend in the 1990s. And while the human mind finds it quite easy to grasp the idea of future change, the change that is grasped is usually an intensification of the present trend.

References

Fayol, Henri (1949) *General and Industrial Management*, London: Pitman.
Gatley, S. and R. Lessem (1995) 'Enhancing the Competitive Advantage of Transcultural Businesses', *European Journal of Industrial Training*, vol. 19.
Hall, Edward T. and Mildred Reed Hall (1990) *Understanding Cultural Differences*, Yarnmouth, Maine: International Press.
Hampden-Turner, Charles and Fons Trompenaars (1993) *The Seven Cultures of Capitalism*, New York: Doubleday.
Hofstede, Geert (1980) *Cultures Consequences*, Beverley Hills, LA: Sage.
Lawrence, Peter (1986) *Invitation to Management*, Oxford: Basil Blackwell.

Lawrence, Peter (1990) *Management in the Land of Israel*, Cheltenham: Stanley Thornes.

Lawrence, Peter (1998*) Issues in European Business*, London & Basingstoke: Macmillan.

Lawrence, Peter; Barbara Senior and David Smith (1998) 'The Anglo-American Contract: a New Look', paper presented at annual conference of Association of International Business, London: City University.

Ronen, Simcha and Oded Shenkar (1985) 'Clustering Countries on Attitude and Dimension: A Review and Synthesis', *Academy of Management Review*, vol. 10, no.3, pp. 435–54.

Trompenaars, Fons (1993) *Riding the Waves of Culture*, London: Nicholas Brealey.

Thurow, Lester (1996) *The Future of Capitalism*, London: Nicholas Brealey.

Weinshall, Theodore (1977) *Culture and Management*, Harmondsworth: Penguin.

CHAPTER 2

Born in the USA

It may seem odd to have an early chapter on business and management in the USA in a book devoted to management in Western Europe, so why are we doing it?

There are a range of overlapping reasons, but the essence of it would be that America pretty-much invented management and has given the world a model of professional management and thereby provided a standard of competence for other countries. It may be helpful to unpack this idea a little.

One should probably start by distinguishing between:

- management as an activity; something people do,
- management as an idea; a consciousness and labelling and analysis of this activity,
- management as a subject; something that is taught, or that people are trained in.

The first of these, management as an activity, has always been with us in the sense that mankind has attempted tasks requiring the coordinated efforts of many people – building the pyramids, and so on. So management as an activity is not the property of any particular society or period. But management as an idea and management as a subject are more American than they are anything else. Management as an idea, the conviction that there is something called management that can be identified, extrapolated, and discussed, seems to have gained an early currency in the USA (Lawrence, 1986). One may speculate as to the reasons for this, and part of it no doubt is the vastness of America, the plenitude of resources and opportunities it offered to those making their home there in the 19th century, where space and opportunity always outran population. This in turn put a premium on certain talents: capability, versatility, managing skills, and the development of mechanization and labour-saving ways of doing things.

Then again by the beginning of the twentieth century America had become the world's largest affluent domestic market. Everything it did – from building railroads to supplying chocolate bars – had to be done on a larger scale than anywhere else. So more capital was required, more capital equipment utilized, more people employed, more output demanded and more robust distribution systems established. There was more to plan, more to organize, more to coordinate – in short, more to manage.

As with the idea, so with the subject. One may quibble about which country had the first business school, but Wharton, Pennsylvania, established in the 1880s, is certainly a contender. But perhaps more important is the speed with which business and management education developed at college level in the USA, such that by the 1950s more young Americans were studying business administration than anything else. America also pioneered the MBA, and dominated the management literature, where until the mid twentieth century nearly all major writers on management were Americans (Henri Fayol, French author of *L'administration générale et industrielle* first published in 1911 is of course an exception). The scientific management movement of the late nineteenth and early twentieth century was American, much of the classical management literature was American, the Human Relations movement was largely American; marketing and business strategy were American inventions, and organized mass production was an American speciality. Even as the twentieth century draws to a close something like 80% of all the books ever written about management have been written by Americans.

Not only were America's companies bigger than those of other countries, but many of them internationalized at an early stage, establishing manufacturing operations in Western Europe, Canada and sometimes in Latin America during the 1920s and 1930s. In some cases the USA achieved this cross-border expansion by acquisition in the same early period, with General Motors, for example, buying Opel in Germany and Vauxhall in Britain in the 1920s.

In the first half of the twentieth century America's status as a world power was implicit rather than explicit, a case of power tempered by distance and isolationism. But the Second World War (1939–45) changed all that, when from the end of 1941 American involvement was total. When in May 1945 the Armistice in Europe was signed, Britain had one million troops on the Continent; the USA had three million. In the Far East it was above all the USA that beat Japan, and at the end of the War only the USA had nuclear weapons. What is more the USA achieved great feats of military-industrial production during the War, not only arming itself but becoming in Roosevelt's phrase 'the arsenal of democracy' and to a significant extent arming its allies in the struggle against Nazi Germany.

At the end of the War there was little competition for American companies. In Europe only four countries had been neutral – Spain, Portugal, Switzerland, and Sweden – and while Sweden in particular did enjoy a marked post-war boom, the economy of the USA was bigger by an enormous degree than that of any of the neutral countries or those undamaged by the War. At the end of the War the USA had some two-thirds of *the world's* industrial output.

American companies were everywhere, American investment (and loans) omnipresent. These post-war American companies had more resources than those of any other country, had a greater R&D (research and development) capability, pioneered new products, opened subsidiary companies across the Free World (that is to say the non-communist world) and dominated markets everywhere. It was a golden age, and one that lasted for more than thirty years. One feature of this golden age was the American presumption of management superiority (Locke, 1996). America spoke of 'the management gap' which like its twin 'the technology gap' was the extent to which America's management (or technology) was better than everyone else's. In the early post-war years indeed America set up what were called Joint Productivity Councils, the essence of which was that thousands of European managers were offered trips to the USA and instruction in American methods of organizing production and managing enterprises.

What is more, others were inclined to accept the American view. At the level of popular thinking, while Europeans might view the USA as short on history, culture, and refinement, no one doubted its efficiency, energy, and know-how. Non-Americans who worked for American companies were for the most part impressed by American resources and drive, systems and efficiency (and they were usually paid more than their compatriots working for indigenous companies).

In short, American practice was seen as exemplary. And as we saw in the previous chapter, until the late 1970s there was little awareness or discussion of cultural and institutional differences between countries that might impact on management. This loose presumption of management homogeneity was very much fuelled by the professional image of American management. America, that is to say, was the model, certainly the way things were meant to be, and any country-based differences could be understood in terms of falling short, for the moment, of this model.

The American decline

This golden age faltered in the 1970s, and certainly for the last twenty years of the century there has been much public discussion, most of it initiated by American commentators themselves, of the presumptive US economic decline.

The first salvo was fired in the pages of the Harvard Business Review in 1980 when two influential articles appeared, by Raymond Vernon (1980) and by Robert Hayes and William Abernathy (1980). These writers variously accused American companies of under-investment, short-termism, and a neglect of the engineering dimension, of trying to force unsuitable American products down the metaphorical throats of other countries, and of an over reliance on finance and marketing. Since those heady days more sustained accounts of the US decline have appeared, including those of Dertouzos (1989), Thurow (1992), Locke (1996), McRae (1994) and Thurow (1996). At the same time the USA remains the world's richest country. While a number of countries score higher on GDP per capita than the USA (Switzerland and all the Scandinavian countries, for instance) whenever the more realistic measure of purchasing power parity is used America still comes out top (McRae, 1994; Lawrence, 1996). So how then is the famous decline to be understood?

The American economic decline is *relative*, and in two senses. First, the USA has declined in relation to its own past, the golden age after the Second World War outlined in the previous section. Instead of accounting for two-thirds of the world's industrial output it accounts for less than one-third; instead of being the richest country on earth by far, it is now simply the largest among a number of rich, developed countries; instead of dominating most product markets on a world basis it now dominates only a few; instead of being a country where ordinary people were much better off than their counterparts in other countries it has become a society where the purchasing power of the blue collar worker has improved little since the late 1960s, and so on.

The second sense in which the USA has experienced relative decline is in comparison with other (competitor) countries, especially Japan and Germany. Both these countries coming from way behind having been the losers in the Second World War have done better than the USA in terms of merchandise exporting and world market share; they are not smeared with the taint of short-termism, nor endlessly driven by considerations of shareholder value; their products are not sold on jazzy marketing but on quality, and value, and attention to detail. To make it worse Japan has actually made symbolic acquisitions in the USA: the Rockefeller Centre in New York and the Columbia and Universal film studios in Hollywood are Japanese owned.

The two senses of relative decline are of course linked. As other countries rebuilt their economies after the Second World War, especially Germany and Japan, they would contribute more to world trade and world industrial capacity, and this would push down the American share. What is more, as companies in other countries became more successful, they would increasingly seek to invest in the USA as the world's richest market both by merger and acquisition and by establishing their own subsidiaries. In terms of America's own past, its recent past, this is a remarkable development. In the 1950s and 1960s FDI (foreign direct investment) was something the USA 'did to' other countries; now they are at the receiving end of foreign investment, with Britain having the largest investment in the USA and Japan being in second place.

The discussion of the American economic decline has gone on for so long now that the thesis is being revised and qualified. One argument here is that the American economy has moved earlier and on a larger scale from manufacturing into services, but it has competitive advantage in many of these service operations, by being a prime mover or by having better productivity in services than other countries, so in the middle term it will succeed. This defence is offered by Michael Porter in his famous *The Competitive Advantage of Nations* (1990) where Porter also makes the point that the USA has military and political power, indeed since the collapse of European communism it is *the* world power, and that somehow or other this political power will be a bulwark against undue economic decline. Or again the present writer while picking over data on the composition of American exports has noticed that while manufactured goods constitute a declining proportion of all US exports, raw materials and foodstuffs constitute a rising proportion (Lawrence, 1996).

Now this is a bit of a back-handed compliment but at least America is rich in raw materials and is a major food producer (the world's cheapest food producer indeed) and in consequence does have this option, that is not, for instance, open to Germany and Japan – if *their* manufacturing loses its competitive edge the consequences will be inescapable. Another line of defence is offered by Hamish McRae (1994) who argues that the USA continues to enjoy the economic advantage of its own culture, in the sense that people want American cultural products, films and videos and TV series that depict American life and are thus attractive and appealing to others – hence America's domination of the world entertainment business. In fact McRae's argument could be extended to cover a range of fashion goods and leisure services – restaurant chains such as Hard Rock Cafe and Planet Hollywood (and MacDonalds, which by turnover is larger than Mazda of Japan or ICI of Britain) are appealing because of their Americaness, while much youth clothing – jeans, trainers, and so on – benefit from an American youth culture image.

So the decline is relative not absolute, and we are now seeing a counter-literature, or at least a range of counter arguments. But one theme which runs through the decline critique concerns the constancy of American management and business practice. That is to say it has been agreed by a variety of people (Hayes and Abernathy, 1980; Dertouzos, 1989; Thurow, 1992) that American management has not changed, has not adapted to new conditions, plays to the same strengths, tries to work in the same way, as though still in the golden age.

If then American management and business practice is marked by this stability and consistency in the second half of the twentieth century, what then are its key features?

First impressions

One might start by posing the question: Suppose one were British and went to work for 'a typical company' in middle America, what sort of things would be noticeable in the first few days? To begin with, one's induction into the company would be more overtly organized and systematic than you would find at home. You would be told all the practical things you needed to know up front, you would get an information pack, would be entered into files and data bases, your remuneration and all your benefits would be organized, they would have door keys, swipe cards and a parking lot all ready for you.

Then you would see differences in the way (the same) language is used. American English is more direct, more forceful, more explicit; nothing that needs to be said is left unsaid for reasons of delicacy. And Americans check that their message is getting across; asking: 'Do you understand that?' 'Am I making this clear?' In these exchanges it is OK to admit that you have not understood, but by American norms you are not allowed to walk away without having understood.

American communication is also more information centred. Both in everyday life and in work situations Americans exchange more information. Trading facts is a kind of small talk, it may fill the social space that in England is devoted to talking about the weather. And in management, information is of the essence; it drives systems, triggers decisions, and fuels the operation of controls.

You may also notice that Americans typically have an ability to instantly fix certain facts in their minds. When an American is introduced to five people in a cocktail bar he or she will actually take on board all their names and be able to use them instantly. An American who asks the way to City Hall and is told:

> Go right out of the lot, left at the first intersection, nine blocks then turn right, turn left at the second stop light, it's on the left!
> Have you got that?

generally will 'have it' and won't need an action replay.

Everyone you are introduced to will call you by your first name and expect you to do the same, notwithstanding any differences in rank. In these first encounters you may find that they are more phased by your accent than you are by theirs, that you know more about America than they know about Britain, and that their understanding of your country is more stereotypical than yours of theirs. If you were from a smaller European country there would be both less stereotyping and less basic knowledge. Americans don't usually have much idea where Denmark, Portugal and Austria are, and would be hard put to name their capital cities. Also if you were from a smaller European country you might well encounter a bit of benign vagueness on the part of your hosts about your native language (you might be asked if you speak Belgian or Swiss at home).

You would notice in the early days that people are generally less deferential. Secretaries, for instance, are much less deferential to their bosses or to managers in general than are many of their European counterparts. They will say bluntly:

I'm going to lunch now.

not:

If it is OK with you I will think about going to lunch.

When offered bits of work they don't think worthy of their capability they will say they are going to pass it on to some office junior:

I'll give it to Sadie.

means don't waste my time with this low grade stuff. But they will also tell you more, in an unvarnished way and not worry about whether you won't like it or will want to 'shoot the messenger'. Everyone in an American company indeed will tend to render less deference to everyone else. You might respect their power, but you don't have to respect their status. So you can answer back, put up opposing views, point out the weaknesses in someone else's position, and most American managers observably do all of this.

This phenomenon often leads Europeans in the first instance to presume that the work situation is more secure, that the hierarchy is of less account. Not so. If you get it wrong, if you go too far, if you become 'a road block' that someone with more power seeks to remove, you will be fired (remember the *bon mot* that America is the easiest country in the world in which to get a job – and the easiest country in which to lose one!). Notwithstanding these realities of power, Americans in the author's experience are still more challenging and outspoken.

The European newcomer may also have the feeling that there are more women in professional and managerial posts, and a man is more likely to find he has a boss who is a woman. At first this strikes you, as an old-fashioned European you find yourself thinking you did not expect to find a woman as financial controller or a woman running the branch office or whatever. Then after a bit you notice it less because the women seem to be less differentiated in style and behaviour from the men: they show the same directness, the same get-to-the-pointness, have the same friendly yet assertive verbal style – and of course they do not defer to anyone either!

In the first few days British newcomers may well find that they adjust somewhat their own speech. Not in the sense of trying to talk with an American accent but by becoming more direct, less circumspect, simplifying the structure of sentences (discarding the adverbs, getting rid of the dependent clauses). British humour is also a bit of a liability since it deals too much in allusion and metaphor (Barsoux, 1993).

In the first week in an American company you are also bound to attend some meetings. American meetings are quite overpowering in their purposefulness. There is not much humour, problem dissection is perfunctory, but the purpose is always to move things forward, to find workable solutions. At the end of a meeting in an American company you always know:

- what we are going to do,
- who is going to do what,
- how long it is going to take,
- when we are going to meet again to review progress.

This is what they do best.

Systems

Underlying many of the points made in an introductory way in the previous section is the American penchant for systems, or as a Scottish researcher on the features of US subsidiaries in Britain once put it, for formalization (Jamieson, 1980). Writing about the many American companies that have a corporate presence in the UK Jamieson observes:

> American firms are more likely to have fixed procedures for a wider range of activities than their British opposite numbers (Jamieson, 1985).

and again:

> This stress on formal procedures amounts to a much greater use being made of the techniques of managerial control. This is especially noticeable in the field of financial and budgetary control, but it is also a distinctive feature of the personnel area (*ibid.*)

Staying for a moment with Jamieson's point concerning formalization in personnel administration the present writer has been struck when visiting companies in the USA by the range of personnel procedures, including:

- elaborate, formal recruitment and selection procedures,
- systems for implementing federal government requirements on equality of opportunity, involving tracking job applications from minority groups and ascertaining the proportion selected for interview or appointment,
- more routine checks on the background of applicants; it is quite common for an American company to check that applicants for professional and management jobs really do have the college degrees they claim; at a lower level checks on driving records with the public authority, checks with prior employers to verify reasons for termination; all this is much more standard practice than in Europe,
- likewise so are standard medical checks on incoming employees (to make sure they do not already have a health problem for which they may later try to sue the company!) and drug checks,
- a systematic gathering of salary data, external to the company so that the

company is able to position itself in local, regional, or national labour markets according to the type of employee,

- elaborate systems for determining salary grades, factoring in dimensions such as level of initiative required, time span of decision, range of responsibilities, and of course quantifying these,
- systematic administration of employee benefits, especially medical benefits; US companies traditionally offer a wide range of benefits including, for example, company administered saving schemes and a variety of counselling services (relationship counselling, counselling to drug or alcohol dependents, and so on).

It is the same with marketing. American companies will be more assiduous collectors of market data. They will put more effort into:

- establishing global market size,
- establishing own company's market share,
- competitor analysis,
- customer analysis,
- gathering of data on markets the company intends to enter.

Now none of this is meant to suggest that this formalization is peculiar to American companies, and indeed European companies have clearly moved in this direction in the last twenty years of the twentieth century. But this formalization, this attachment to systems, is a traditional American strength. Americans just like to have everything codified, quantified if possible, and 'nailed down' so there can be no argument about it afterwards (three-quarters of the world's lawyers live in the USA).

This penchant for systematization also probably has its origins in the nineteenth-century phenomenon referred to earlier to explain the emergence of the idea of management, namely the excess of resources and opportunities to population. In other words you can make few people 'go further' (get more done) if you can systematize their tasks in the sense of disaggregating the task and re-configuring the elements in an easy to follow systematic way.

It has also been argued (Thurow, 1996; Lawrence, 1996) that formalization has come to mask the inadequacies of a poorly educated workforce. As Thurow (1996) puts it, the American workforce has been 'dumbed down' by systems that require little thought for their operation that were designed in the first place by cleverer people. In support of this view Thurow gives figures showing a higher ratio of professionally qualified staff (managers, engineers, computer scientists) to ordinary workers in America compared with Germany and Japan.

At the same time it has to be said that these systems have, certainly in the past, given American companies a competitive edge and given American managers a professional image. They have also been the substance of the cross-border transfer of management know-how, and these systems have often enjoyed the respect of Europeans and others working in American subsidiaries.

Proactivity

Being proactive is a state of mind as well as a set of behaviours, and American management exhibits both. The vastness and richness of America, the circumstance of it being settled by immigrants seeking personal betterment, the ability of this entity to offer 'happy endings' to so many people – all this tends to ingrain optimism in American society. And the optimism combined with individualism and the belief in the 'right to happiness' enshrined in the 1776 Declaration of Independence, in turn leads to a proactive disposition. One should, in short, take action to secure the success and happiness which is one's right.

This proactive disposition is generally characteristic of American management. Its implicit starting point is that whatever the aim is, it is capable of accomplishment – it is just a matter of setting objectives, allocating resources, organizing for action. To put it another way, American management is imbued with a bias for action, and in this matter it tends to contrast with Europe. There are some situations where it really is not obvious what one should do, whether one should do a particular thing or pursue a particular course of action. There may be arguments for, and against. In such situations Europeans may do nothing for fear of making things worse, and Americans will always do something!

Another element in this bias for action in the American case is the way Americans connect means and ends. In their view there must be available means for the achievement of desirable ends, and this conviction leads them to define certain actions as appropriate, and they get on with it. Europeans are not so sure.

This American disposition is also manifest in a concern with solutions rather than with problems. It is all quite clear in meetings at American companies where the analysis of the problem is often rather perfunctory by European standards, especially if the problem cannot be formulated in financial or other quantitative terms. But this problem discussion is simply a preliminary to the advocacy of some solution. Again the solution does not have to be perfect, it has to be doable; it does not have to guarantee success, just have a passable chance of working. Americans are much less worried about attempting solutions that fail. Where Europeans may feel abashed at this outcome, feel it leaves them open to charges of having slighted the problem analysis or been too hasty, Americans just don't care – they will try something else, and keep trying until they find something that works. The author once sat in on a meeting chaired by an Operations Vice President aiming at the solution of a substantial problem in their manufacturing programme. The group put together a possible solution and went through the 'who is going to do what, when, and how much will it cost routine' and then he signed it off with the remark:

> It may have some holes in it, it may work better than we think. It is a question of getting in and trying.

The same proactivity that we have indicated as a feature of American management in general is also typically observable at the level of the individual manager. First of all there tends to be a positive attitude to work and ambition, or at least lip service is paid to these. There is a lot of coming in early, staying late, starting or finishing business trips during the weekend; furthermore, meetings scheduled at weekends, say task force meetings or big decision presentations to higher ups, are by no means unknown. Second, everyone acts as though they want to get up and get on, there is little in the way of modest concealment or denial of ambition so often encountered in Europe. And salary hierarchies tend to be steep, so that being promoted means an estimable financial reward. Third, one manifestation of this drive to succeed by individual managers is mobility between companies. Not all American managers have changed jobs and employing organizations frequently, but in the author's experience many have done so, and these individual careers often show a level of inter-company mobility that would be regarded as exceptional in Europe, especially in the more stable countries such as Sweden or the Netherlands. Fourth, when individual American managers review their careers it sometimes emerges that drive has predominated most restraints. These managers will describe with zest how they moved around between employing organizations, dragged their families from place to place around the USA, grabbed every opportunity, sometimes 'sailed close to the wind' – claimed things they did not have a right to, bluffed mightily to get hired, played a thin hand well when they had to – and with all that they seem to be saying 'Well I made it, didn't I?', and no further justification is required.

Strategy

The growing interest and concern with corporate strategy throughout the developed countries of the world in the last twenty years or so of the twentieth century, should not blind us to the fact that strategy was pretty much an American invention. As has been noted earlier, the USA has had bigger corporations than other countries, there are more of them, and they internationalized at an earlier stage. When this is crossed with the intense interest in business and economic success, long recognized as a feature of American society, then the central importance of corporate strategy is the result. For what is strategy but a set of programmatic intentions and decisions aimed at ensuring the future success of a given company?

Now clearly we are not making a black-and-white contrast between the USA and other countries in the matter of the importance accorded to strategy, but in the case of America the concern with strategy is stronger, more explicitly recognized, and has been in place longer. The contrast shows in a variety of ways with senior managers in American corporations.

First of all, these American companies always seem to have objectives: explicit, often bold, typically quantified. Second, American executives take the responsibility for strategy seriously and consciously. If asked open-ended questions about the nature of their job, their priorities, and so on, strategy typically predominates (this is not to say that there is any corresponding neglect of operations or implementation, just that strategy figures large). Third, American executives are invariably ready to articulate this strategy for the benefit of inquirers with an ease that implies that communication of the strategy is the norm.

What is more, American executives tend to exhibit a high level of industry knowledge, especially quantifiable knowledge. They will know the overall value of sales for the industry in which their company operates, know how the industry is stratified – into big, medium sized, and small companies – and what their market share is. They will be able to distinguish between markets and segments, know which are expanding and which are contracting, they will put numbers to all this, can manipulate this knowledge to produce future scenarios, speak knowledgeably about developments in the industry – whether technical-production matters, issues of taste, demand, or fashion, or changes in the configuration of the various corporate players.

Now again no black-and-white contrast with executives in other developed countries is intended; it is simply that in the present writers' experience Americans do this better, with more conviction, more easy familiarity with the detail.

In the same vein American executives seldom have any difficulty with the idea of key success factors (KSFs) – factors that are essential to the success of companies in a given industry, but which of course vary from industry to industry. If asked about KSFs they are typically able to rattle them off in a way that suggests it is always in their minds, they have not had to think it through to respond to your question. Similarly if one asks senior executives to name any particular decisions that stand out in importance that they have made in their years of office they are prone to cite decisions of a strategic nature – changes in the product mix, entering new markets or withdrawal from existing ones, merger and acquisition , reconfigurations of the company's value chain, major changes in distribution arrangements, physically relocating plants, and so on. Incidentally a frequent European response to this question about 'most important decisions' is to say that there are not any, that the senior management task is not like that. Again in the American case one has the impression that all this is in the front of their minds, that these issues have an insistent reality.

Professionalism

If we take the concerns of the last three sections of this chapter – systems, pro-activity, strategy – they seem to be the essence of American management, and to constitute its claim to professionalism. It is these features and qualities that have commended American management in the past, engaged the respect of Europeans and others working for American companies, and raised American management to the status of a model. But it is only fair to ask: Are there any 'buts'? There are two, and we will explore one for the sake of completeness, and the other since it is central to the present book that seeks to compare management style and practice in different (European) countries.

The first of these 'buts' is to say that if American management has these positive features why is it that for twenty years there has been a debate about America's relative economic decline? And part of the answer must be that those who control and direct American companies have shown too little aptitude to adjust to changed world conditions. They have continued to play the same strengths, operate in the same way, as though still in the golden age. To give this argument more focus consider the case of key success factors in manufacturing. In the old days it was about scale of operations, cost-efficiency, large throughputs, large domestic market, little foreign competition, product promotion backed by financial and marketing muscle. All this played to American strengths. Now much of this has changed to an emphasis on quality, customized design, environmentally friendly products, shorter production runs, quicker new product introduction, more manufacturing flexibility, more downwardly delegated responsibility in the factory, more empowerment. All this plays rather less to American strengths, but it plays for example to German and Japanese strengths, with a better-educated workforce, better vocational education, better workplace training, and less reliance on systems to compensate for, in the words of Lester Thurow, a 'dumbed down' workforce in the USA.

It should be added that this argument is not necessarily decisive. Not just in the sense that the USA may overcome these limitations, but that the game may continue to change in a way that takes the focus off competence in quality manufacture. The issue here is the move away from manufacturing and towards services, how far will it go, and what will be its implications for countries with relative strength or weakness in manufacture – and this is unknowable.

But consider that services already constitute a bigger proportion of GDP for the USA than for other developed countries. The USA is already the biggest exporter of services. And in so far as there are reasonable inter-country comparisons the USA has better productivity in service provision than competitor countries. Keep in mind that the essence of service provision is systems and interfacing with the customer. These are American strengths.

The second and final issue concerns American perception of cultural difference, and this tends to be weak. Americans are not particularly well informed about other countries, and not well attuned to cultural difference. While they may recognize that European countries may be different from America they tend to lump them together and fail to realise that many of these countries are as different from each other as they may be from the USA.

When it comes to management Americans often have difficulty with the idea that departures from the American norm do not necessarily constitute failure or inefficiency; that management practice in other countries may be shaped by a different configuration of beliefs and a different ensemble of national institutions. Nonetheless it may well be the case that it works for them.

Notwithstanding these qualifications it has been desirable to review American management at an early stage in the present book. The USA has come to represent a model of professional management, albeit a somewhat acultural one, and it does offer an extra-European reference point. In some of the following chapters indeed it will be helpful to make comparisons back to the USA and to be able to take for granted some understanding of the management dynamics of that country.

References

Barsoux, Jean-Louis (1993) *Funny Business*, London: Cassell.

Dertouzos, Michael *et al.* (1989) *Made in America*, Cambridge, Mass: MIT Press.

Hayes, Robert H. and William Abernathy (1980) 'Managing our way to Economic Decline', *Harvard Business Review*, July/August, pp. 67–72.

Jamieson, Ian (1980) *Capitalism and Culture*, Aldershot: Gower.

Lawrence, P. A. (1986) *Invitation to Management*, Oxford: Basil Blackwell.

Lawrence, P. A. (1996) *Management in the USA*, London: Sage.

Locke, R. R. (1996) *The Collapse of the American Management Myth*, Oxford: Oxford University Press.

McRae, H. (1994) *The World in 2020*, Boston, Mass: Harvard Business Press.

Porter, Michael (1990) *The Competitive Advantage of Nations*, New York: The Free Press.

Thurow, Lester (1992) *Head to Head*, New York: William Morrow.

Thurow, Lester (1996) *The Future of Capitalism*, London: Nicholas Brealey.

Vernon, Raymond (1980) 'Gone are the Cash Cows of Yesteryear', *Harvard Business Review*, December pp. 150–5.

CHAPTER 3

France

The American economist Lester Thurow begins his book *The Future of Capitalism* by posing the question: Why is capitalism interesting, why should we be thinking about its future? In effect he suggests three answers to this question, which tend to intermingle (Thurow, 1996).

First of all, capitalism has survived. European communism failed, and the former countries of Central and Eastern Europe are doing their best to emulate the Western market economy, and hopefully to enjoy the political freedom and relative affluence of the West. What is more, some of the non-European communist states failed too, for instance Mongolia, or like Cuba, appear to be failing. And even China, that bastion of intact communist power, has made significant moves towards a market economy system.

Second, Thurow suggests that among the capitalist states, those deviant ones that sought to mix capitalism with socialism, such as Sweden, ended up spending too much on welfare, borrowing too much, and being unable to service their debts and maintain their welfare provision simultaneously, especially in the face of ageing populations. So around the capitalist world from the 1980s on, there has been more emphasis on a kind of traditional 'pay as you go' economics; governments have sought to reduce public sector borrowing, public expenditure, and to find ways of privately funding welfare. The balanced budget has become a virtue, and in some cases a reality. No one doubts the desirability of fiscal restraint, it has become a primary goal. Consider as a little indication of this state of mind that as 1997 drew to a close the Canadian government announced with quiet pride that the two Canadian provinces which had eliminated the gap between revenue and current expenditure, and had put in hand measures for the reduction of public debt accumulated in the past, these being Manitoba and Saskatchewan, had the lowest unemployment rates in Canada (Canadian High Commission, 1997). This finding was stated simply, as though self-evident, though the weight of (Keynesian) twentieth-century evidence is that you reduce unemployment by means of public spending.

The drift of these two arguments is that there is a certain convergence going on in capitalism, where the communist deviation has (largely) been eliminated, as has the spendthrift-welfare deviation. Thurow's third argument, however, is superficially rather different. It is to say that the future of capitalism is worth discussing because capitalism is unpredictable. Yet while at this point Thurow offers one or two idiosyncratic examples, the overall thesis of the book is that there are general patterns of change, perceptible world-wide, or at least in a variety of countries or regions. So it would be fair to say that running through these speculations of a leading economist is the idea that the countries of the world are converging on capitalism, and that the capitalist system is coming to display greater homogeneity caught as it is in the grip of universal dynamics.

This thesis is of particular interest with regard to France, since:

- outside a small group of specialists there is no general recognition that capitalism in France is different,
- but it is!
- and whether or not this difference is being eroded is an interesting speculation.

But let us start with some of the ways in which French capitalism has differed from the Anglo-Saxon norm.

Vive la différence

In France the critical difference has always been the role of the state. This idea is starkly expressed in the first sentence of Colin Gordon's authoritative book on French business:

> More than any other OECD country, the state has played a crucial and all pervasive role in France in determining the major directions in which business activities have moved (Gordon, 1996:1).

If one asks how this state influence has been expressed then the answer has several ingredients, some of which are easy to get hold of while others are of a more subtle, processual nature. Let us start with one of the more straightforward factors.

When France was liberated from the Nazi occupation in 1944 the period of post-war reconstruction revolved around a series of five-year (economic) plans. Indeed these five-year plans still exist at the end of the twentieth century though they are now more of a political ritual than an economic reality. But in the early post-war days these plans mattered. They set industrial priorities, and put the power of the state behind them. This exercise, *planification* as it is called, also had the result of bringing civil servants and industrialists into closer contact, a theme that will recur in this chapter. What is more in a later period, approximately 1960s to 1980s, the French government had the discernible policy of seeking to foster in France a number of 'national champion' companies that would have critical mass, would be big enough to face European (especially German) competition; this policy was pursued via state-sponsored mergers with government (facilitated) finance, and sometimes contracts helping to make a reality of the aspiration.

Or again, the French government has been consistently committed to the European Union (EU), feeling this would enhance the Europe-wide exportation of French goods and services. So that France was a founder member of what was then called the European Economic Community in 1958; was a later enthusiast for the Single European Market initiative of 1992–93 that sought to eliminate non-tariff barriers between the EU partners; and later still, unlike Britain, was committed to first wave membership of the European Monetary Union (EMU).

Another tangible way in which the French state has intruded on the economy is by owning a larger share of it than has been usual in Western states. Some of this state ownership is historical; tobacco, for example, has been a government monopoly since the seventeenth century. And the post Second World War period saw further nationalization, inspired in part to punish industrialists who had collaborated with the German occupation and its puppet Vichy regime – Louis Renault was the most famous example of a collaborator whose company was expropriated. And then again in the early 1980s under socialist president Mitterand more nationalization occurred. According to Colin Gordon (1996) the high point occurred in 1984 by which time the public sector represented 16 per cent of the working population, 28 per cent of turnover, 36 per cent of investments, and 91 per cent of bank deposits. Since this high-point was achieved there have been waves of privatization, and privatization-deregulation is still (1998) the order of the day. Yet one must not assume that privatization in France means the end of government influence. The state decides what and when to privatize, it will choose the CEO (chief executive officer), and may well affect the capital structure of the 'newly privatized' company by arranging or guaranteeing finance. It should be added that France tends towards a model of large-scale capitalism with financial empires structured around banks and lending companies. Shareholding by British style financial institutions such as pension funds and unit trusts is relatively absent, and private households own a smaller proportion of shares than in Britain. The other principal peculiarity of company ownership in France is that more companies are owned by individuals or families. As everyone knows, France has a lot of small, family companies, more absolutely and proportionally than Britain. Rather less well known is that there are a lot of large companies in France, for example Michelin or L'Oréal, where a family is the principal shareholder.

To this litany of patterned difference we might add the fact that France at the time of writing (early 1998) has a rather high rate of unemployment, more than double the British rate, in spite of having a favourable trade balance from 1994 on when France emerged from the early 1990s recession. Finally, France has a low trade union membership rate, the lowest in the EU and probably the lowest in the industrial world. According to British Trade Union Congress figures for 1994 the French rate is 9 per cent, compared with 29 per cent for Germany and 34 per cent for Britain.

This brief account of some of the distinctive features of capital and business in France will hopefully set the scene for a discussion of French management. We will return to the issue of convergence à la Lester Thurow at the end of the chapter.

Les cadres

The standard word for managers/management in French is a collective plural, *les cadres*. It can be used in the singular, one can speak of *un cadre*, a manager, but it is typically used in the plural. One can also qualify the term to indicate sub-categories of managers, as in *cadres supérieures*, senior managers, or *cadres moyens*, middle managers. And *cadres* has a distinctively male connotation; *un cadre* is automatically assumed to be a man, a female manager being designated as *une femme cadre*.

Both the term and the derivation are indicative. *Cadres*, while designating managers, does not have an *exact* equivalent in other languages, with the exception of Italian where the term *quadri* is sometimes used. Both *cadres* and *quadri* have the original meaning of designating some military entity, an ensemble of commissioned and non-commissioned officers. The fact that a military term is used, metaphorically, to designate a non-military group is itself instructive. It is lending to management a policing and control orientation, in the French case palpably manifest in a concern with the rigours of formal authority (and in a later chapter on management in Italy we will introduce survey data from the late 1990s to illustrate the 'law and order' orientation displayed by Italian managers as well).

The introduction as well as the derivation of the term is also significant. The expression *cadres* was first used in France in the 1930s, in a period of considerable labour unrest. In this context the expression *cadres* was first commandeered to indicate professional managers, typically engineering graduates, who were seen as a third force, neither workers nor *patrons* (business owners). While other countries have been inclined to blur this distinction between business owner and manager, between industrialist and executive, the clear thinking and typology-loving French are concerned to highlight the manager versus owner distinction. And of course the separateness of the French manager from the class of business owners is sometimes substantiated and authenticated by means of his education – of which more in a moment.

The notion of *les cadres* is also more bounded than the looser Anglo-Saxon term management; it conveys more categorical precision. Employees of French business organizations are never in any doubt as to whether or not they are *cadres*. There is no fudging or blurring, no discussion as in the Anglo-Saxon world about whether or not this first line supervision is part of management. *Passer cadre*, to be appointed a *cadre*, is a standard expression in French; you know when it happens without being dependent on the rear view mirror. Incidentally *les cadres* have some features that distinguish them in a legalistic sense, including their own retirement scheme and their own placement service.

While there are different ways in which *cadre* status may be achieved, and indeed a certain malaise is characteristically attributed to *les cadres*, several constituencies treat *les cadres* as a unitary group. One of these constituencies is politicians, who both praise *les cadres* for their contribution to modernization and to national economic well-being, and speak of trying to represent them, of winning their support, of going for 'the *cadre* vote'.

The media also tend to treat *les cadres* as a unitary group, speaking of *cadre* opinions, wishes, grievances, aspirations, and so on. And indeed there are a plenitude of magazines devoted to the presumptive interests of *les cadres* – *L'Express*, *L'Expansion*, *Le Nouvel Economiste*, *Capital*, *Challenge*, *L'Essentiel du Management*, and more besides. Furthermore *les cadres* are the target of a great deal of consumerist advertising. The key consideration here is that *les cadres* have both a high disposable income *and* they constitute an educational elite which in turn has implications for their taste and discrimination.

Finally in this discussion of quasi-unitariness it might be added that this idea of *les cadres* as the agents of modernization and national economic achievement seems to be timeless. To put this remark in context one should say that the industrialization of France in the nineteenth century lagged behind that of say Britain, Germany, or the USA. Furthermore, relative industrial weakness was seen by the French to be a factor in their vulnerability to German attack from the time of the Franco-Prussian War (1870–71) to the Second World War (1939–45). It was only after the Second World War that France completed the process of industrialization, caught up with the more prosperous countries of Western Europe, and came to enjoy during what were called *les trentes glorieuses*, the thirty glorious years of post-war economic development, growth rates that surpassed those of West Germany in that country's 'economic miracle' period. In this period, the 1950s and 1960s, it is only natural that *les cadres* enjoyed the status of national heroes. What is interesting is that the veneration seems to have continued into the 1980s and 1990s.

Malaise

Notwithstanding these unitary perceptions of *les cadres* as a group, for decades now a certain *malaise* or *crise* has been attributed to them. The original *leitmotiv* running through the idea of the *malaise des cadres*, pretty much a standard expression, derives from their intermediate buffer position between workers and business owners, something that would worry the French with their penchant for remorseless clarity of thought more than it would worry Anglo-Saxons. The implications of this dubiety were highlighted in *les événements* of 1968 – the student uprising, worker protests – where some *cadres* joined the striking workers while others were taken hostage by them as representatives of the 'boss class'.

In the 1990s, however, the almost ritually ascribed *malaise des cadres* has taken on a new meaning. The 1991–94 recession saw downsizing, delayering, and process re-engineering, leading to significant *cadre* unemployment for the first time – a tremendous psychological blow. While this unemployment among *cadres* is way below the national unemployment rate, it is without precedent for this hitherto privileged group. And it is recognized as impacting on the relationship between *les cadres* and their employing organizations, making the *cadres* more circumspect, less loyal, and less devoted, as well as more cynical about their prospects. Employers now recognize that they cannot as before demand unconditional loyalty in return for implicitly guaranteed status and security. The new mood is nicely caught by a French manager working for Philips, quoted in *L'Expansion*:

> *Philips, je me disais, c'est du costaud, j'en aurais jusqu'à ma retraite. Quelle illusion!* (*L'Expansion*, 25/1/96, 44)
> (Philips, I thought that's nice and solid, that will see me through to retirement. What a joke!)

There is, however, a sense in which this discussion of the malaise is premature, in that we have not yet made clear the various routes into management or the determinants of management career success.

Becoming a *cadre*

Let us begin by describing the system that applies to the majority, sets the tone, and expresses peculiarly French convictions regarding the nature of individual worth and difference. To put it simply what the French esteem is cleverness.

Being able to do intellectually demanding things better or quicker than most people, passing exams with high marks, gaining admission to exclusive educational establishments via competitive entry exams – all this matters more, will take you further, indeed is more indispensable in France than in most countries. The worst thing that can happen to you in France is that you are thick, and cannot pass exams. If this is your fate, then character, motivation, looks, luck, and inheritance, while they are all worth something, will be less of a compensation in France. France is run by its star pupils, those who did best in the educational system, and this applies to French business as well as to the French state. Indeed one of the interesting things about France is the unity of the national elite. And this unity is based on shared educational antecedents, of a mind-stretching rather than character forming kind. This is how it works.

After a sojourn at a comprehensive high-school those who matter proceed to a selective secondary school establishment, the Lyceé, where they will eventually take the baccalaureate exam at the age of 18. The baccalaureate is the examination that admits to university; it is the French equivalent of 'A' level in England or Abitur in Germany. But the baccalaureate, or *le bac* as it is popularly known, is not a unitary exam, and does not lead in a single direction.

First of all there are a number of *bac* options, in the sense of groups of subjects. The most important one is Bac S, the natural science option, and it is the most important, most prestige conferring, because it includes most maths, where mathematics is seen as the purest test of abstract mental powers. Anyone who is ambitious and clever enough will go for Bac S. There may be other subjects, or *bac* options that they enjoy more. There may also be *bac* options that appear more occupationally relevant; there is for example an economics and business studies option, but it will be avoided by anyone seriously considering a career in business and management so long as they are bright enough to do the Bac S. Demonstrating cleverness and being in the right (and narrowly defined) educational career track, is more important than interest, enjoyment, or presumptive relevance.

A further anomaly is that although *le bac* admits to university the most able and ambitious, Lyceé students will not choose to go to university. Instead they will aim for entry to the top tier of France's higher education system, the *grandes écoles*.

There are between 140 and 160 of these institutions (the approved list of *grandes écoles*, varies from time to time, and so does the rigour of the description). There are in essence two kinds – engineering schools and commercial schools. Most *grandes écoles* belong to the first category; they are schools of engineering, both generalist and specialist, the oldest dating from the time of Napoleon and many founded in the nineteenth century. The commercial schools are fewer in number but have come to enjoy considerable prominence in the later twentieth century. The first, and pre-eminent in the group, is HEC (Haute Ecole de Commerce) founded in 1881; HEC is of course in Paris, and significantly in so centralized a country as France HEC and the two other commercial *grandes écoles* in that city are known as *les trois grandes parisiennes*. Commercial *grandes écoles* in the provinces usually have the city name preceded by the letters ESC, standing for *école supérieure de commerce;* for example ESC Lyon, which in an institutionally status conscious society would rank number four nationally, after *les trois grandes parisiennes* of course.

The *grandes écoles* differ from the universities in a number of ways:

- They are perceived as better, or more intellectually elitist, as attracting cleverer people.
- They are smaller; in the late 1990s the average size of the *grandes écoles* is around 400 whereas the universities have thousands of students.
- The *grandes écoles* are better connected – with government, companies, employing organizations of all kinds.
- The *grandes écoles* are, to use the North American expression, 'front-end loaded'; that is to say, they are difficult to get into; if you can get in, you will assuredly 'get out' (graduate), and live happily ever after in a career sense; most managers in most French companies are *grande école* educated.

To get into a *grande école* one has to pass a nationally competitive exam, the *concours*. To prepare for the *concours* one spends two years or more *after* passing the baccalaureate, at an *école préparatoire* – these latter institutions are known colloquially as *les prépas*. It is well understood in France that the time spent at the *prépa* getting ready for the *concours* will be the toughest experience you ever have; you will work harder, be more focused on study, more committed to striving for 'final victory' than at any other time in life. Once arrived at a *grande école*, the rest will be relatively easy. Throughout the post Second World War period French companies and foreign-owned subsidiaries located in France have recruited their *cadres* directly from the *grandes écoles*, many have recruited exclusively from the *grandes écoles*, and indeed some companies have a known predilection for graduates from some particular *grande école*. In French companies, young management recruits who have a *grande école* education behind them are said to be on *la voie royale*, the royal route to career advancement.

To offer a broader picture it should be said that not all French managers are ex-*grande école*. SMEs (small and medium sized companies) will for the most part not be able to attract illustrious *grande école* graduates (or be able to pay them appropriate salaries). Or again some graduates of the university as opposed to the *grande école* sector find employment in French companies; this is particularly likely where the company wants to hire staff in some subject that is not part of the *grande école* curriculum but that is taught at university level, for example information technology. It has also been the case that service sector companies generally (excluding financial services) and retailing in particular are not attractive to *grande école* graduates, and companies in this sector have typically recruited less augustly qualified trainees, especially the graduates of the IUT (Instituts Universitaires de Techologie) sector. The IUTs offer courses that are shorter than those of traditional universities and are more vocationally oriented – both with regard to engineering and commerce specialisms. Again as noted at the start, France is a country with a high proportion of small, typically family-owned firms; it is also a country where rather a lot of large companies have a particular individual or family as the principal shareholder. In consequence inheritance, being born into the right family, will lead relatively more people into the reaches of owner-management in France than in say Britain, and particularly in the case of smaller firms where people are unlikely to be *grande école* graduates.

Strengths

The dominant system of *cadre* recruitment via the extremes of educational attainment distinguishes France. While educational credentials play a role in manager selection everywhere, the near exclusive weight given to these considerations in France is in contrast with, for example, the American emphasis on drive and performance, the British emphasis on social skills and personality, the German emphasis on specialized knowledge and understanding, and so on. These contrasts sometimes lead foreigners (non-French people) to make a bit of a pastiche of the French system. There is a critique to be offered, but it is important at this stage to underline the strengths of the system:

- French managers are undoubtedly bright, when it comes to formal educated cleverness they arguably have more of it than managers anywhere else in the world.
- The arduous years of study, especially at the *prépa*, develop a capacity for sustained hard work and concentration.
- The French education system is particularly good at developing intellectual qualities such as rigour, analysis, synthesis, logical consistency; this shows in later life in the sense that French thinking, French exposition, French argument tend to be lucid, sequential, consistent.
- The educational *élan* of the French manager implies greater powers of communication, written and oral; in particular, levels of verbal fluency are high; for the French manager the language is not a tool but a cultural benefit and a vehicle for demonstrating style and wit.
- French managers tend to be numerate (remember the tyranny of the Bac S with the heavy diet of maths!).
- What one might call 'engineering appreciation' is widespread among French management; remember some two-thirds of the *grandes écoles* are engineering schools; people trained there may not have all the practical prowess of a German *Fachhochschule* trained engineer, but they will have understanding and appreciation.
- French *cadres* are likely to be strong on *culture générale*, be interested in and able to talk about literature and drama and politics and philosophy,

in contrast to the often narrow focus on business in the Anglo-Saxon world.

- Success in the educational contest will endow the French manager with a high level of self-confidence; the *voie royale* and all that!
- Each *grande école* is a magnificent contact net, and the *grandes écoles* considered collectively produce a unitary elite who 'speak the same language', prize the same qualities, have the same approach.

A unitary elite

It may be helpful to elaborate on this idea of a unitary elite, which again is distinctively French. It has been made clear that the majority of senior managers in high profile companies have a *grande école* background, and that this is the dominant model that colours the whole system. But it is also the case that pretty-well every elite in France – intellectual, political, and administrative, as well as business and industrial – is predominantly *grande école* educated. So that most French presidents went to one or more *grandes écoles*, as did most prime ministers, party leaders, government ministers, and above all civil servants.

These shared educational antecedents make for rapport, shared values, ease of communication, and the relative absence of mutually hostile stereotypes between elite groups which are common in other countries. In consequence France has been at its best at the interface between engineering and government in the post Second World War period. A lot of successes in this period, for example the TGV train, nuclear power, military aviation, helicopters, telecommunications, and so on, have occurred where the French state took the lead while cooperating with leading companies; the latter supply the research, development, and manufacturing capability while the government commissions, encourages, facilitates, organises credit, and provides a market.

There is indeed a further twist to this 'common ancestry' argument via the institution of *pantouflage*. The essence of *pantouflage* is that individuals will make a mid-career move from prestigious posts in the government service to commerce and industry, starting their new company-based careers at or near the top. This will typically happen to people in the most prestigious part of the French civil service, the so called *grands corps*, and is something that may occur when people are in their late 30s to late 40s. While *pantouflage* is most likely in the defence industry, or into companies which are in the state sector or are contractors to the government, it is not limited to such cases. Traces of *pantouflage* may be found in other countries but France is unusual in the scale of this phenomenon and in the fact that it is largely taken for granted. Thus the unitary elite model may be so depicted.

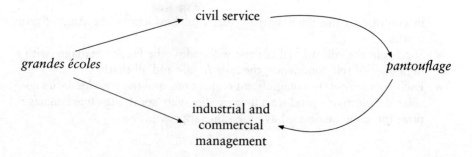

The fact that this one-way movement from the *grands corps* to senior management does occur leads to another kink in this education–occupation system. It is quite common for high-flyers to go to more than one *grande école* to demonstrate their fitness *par excellence* for elite membership. So for instance one might go to both a general engineering school and to another specialising in some particular branch of engineering. And particularly sought after as 'a second stay' *grande école* is the Ecole Nationale d'Administration (ENA) which in turn is a jumping off ground for the *grands corps*, which in turn may lead, as we have seen, to a top job in banking or industry. So if one sought to end up as the head of a company an ideal route would be:

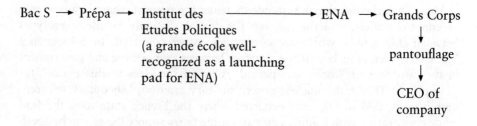

The irony is that one's best route to top management is based on avoiding any prior contact with industry in favour of the civil service and its training college!

A French understanding of management

It should be clear that the French understanding of the nature and challenge of management differs in emphasis and priority from the Anglo-Saxon norm. In the French scheme of things management is an intellectual task: it is about analysis and formal decision-making, about the ability to master complicated issues quickly and make rational judgements upon them, it is about understanding and synthesis and the logical demonstration of imperatives.

Now while these elements are not absent from the understanding of management in other countries they are more prominent in the French mind, and are emphasized in preference to the more down-to-earth issues of 'selling decisions', implementation, removal of 'road blocks', sustaining motivation, and getting people to 'buy into' projects.

This different conception of management is reflected in advertisements for management posts. These give special prominence to the fundamental educational requirement, using a 'bac +2/3/4' or whatever formula to indicate the number of years of full-time study beyond the baccalaureate exam that is needed to reach the appropriate level of education – a formula that is instantly meaningful to French applicants. Executive adverts indeed sometimes name the particular *grande école* or more often a group of status-equal *grandes écoles* from which they would deem applicants to be suitable. What is more while the advertisements do increasingly carry references to energy, performance, and self-starter qualities, this is a fairly recent development, first observable in the 1990s. On the other hand French management adverts often include a reference to more cerebral qualities of brilliance, rigour, powers of analysis and synthesis.

The same phenomenon, the preoccupation with educational qualifications, often pervades the French CV. By Anglo-Saxon standards a French CV is short, dry, and incomplete. For a person starting out on a management career at the end of a lengthy period of formal education, the CV will do little more than note these educational milestones – which baccalaureate exam (ideally Bac S of course), grades if honourable, *concours*, *grandes école*, and dates. If the applicant has any work experience, either in terms of internships or first job, these will be recorded – but rather dryly – there is seldom any American-style attempt to 'talk up' these experiences, to make them sound good. Also typically absent is the British style enumeration of leisure interests and activities and voluntary organization memberships that are meant to indicate balance, social skills and extrovert competence.

Clearly if you have done the right things educationally, no 'talking up' or 'fleshing out' is required. Doing well in the *concours* and attending a decent *grande école* says it all.

Making careers

For the typical *grande école* entrant to management, career development will largely take care of itself: there are few choices in the hands of the new graduates. First of all only big companies are acceptable; there can be no trade-off of greater responsibility earlier against lesser corporate standing. Second, retail must be avoided like the plague (demeaning for a *grande école* graduate, they might want you to have a spell on the shop floor, proving yourself among ordinary people – a Frenchman does not spend two years at the *prépa* study-ing seventy hours a week to end up working with ordinary people). Third, there is a general bias in favour of high tech companies, companies whose customers are other companies, organizations or the government; a *grande école* graduate does not choose the food processing industry or a consumer products company. Fourth, it goes without saying that the company chosen must be headquartered in Paris – though pretty well every company one has heard of, apart from Michelin, is. Finally one will choose functions and activities which are concep-tual rather then tangible: Marketing which is about concepts and analysis is better than sales which simply 'moves produce'; finance which is nicely abstract is better than manufacturing; human resource management (HRM) is better than purchasing, and so on.

But aside from such basic and initial choices *grande école* graduates can, to a large extent, sit back and let the company do it for them. After all the company knows what it wants and where to get it – that is why it recruited from the *grandes écoles* in the first place. It has paid a lot for these elitist entrants to corporate life and given them early *cadre* status. Their development will be a prime concern of the HRM department. They will be given interesting assign-ments, sent out to the provinces or abroad on missions, attached to senior people in PA roles – generally allowed to display their strengths; cleverness and confidence.

Generalism, specialism and mobility

In attempts to characterize management in different societies one may distin-guish between a generalist and specialist orientation. Britain is clearly general-ist. The presumption is that management is a matter of personality, social skills, leadership qualities, getting on with people. A person who has these will make good as a manager, and such qualities are required in the management role whether one is running a brewery or a machine tool company, whether one is working in personnel or marketing. The American view is similar stressing the need for drive, ambition, energy, social competence, and an understanding of management systems.

Germany on the other hand, and countries influenced by the German mode, take a more specialist view of management, seeing discrete jobs each requir-ing special, and different, knowledge and training. In Germany managers are largely recruited, placed, and advanced in terms of specialist knowledge and experience.

If we ask how management in France is to be classed on the generalist versus specialist continuum, the answer is that France has a generalist view of man-agement. But it is important to note that the French view is not a replication of the British and American. The French concept is rather one of intellectual generalism; the challenges of business and industry, and for that matter of government and administration, require the response of a trained mind, the product of educated cleverness.

Mobility in the primary sense of the mobility of managers between different companies, leaving one company and joining another, or not doing so, is known to vary from country to country, and there is some pattern. Commitment to a specialist view of management tends to go with low rates of inter-company mobility. If one believes management jobs to be discrete, to require particular competences and specialised knowledge, then inter-company mobility makes little sense; at least any such mobility would have to be between different companies in the same industry.

On the other hand countries committed to a generalist view of management may or may not have higher rates of inter-company mobility. Japan has a generalist understanding of management, but as is well known, very low rates of inter-company mobility. Whereas the USA, another generalist country, appears to have high mobility rates, and more importantly, takes a positive view of mobility seeing it as evidence of energy and ambition.

In this connection France is an interesting case, in that mobility is uneven, a little patchy, rather than something about which one can generalize in a confident way. For the most part mobility occurs:

- in particular functions or industries, for example in the sales function, in advertising, in PR (public relations) in IT (information technology),
- in the subsidiaries of American MNCs (multinational corporations),
- in the early stages of a management career,
- at the very top, with *pantouflage* and (often state sponsored) moves between top jobs in different companies.

But on the whole the French tradition does not favour high rates of inter-company mobility. It has certainly been frowned on in heavy industry, banks, and government-owned companies. As with so much else in France, a clue to this traditional orientation is to be found in educational qualifications. If one is a *grande école* graduate mobility is not necessary; if one is not, mobility is not for the most part possible – one's best chance will be to advance in one company through proven competence and loyalty.

Work relations

There is general agreement that work relations in France are more formal, often more impersonal, and arguably more hierarchial.

First of all French people are more likely to draw a clear line between work and non-work than are either the British or the Americans. Relationships at work, that is to say, are less likely to be carried over into leisure time, there will be less 'slipping out to the pub' at Friday lunch time, less meeting up out of working hours to some social or recreational end. Similarly, French people at work will be more likely to keep their private life private, will volunteer less in the way of autobiographical information. And they are less likely to relish questions about their out-of-work lives, their husbands or wives, or what they did over the weekend.

Second, there is rather less humour in the French workplace than in say the typical British one. And what humour there is will be less likely to serve a bonding, or 'including-in', function. Indeed the French penchant is for wit rather than humour, and wit of course requires brains and verbal fluency and the power of allusion. So the quality of wit in a French company will rise as one goes up the organizational (and educational) hierarchy. As Jean-Louis Barsoux once remarked, understanding a joke in France is like passing an intelligence test (Barsoux and Lawrence, 1997).

Third, the hierarchy is more self-conscious, predominates, and there is less mixing across ranks or levels. A French employee who has a problem will be more inclined to pass it up to the next level for resolution. Interestingly a multi-country study of manager values conducted by André Laurent found that French managers were inclined to agree with the statement:

A manager must have to hand precise answers to questions subordinates may raise about their work.

Of the national groups in the survey 13 per cent of the American managers accepted this, 30 per cent of the British managers, and 59 per cent of the French (Laurent, 1986).

French managers rely more obviously on the authority of office, rather than on personal qualities or pull, when they decide, instruct, give directions. They are inclined to take themselves and their authority more seriously. And rank will be protected. French managers will not be expected to work in open plan offices, eat with manual or even clerical workers, go on works outings or receive feedback from subordinates. Indeed it is not uncommon for French managing directors to have offices with sound-proof doors.

Meetings are also part of French management formality. Meetings are an indisputable part of management work the world over, and yet in most countries managers individually claim that meetings take up too much of their time. French managers, on the other hand, are inclined to take a positive view of formal meetings, see them as the essence of the management task, as the only way to get things done. French meetings are also distinctive: there is more eloquence, more analysis, more intellectual point scoring, and more ready discussion of general ideas.

Finally there is something different about the quality of work groups in France. Groups do form, but they tend to be based on a perception of common interests, on the defence of *droits acquis* (acquired rights and privileges) rather than on natural affinity or sociability. Work groups are job-specific, section-specific, function-specific. Groups are not likely to include people from *different* hierarchical levels or different management departments. The American idea of the task force, where people from different departments and different levels come together, pursue some one-off objective for a time with every appearance of cooperation and conviction, and then disband when the objective has been achieved, is deeply disquieting to the French – they just know this is a con!

While this short section has drawn attention to the more formal and hierarchical nature of work relations in French companies, it should be said that this is not the whole story. Running through all this are elements of irreducible individualism, confusion, and creativity.

So that while French organizations are more rule-focused there is probably more infraction of rules. While there are more procedures, these are external to the individual, at most a little constraining, but not something you have to believe in. While there are more meetings, these offer more scope for the expression of ideas and are less constrained by agendas. In short some creative informality is counterpoised to the dominant formalism.

Assessment

Already in this chapter we have been concerned to draw attention to the strengths of the French system including:

- the undoubted quality of the *grandes écoles* graduates,
- the symmetry between the French understanding of the management task and the selection and recruitment system,
- the advantages that derive from a unitary elite with common educational antecedents,
- the positive effect through much of the post-Second World War period of cooperation between industrial, political, and administrative elites.

But it is also necessary to face up to the question: Is there a downside? We would like to suggest three possible lines of criticism.

First, while in the late 1990s there have been a few well-publicised cases of French companies announcing that they will cast their recruitment net more widely, take (some) candidates from the universities, the IUTs, and elsewhere, the bulk of the *cadre* population is still recruited from the *grande écoles*. This is quite simply demotivating and limiting for everyone else, and tends to downplay by implication non-ratiocinative abilities.

Second, at the risk of being a bit flippant, one might say of French management that if it helps to be clever they will do it well, and if it doesn't they won't.

So:

- French companies tend to do big things well and small things badly, because all the brains are concentrated at the top, the 'lower downs' are more alienated than their counterparts in other countries and are not going to 'buy into' the system.
- Implementation is not a French strength; it is an unprogrammable, messy, hands-on, compromise-driven enterprise best delegated to somebody more junior.
- Teamwork does not come naturally to the French for reasons already explored including individualism, formalism, hierarchialism, and a system of elite recruitment and advancement likely to alienate the non-selected.
- Motivation is problematic for French managers, because it is difficult to 'get close to' subordinates, difficult to appeal to them, difficult to overcome their reluctance to surrender too much of themselves to any employing organization, or even to pretend to do this – a facility that comes naturally to Americans; in consequence French managers over-rely on their formal authority, and pull rank when necessary; they are also forced into an over-reliance on objective rationality.

Some of these strands may be identified in a *cause célèbre* of the late 1990s, the closure of the Renault plant at Vilvoorde in Belgium. This gruesome little narrative began in March 1997 when Renault President Louis Schweitzer announced the intended closure of their Belgian subsidiary plant employing 3180 people to make the Clio and Megane models.

The reasons given for this move were company and industry over-capacity, falling sales and profits, and the need to cut costs. We should say straightaway that our concern here is not to question the objective rationality of the decision but to draw attention to other considerations.

Schweitzer's decision caused an uproar. This was made worse by the fact that the Vilvoorde plant was located in the Belgian prime minister's constituency! The prime minister apostrophized the decision as 'brutal' and slammed Renault for lack of consultation. It was also rumoured that Schweitzer tried to get local management to drive completed cars out of the factory compound lest they were impounded or vandalized by Belgian workers.

But perhaps most interesting is the effect of the announcement on Renault's *French* workforce. One might have expected that the French employees would be at least secretly relieved that it was the Belgians who were being sacrificed while French jobs would be secure. But no, Renault's French employees made common cause with their Belgian colleagues and after a demonstration in Paris, not Brussels, in June 1997 Schweitzer was obliged to rescind his decision, and offer an independent committee to examine the viability of the Belgian plant (it did not make any difference, of course, except to Schweitzer's reputation as a macho manager).

Now we would reiterate that the rationale for closing the Belgian plant is not the point at issue. Schweitzer's original decision was received favourably by the financial press, and eventuated in at least a short-term boost in the Renault share price. But the Vilvoorde story does raise issues of human concern, political feasibility, and implementation that go beyond the imperatives of corporate strategy. In the history of industrial man, no one has ever been persuaded by objective rationality when it put them on the street!

And what of Louis Schweitzer? His career exemplifies the forces discussed in this chapter, namely:

ENA (very prestigious
grande école)

↓

*Inspecteur des Finance
Grand Corp*, high status
job in French civil service,
chef de cabinet
for Budget Minister

↓

chef de cabinet
for Industry & Research Minister

↓

top management team at
Renault, at age of 43
i.e. *pantouflage* as described
earlier in the chapter

↓

PDG (managing director)
of Renault, 1994

↓

'World famous in Belgium' 1997

The underlying issue here is that a society that recruits its elite exclusively on the basis of educational brilliance is asserting the priority of objective rationality over other considerations: this will not always be good news.

The third general criticism of the French system that we would like to run concerns the unitary elite. There are advantages in recruiting a national elite in an objective fashion that commands respect and acceptance: to put it bluntly there is much to be said for picking the elite in terms of brains. But there is a corresponding disadvantage. It is not that the French elite lack strengths, but that they all have the same strengths. They are all bright, they all come from the *grandes écoles*, there is mobility between the different sectors of the elite, they all know each other or can at least 'access' each other, and they are all centred in Paris.

An elite so constituted poses the problem of necessary variety. A national elite has to relate to the environment and its changing demands. For this it needs a *variety* of abilities – including the possibility of alternative perceptions of reality and rival responses. This necessary variety is precisely what the French elite lacks.

Change?

It is probably desirable to pose the question: Is there any reason to expect that the key elements of French business and management outlined in this chapter are changing? It is a difficult question to answer, because we do not know how far certain trends apparent in the late 1990s will go, nor the extent to which the French state may be able to neutralize certain pressures for change from the outside (they have been pretty good at it in the past!). It is also the case that there seem to be developments pointing in different directions.

First of all one might note a general paradox. This is that in the ten years or more in which I have been interested in French management, it seems to have stayed remarkably the same – that is to say, same recruitment patterns, same style, same mix of strengths and weaknesses, same articulation via the *grandes écoles* to other national elites – and I have discussed this judgement with French people in a position to know, and had it confirmed.

At the same time, the 1990s have seen significant change in international and business relations, including:

- the fall of European communism in the first part of the decade, and the progressive opening up of the former command economics of Central and Eastern Europe (Lawrence, 1998),
- the Gulf War of 1991, and continuing tensions in the Middle East,
- the advent of the Single European Market in 1992–93, the package of measures to eliminate non-tariff barriers in the European Union (EU) (Lawrence, 1998),
- the enlargement of the EU with the accession of Finland, Sweden, and Austria in 1995, and pressure from Central European states to be admitted,
- growing internationalization of business,
- privatization and deregulation favoured by many Western governments,
- the progressive withdrawal of the USA from world economic leadership even though the American economy has boomed for much of the 1990s.

So the question with which we started might be reformulated as: Will any of this affect specifically business and management in France?

The rational answer would appear to be that France will be affected. We showed at the outset that capitalism in France is different. But it is now likely that:

- the growing control by the EU of the affairs of its member states,
- the growing internationalization of business,
- the result of privatization and deregulation,

will all serve to limit the options of the French state, and to reduce the distinctiveness of French capitalism.

There is another angle. We have noted in the earlier discussion of the *malaise des cadres* that downsizing and delayering are leading to *cadre* unemployment, and at the same time intensification of competition will push the trend further and lead companies to recruit and appoint fewer *cadres*, and to do it on the cheap. And one can certainly save money by recruiting people who do not have a *grande école* background.

The personal care products company L'Oréal, for example, caused a stir in the Spring of 1995 when it announced that it would pay particular attention to applications from *autodidactes* (it means people who are self-taught, the French euphemism for those lacking higher education). Or again Andersen Consulting in 1996 announced that it would allocate 75 posts to university as opposed to *grandes écoles* graduates.

French companies that engage in initiatives of this kind tend to be seen as reformers, taking forward the egalitarian spirit. But it may be the case that all they want to do is save money, and an *autodidactes* is a whole lot cheaper than someone who went to ENA.

Put more broadly the hypothesis is that business change may cause management change, and even some reconfiguration of French capitalism and the French elite. At the time of writing (early 1998) these are speculations rather than prophecies.

References

Barsoux, Jean-Louis and Peter Lawrence (1997) *French Management: Elitism in Action*, London: Cassell.

Canadian High Commission (1997) *Canada Focus*, Vol. 5, Number 41, 12 December.

Gordon, Colin (1996) *The Business Culture in France*, Oxford: Butterworth Heinemann.

Laurent, André (1986) 'The Cross Cultural Puzzle of Global Human Resource Management', *Human Resource Management*, Vol. 25, No. 1, 133–48.

Lawrence, Peter (1998) *Issues in European Business*, Basingstoke and London: Macmillan.

Thurow, Lester (1996) *The Future of Capitalism: How today's economic forces shape tomorrow's world*, London: Nicholas Brealey.

CHAPTER 4

Italy

Two of the major European countries discussed in this book, Germany and Italy, achieved political integration at a late stage, namely in the second half of the nineteenth century. The general view is that both have been affected by this late achievement of statehood, albeit in different ways. In the case of Italy the principal effect appears to be a relatively low identification with the nation state, something that is manifest in both positive and negative ways. The latter would include:

- a diffusely cynical attitude towards the state, a feeling that it is there to be deceived, outwitted, and if possible ripped-off,
- widespread tax evasion,
- organized lawlessness in the south in the form of the Camorra and the Mafia,
- a somewhat exploitative attitude to employment in the state bureaucracy, with over-staffing matched by underperforming and both of them topped off with moonlighting.

Perhaps ironically this bundle of negative civic attitudes is reflected in the views regularly expressed by Italian managers in attitude surveys in which, as we shall see, there is a striking emphasis on order, structure, and authority, an emphasis that is no doubt compensatory.

The positive manifestations:

- strong local and/or regional loyalties (as opposed to national identification),
- a stronger attachment to the institution of the family than is the case in most other European states,

also have implications for business and industry.

In Italy the family is the primary focus of affectivity and loyalty: everyone else and every other institution, including the state, are fair game. This idea is nicely caught by Tim Parks, an Englishman with an Italian wife living near Verona, who speaks affectionately of an acquaintance, one Francesco who is an adjuster for a car insurance company. Francesco knows that people will try to include in the accident repairs to be paid for by the insurance company all sorts of prior mechanical defects and bodywork blemishes that have nothing to do with the accident in question. He knows all that, but his company will pay anyway. But says Parks reflectively:

> After all that is why car insurance is so expensive. So everyone can exploit it.

And Parks draws the moral:

> Clearly, Francesco is infinitely better equipped than I am to give an Italian child an education (Parks, 1996:89).

Not only are families stronger in Italy, but the family is more frequently a unit of economic production as well as consumption. So there are more family firms in Italy than in most European countries, there are more small firms, the family is more often the source of working capital, a family ownership stake in large companies is more common than elsewhere (for example Fiat), and the role of share capital in economic life is relatively slight. On this point, according to William Brierley, the total market capitalization of the Milan stock exchange is only 16–17 per cent of GDP as against 55 per cent for the Wall Street exchange and 98 per cent for the London stock exchange (Brierley, 1993). This striking statistic also reflects the size of the state-owned sector in Italy, of which more later.

The other positive manifestation, the nexus of local–regional attachments, is something of a *cause célèbre* among both Italians and others writing about Italy. Luigi Barzini in his famous monograph on Italian society waxes lyrical on the minutiae of local differentiation (Barzini, 1964). Or again John Haycraft, an Englishman who lived expatriately in Italy and ran a language school, speaks with conviction of every town having a distinct identity, together with its own cuisine, festivals, saints, fairs, and so on.

Most famous in the matter of regional differences is the famous north–south divide. The north is more prosperous, has low unemployment levels, is generally industrialized, and has more sizeable towns. And in the mid 1990s it even came to espouse breakaway ambitions of seceding from the 'Italian nation' and developed a political party dedicated to this end. In contrast the south is traditionally agricultural (with a few implants of large northern companies such as the Alfa Sud works at Naples), is much poorer, has been plagued by the Mafia and similar organizations, and as of 1997 reported an unemployment rate of 22 per cent (it is about 7–8 per cent for northern and central Italy). Employment with government organizations, civil service jobs in conventional English, are particularly popular in the south, where the excesses of an over-manned but rather inefficient bureaucracy are most in evidence.

The north–south problem is not new, and it has been well documented in fiction and memoires. In the 1930s Carlo Levi, a middle-class Turin Jew, was rusticated to the south for political activity during the Mussolini period. In his account *Christ Stopped at Eboli* (Levi, 1947) he has left a searing picture of southern backwardness – not just of poverty but of a lack of civic amenities, a grotesque survival of personal power among the privileged, and of a primitiveness of relationships. Ignazio Silone's *Fontamara* originally published in 1934 shows the repressive use of political power against the southern poor (Silone, 1946). At a somewhat later stage an American woman, Ann Cornelisen, describes in her book *Torregreca: A World in Southern Italy* her attempts to act as a change agent and quality-of-life improver in a remote southern township (Cornelisen, 1969). The captivating thing about her account is how far removed this world is from the modernities and prosperity of north-west Europe at that time.

In the 1950s and 1960s when Italy experienced massive economic growth the unemployment and underemployment problems of the south were in a sense eliminated by migration to the more prosperous north. But in the late 1990s this migration has largely ended, as the demand for unskilled and semi-skilled blue collar workers has receded, not just in northern Italy but world-wide. Today (late 1990s) it is only the more talented and qualified southerners, young people for the most part, who exit the region for reasons of career opportunity. According to *The Economist* survey (November 1997) the pattern of unemployment has changed somewhat in the south. The numbers unemployed remain high, and they have for the most part been unemployed for more than a year, but they seem reconciled to their fate, getting along as best as they can with social security benefits and a bit of remunerated employment in the black economy, but above all being supported by their families long term, where at least one family member will have a decently paid job, probably with the state. (Note the role of the family again, as a counterpoise to the state).

This persistent though not unchanging north–south divide does impact on the economic map of Italy, where:

- large private sector companies are concentrated almost exclusively in the north,
- the government is the largest employer in the south,
- there are different income and unemployment rates as between north and south,
- a more thorough-going industrialization of the south is impeded by poor infrastructure and the fear of (northern) companies that they will face Mafia extortion and perhaps executive kidnappings if they relocate to the south.

What is more the birth rates are different as between north and south, with reproduction rates being higher in the south. Again *The Economist* survey of November 1997 suggests that two positive developments in the south are firstly the declining influence of the Mafia, the view that northern public opinion has been outraged by Mafia minders and this is serving as a brake on Mafia influence, and that government funds to the south are now being channelled into more specific projects with a possible enhanced benefit to the region.

But with all, the fact remains that the north, and to an extent the middle, is where industry is. And as with industry, so with management. Using admittedly 1980s figures Claudio Pellegrini asserts a global population of 135 221 managers in Italy, distributed unevenly between the regions (Pellegrini, 1989):

67% in the North
22% in central Italy
11% in the South

Society and economy

So far we have canvassed three key themes:

- alienation from the (nation) state,
- the importance of region and locality,
- the effective centrality of the family,

and noted that these have some shaping effect on the economy.

But Italy is differentiated in other ways. By the standards of Western Europe it would probably be adjudged the country of natural disasters. Floods and mud slicks abound, earthquakes are not uncommon, Italy has active volcanoes, and of course Venice is always sinking! Some writers, John Haycraft for instance, suggest that the hovering threat of natural disaster induces a certain fatalism in Italians that in turn finds expression in the superficial hedonistic 'live for the moment' disposition popularly associated with the Italians. It is also possible that co-existing with this is a certain preventive cautiousness surrounding insurance, house purchase, provision for family members, and so on.

We have noted the importance of the government as a source of stable and (early) pensionable employment. It would be right to add that non-family life is experienced by Italians as more constraining – at least in theory; there are quite simply more regulations, prohibitions, and forms to fill in. Tim Parks again writes entertainingly of a mercy dash to the maternity hospital with his wife experiencing frequent and painful contractions. On arrival however, a scene from ER does not ensue, but a lengthy form-filling ordered by a man at the reception desk! On reaching the labour ward there is another form to fill but the happy couple's second child is born before the form is completed (Parks, 1996).

This bureaucratization of everyday life, conjoined with the alienation from the state, induces a certain ingenuity in attempts to beat the system. Parks again tells an engaging story of buying a house, for which he signs two contracts – one specifying a modest purchase price for the benefit of the authorities, another specifying a higher price to be actually paid to the builder, with the stipulation that the second contract has to be torn up after payment, and this done before witnesses, so that no one will ever know what the real price was (Parks, 1996). Some of this ingenuity doubtless finds its way into business life.

Again in Italian organizations while communications are formalized at one level, at another they are marked by an immediacy and intimacy. This in turn is sometimes thought to relate to the lack of a British-style class system in Italy. While there may be some general snobbery there is not much innate sense of class. Communicativeness and sociability transcend the social hierarchy. The sharp-witted worldliness of Italians to which we have drawn attention is sometimes thought to be somehow inversely related to the influence of the Catholic church – even if only 30 per cent of the population claim to be practising Catholics and divorce has been allowed since 1970. The idea is that the Church offers some 'division of labour' when it comes to contemplativeness and action. The Church does the soul-searching for you, while the citizenry are freed for money-making and the robust enjoyment of beating the government system.

Italy not only has a spectacular past – Etruscan civilization, the Roman Empire, the Renaissance, and so on – it also has a strong sense of the past. John Haycraft suggests that Italians tend to talk about historic events as though they had witnessed them, tend to cite historical events as causes of present states. At a more humble level foreign tourists in Italy are often struck by the way the locals interrogate them as to which historic or cultural attractions they have visited, implicitly suggesting a pride in all this on the part of quite ordinary people. This sense of past glories no doubt feeds a tendency to grandiloquence which in turn is exhibited quite strikingly in surveys of management attitudes.

Italy was not among the countries of Europe that industrialized early or comprehensively. And setting aside agriculture Italy was handicapped in the first wave of industrialization by its relative lack of raw materials. While Italy produces around a third of the world's supply of mercury, and there are some zinc and lead deposits on Sardinia, there is practically no coal and not much else. Nonetheless Italy was among the six founder members of what is now the European Union, and experienced massive growth attendant on EU entry: in the ten-year period 1957 to 1967 production increased 91 per cent – that is to say economic growth was faster than in Germany or France at that time, and by 1967 Italy had become the world's seventh industrial power, and is today of course a member of the G7 group.

Products and produce

Since Italy's industrialization is largely a phenomenon of the post-war period, and its industrial standing is perhaps not a part of its popular image, it may be helpful to indicate some of its strengths.

First of all Italy is a major producer of a whole range of food and drink products. It is one of the world's greatest wine and cheese producers, a leading producer of olive oil; oranges, tomatoes, and avocado pears are widely grown, indeed Italy produces a whole range of fruit and vegetables. Its ice-cream is famous, it has a number of confectionery specialities, and the company Ferrero Rocher is among the world's 'big six' confectionery companies along with Mars of the USA and Cadbury of Britain. Italy brews most of its own beer, though most Italian breweries are wholly or partly owned by brewers headquartered in the more traditional beer drinking countries.

Second, Italy is a major car producer. Amalgamations in the 1980s made Italy a one-car-company country, that company of course being Fiat, with former independent companies living on as marques or models within Fiat. In fact Italy is third place in Europe for number of cars produced, coming after Germany and France (Spain is in fourth place, Britain in fifth, and Sweden in sixth). What is more, Italian made cars tend to dominate the domestic market – something Italy has in common with its neighbour France, but which is less common in northern Europe.

Third, Italy is a significant producer of machine tools: Florence Vidal puts Italy in fourth place in the world for volume of machine tool production after Japan, Germany, and the former Soviet Union (Vidal, 1990). She particularly highlights the flexibility and adaptability of Italian machine tool manufacturers, and their willingness to engage in creative dialogue with customers, to adapt products to customer's particular needs, and to do this free: '*Cette adaption n'entraine pas de côut supplémentaire*' (Vidal, 1990:51).

Fourth, Italy makes textile machinery, and using 1980s data Vidal speaks of production in this industry as growing at 14–15 per cent per year. In the industry Vidal notes that Italy makes the whole range of textile machinery, and is in fourth position worldwide after Germany, Switzerland, and Japan in that order.

Fifth, Italy is a major producer of electrical consumer goods – dishwashers, washing machines, tumble driers, fridges, freezers, and so on – and there are a number of national champions in this industry. Interestingly the company that is probably best known abroad, Zanussi, was acquired in the 1980s by Electrolux of Sweden. This in itself is something of a national achievement in that by common consensus it has been a successful acquisition despite popular presumptions of cultural difference between the two countries concerned. Indeed Electrolux-Zanussi has found its way into the corporate strategy case books as something of a model for successful acquisition.

Sixth, Italy is also an armaments manufacturer, again with a variety of companies active in the industry, some of them in the state owned sector. Florence Vidal puts Italy in sixth place world-wide for armament exports, while noting that the end of the Iran–Iraq war depressed demand somewhat.

By general consensus Italian banks are the worst in Western Europe; poor service, low productivity, weak in terms of technology and systems, very slow to clear cheques, and living off high interest rates. On the little matter of cheque clearing Florence Vidal tersely remarks: '*il faut dire que les operations de clearing battent tous les records de lenteur*' (Vidal, 1990:93). Vidal also goes on to demonstrate that Italy is a country with a low number of personal bank accounts per head of population in relation to other Western countries; that is to say, it is under-banked. At the end of the 1990s, it is suggested that some improvement is at last occurring.

In contrast Italy clearly has strength in textiles, though the term is too staid to do justice to Italian elan. What Italy excels at is fashionable clothes, and a variety of accessories – jewellery, handbags, briefcases, belts, sunglasses, swimwear, scarves, ties, and more besides. One of these operations, Benetton, has become a world household name (try to think of a major city anywhere in the Triad – Western Europe, North America and Japan, the world's three richest areas – that does not have a Benetton), yet much of the manufacture takes place in small companies, often family companies, in what are known as industrial districts (Bull *et al.*, 1993). Something that Italy has done in this industry better than any other country in the world is to develop fashions for men, *changing* fashions. Any reader who would like to put this to the test is invited to take a stroll down Milan's Monte Napoleone and check out a few shops selling men's clothes: you are likely to find separate racks of ties, of the same quality, with the same fashion labels, but exhibiting 100 per cent price differentials – this year's and last year's models.

The itemization of particular industries in this section is not meant to be exhaustive but to 'put up on the screen' a mix of things that on the one hand belong to the popular image, for example fashion goods, and on the other, things that might not be widely known outside the circle of industry specialists, for example machine tools and armaments and textile machinery. It should be added that there are of course companies operating in chemicals, pharmaceuticals, petroleum refining, steel-making, computers and office machinery, and of course, ceramic tiles. This last named again achieved fame in the corporate strategy literature by being celebrated by Michael Porter as a leading example of structurally determined competitive advantage (Porter, 1990). Incidentally at the time of Porter's researches in the late 1980s Italian companies produced 30 per cent of world output of ceramic tiles and 60 per cent of world exports.

Finally there is the matter of tourism. In the popular mind Italy would be a top tourist country. In fact it is the third most visited country in Europe after France and Spain – Britain is in fourth place (*The Economist*, 1997). When one considers that Italy has not only the sun-sea-sand ensemble but also incomparable artistic and architectural attractions, then third place is rather disappointing (in fact France has something like 60 million visitors a year and Italy little over 30 million). *The Economist* survey suggests that part of the shortfall is the burden for Italy of maintaining its cultural treasures (plus some touristic under-development in the south).

State holdings in industry

A significant portion of the Italian economy is in the state sector. A number of quite large companies are grouped under several state holding organizations, of which the most important is IRI (Instituto per la Ricostruzione Industriale) set up in 1933 to rescue banks whose industrial investments were going wrong. IRI ended up taking over their investments, and by 1936 it had considerable holdings in steel, ship-building and telephones. IRI again took part in the post-war boom, and its initiatives included:

- starting the new steel plant of Taranto in the 'deep south',
- sponsoring some 5900 kilometres of autostrada (motorway) system,
- ditto the Alfasud factory outside Naples.

By the 1980s IRI controlled among other things, Finsinder (the national steel industry), three official TV channels, and the national carrier Alitalia. By the mid-1990s IRI companies employed 350 000 people (Edwards, 1996).

All this has certain consequences for management in Italy. First of all, as in France, a significant number of managers are employed in public sector companies (or at least companies that have been in the public sector). Second, there is at least a presumption that the ethos of these companies will be somewhat along the lines of the civil service rather than typical of private industry. Third, top management positions in these state sector companies are political appointments, and the constituent companies may in a literal sense be following a political agenda rather than a corporate strategy. One of the findings to emerge from André Laurent's research on the attitudes and values of managers in different countries is that a high proportion of the Italian sample regarded themselves as having a political role (and the same was true of the French managers); 'high' here means high in relation to the groups of managers from other countries (Laurent, 1986). Finally, employees may choose to work in organizations in this sector primarily for job security.

Big and small

A distinctive feature of the Italian economy is that while there are some big companies in the private sector – Fiat, Pirelli, Olivetti, for instance – they are not very numerous. Because there are few of them, what they do tends to be highlighted. And companies in this sector, especially Fiat took the lead in what is known in Italian industrial relations lore as the 'hot autumn' of 1969 when Fiat began to implement measures to reduce trade union power. Since then private sector large firms have led the way in rationalization, downsizing, and particularly outsourcing or subcontracting of services and supplies (Magrino, 1989). Another feature of this sector is that particular families are often principal shareholders or owners, even of the large companies – for instance the Agnellis and Fiat, the Benettons, and the Pirellis.

But what is regarded as the most distinctive feature of the Italian economy is the superabundance of small firms, most of them family firms. Indeed it does not end with manufacturing but extends to retail. As Edwards has pointed out Italy has more shops – small family-owned stores in particular – than anywhere else in Europe. So Italy may be under-banked (Vidal, 1990) but at least it is over-shopped (Edwards, 1996). These small firms flourish in such areas as fashion goods, furniture, and of course the famous ceramic tiles. The formation of small firms received a further thrust from the 'hot autumn' of 1969 as a result of large company lay-offs and more particularly outsourcing. The small firm sector is attractive to Italians because these little companies are less subject to the regulations of the Italian state, and the sector overlaps heavily with the black economy, said to account for 30 per cent of Italy's GDP.

There is a further twist to the small firms story. This is that in some cases they are grouped by industry in particular regions known as industrial districts, consisting of both competing firms doing the same thing, and other firms related to them as suppliers or by design input, sometimes sharing facilities or represented by product specific trade associations. This phenomenon is caught very nicely in an earlier account by Edwards:

> A key factor in this success has been security: rather than the small firm standing alone, it is a component in an overall system. The system comprises a group of companies in a specific geographical area that specializes in various aspects of the total production process (for example, the components, the final product and machinery required to manufacture the product or its components) (Edwards, 1996:2920).

Exchange of ideas, logistical simplicity, the mix of cooperation and competition are all claimed as virtues of the system, and as Edwards again puts it:

> Positive responses to customer demand result in upstream developments and innovations which help to ensure the overall viability of the system (Edwards, 1996:2921).

Or again Anna Bull and her colleagues work out the theme of the industrial district in a fascinating case study comparison of textile production as between Como, Leicester, and Lyon (Bull *et al.*, 1993).

Order and individuality

Running through any characterization of Italian management is the tension between order and individuality, and perhaps too between reality and appearances. This is compounded by the difficulty of generalizing across the three corporate sectors:

- big private sector companies,
- state owned firms reporting to government holding companies,
- SMEs (small-medium sized enterprises) mostly in the form of smallish family firms,

and indeed we have referred to some of the sector specific features at various points in the foregoing discussion. But it remains the case that the adage 'every study is only as good as it's sample' is more poignant for Italy than say for Britain or the USA.

In progressing the characterization in a more general way we are drawing on the Bocconni survey which has already been cited with reference to the outsourcing proclivities of large Italian companies (Magrino, 1989), the study of management attitudes in different countries carried out by André Laurent's survey of samples of managers from a range of countries attending post experience courses at his base at INSEAD (Laurent, 1986), and a similar study carried out by Barbara Senior and Peter Lawrence from the base of Nene College, Northampton in the late 1990s; some of this last research has been published in an earlier book by one of the present authors (Lawrence, 1998) and we will call it the Nene study. Both the Laurent and Nene studies are in the form of confronting managers with propositions about management work with which they are invited to agree or disagree: in both these studies the Italians have a distinctive profile. We have also 'plugged in' where possible to British and American managers with expatriate experience in Italy: these are good for telling you what is different.

Organizations as families

Writing elsewhere Vincent Edwards makes a strong case for organizations in Italy having a family character (Edwards, 1996). Now in the case of these very numerous small companies that have already been discussed that is of course literally true. The management team will be family, in many cases all the employees will be family, the capital may well be family savings, and patterns of influence in the firm are likely to reflect those of the family. Going beyond those companies which are literally family firms, however, the organization-as-family idea seems to have some metaphorical truth for larger companies, and there are three principal manifestations of this.

The first is that subordinates, managers and others, often behave in an unruly way, competing for attention and 'parental favour!' Meetings in Italian companies are often more tempestuous: people raise their voices, express themselves more dramatically, are more inclined to cut in on each other, than is common in northern Europe. This is often remarked upon by British and American managers visiting their corporate subsidiaries in Italy.

The second is that 'the children' expect their parents to keep them in order, and tell them what to do. This comes out very clearly in the Nene study, where several of the propositions throw up contrasts between Italian managers and their British counterparts. For instance the proposition:

Most employees like to be told what to do

was accepted by the Italian managers but rejected by the British. It does not get any more straightforward than this! But the proposition:

Employees at all levels should be consulted on matters of company policy and operation

and:

Employees should be able to challenge the views and decisions of management

and:

Employees should be represented on the boards of companies to protect workers' interests when policy decisions are made

were all rejected by the sample of Italian managers, but accepted by their British colleagues. You cannot in the Italian scheme of things have workers' reps on the board of directors: it would be like having kids on the PTA!

Third, in the family it is the parents who get to make the decisions no matter how much the children input their wants and wishes. What this gives you in Italian organizations is decisions being pushed upwards for ratification or approval. Again Anglo-American testimony is eloquent on this point. Managers from companies headquartered in the USA or UK visit Italian subsidiaries to help with tasks such as the implementation of IT systems or financial control measures or to extend the scope of BPR (business process re-engineering) schemes, deal with their opposite numbers, think they have got a deal, and then find it being referred upwards. One expatriate we interviewed spoke of the Italian company as 'putting in a buffer' between himself and the real decision-makers.

Personalism

In the literature in English on society in Latin America the terms personalism and clientism are used to signify a set of relationships that would be regarded as purely contractual-bureaucratic-impersonal in the West; but are never without a personalized element often in the form of protection for dependence, respect for favours, leader-cum-followership in South America. Now the similarity should not be forced but there is an element of this personalism in work organizations in Italy. As Edwards has argued, authority and communication tend to follow personal linkages rather than the mechanics of the organization chart (Edwards, 1996). Some of this is caught again by the Italian responses, contrasted with those of their British counterparts, in the Nene study. For example the proposition:

> At the end of the day, most managers want subordinates who are loyal rather than critical and challenging

expresses this idea of leader–follower, with personal devotion taking priority over professional competence. The Italian managers accept this proposition, but the British reject it. Similarly the proposition:

> Managers, because of their status, are entitled to respect from their subordinates

is also accepted by the Italian but rejected by the British managers. There is also evidence from the Laurent study (Laurent, 1986) of thinking in power terms. Laurent's proposition that hierarchy is about who has power over whom, is accepted by 50 per cent of the Italian managers, the highest proportion of all the national groups, with France second at 45 per cent (the USA was lowest at 18 per cent).

It is also suggested by Edwards that this personalism operates *between* organizations, or between the company and its environing society. So these personal linkages affect sales and purchasing decisions, and the allocation of contracts. In essence when you want something you do not turn to the Yellow Pages but to someone you know.

Individualism

Accounts of Italian society tend to emphasize a certain brand of individualism. It is not quite in the form of American style achievement drives and yearning for economic success, but something rather more difficult to characterize. Part of it is an ethic of personal responsibility. Both Barzini (1964) and Haycraft (1985) allude to an Italian readiness to assume responsibility for their fate in what is a presumptively hostile environment, at least outside of the supportive orbit of the family – by being worldly, cynically alert, ever watchful; ready to 'call in the chips' whenever necessary (and having an instinctive understanding of how these chips are to be created in the first place). Tim Parks, who loves them dearly but does not wear rose-tinted spectacles, pays tribute to the self-interested worldliness of Italians who are 'ready to fight for their gravy train' (Parks, 1996).

This individualism is registered by Hofstede in his famous study of IBM employees in a variety of countries, where the Italian sample register a high score on his individualism versus collectivism dimension (Hofstede, 1980). Or again one of André Laurent's propositions is to the effect that managers may be motivated more by the desire to gain power than by the wish to achieve corporate objectives. 63 per cent of the Italian managers accept this proposition, that is, vote for power rather than objectives; France has the second highest score on power with 56 per cent; Denmark is lowest at 25 per cent (Laurent, 1986).

Innovation and flexibility

Various authorities on Italy have drawn attention to an Italian esprit for innovation-creativity-flexibility, and this in particular is the main contention of Florence Vidal's monograph on Italian management (Vidal, 1990). She cites the machine tool and textile machinery industries as examples of this flexibility in action in the service of customers. The creativity of Italian fashion designers is legendary. Or at a different level, one of the present writers has paid tribute elsewhere to the ability of Italian executives to re-configure the strategic imperatives of an industry (Lawrence, 1998). This flexibility and speed of response is also generally attributed to Italy's host of small firms (Edwards, 1996).

In the face of the ensemble of praise a word of warning is perhaps in order. It is not the case that Italian industry is distinguished in the sense of a high R&D (research and development) spend; and Italy has also been criticized from within for relative weaknesses in innovative industries such as IT and telecommunications (Celli, 1997). It is rather the case that there is a link between the flexibility-creativity asserted here and the individualism explored in the previous section. Italians have excelled in thinking the unthinkable and designing the inconceivable. A nice touch might be added to this discussion with reference to the Bocconi survey (Magrino, 1989) which draws attention to the absence of personnel procedures in the majority of Italian companies. This may be interpreted as a rejection of measures that would be confining rather than ennobling, a tribute to Italian belief in its virtuosity.

Qualificational levels

Italy is not Germany or Switzerland, it is not the land of apprenticeships and vocationally oriented courses at a level between secondary school and university: it is the land of formal, university level education. This emerged clearly in the Bocconi study where 70 per cent of the sample were university graduates, and 93 per cent of the managers had studied at university (Magrino, 1989). The pattern of subjects studied tends to be what Anglo-Saxons think of as continental European, namely engineering, economics and law, typically in that order. In fact three-quarters of the Bocconi sample who were graduates had studied engineering or science subjects, a fact that finds some confirmation in the Nene study where the proposition:

> The engineering function should be a path to senior positions in manufacturing industry

was accepted by the Italian managers but rejected by the British. Another nice insight is offered by André Laurent whose proposition that managers should have precise answers for questions that subordinates might pose, was accepted by 66 per cent of the Italian managers, the highest score for any national group. A splendid testimony to the Italian belief in the authority that is confirmed by formal knowledge.

Mobility

Evidence on the mobility of Italian managers between companies, and even between functions/departments of the same company is not as abundant as one might wish, but still the consensus is that Italy is a low mobility country. The managers who figured in the Bocconi survey are a case in point, where 60 per cent of the sample had worked in only one company and 50 per cent plus in only one function. Furthermore very few had worked in more than one industry, and even fewer had worked abroad. Yet in contrast one-quarter of the top managers in the Bocconi survey had postgraduate qualifications, mostly from abroad.

It is easy to see a number of constraints on mobility in the Italian case, which clearly include:

- the numerical predominance of small, often family firms,
- the semi-dependent nature of management appointments in the government sector companies,
- the fact that there are simply not that many big firms in the private sector, such that in many industries there will not be *alternative* employers, as in larger economies such as those of Germany or Japan.

Then again there is the mildly specialist orientation of Italian management – the predominance of science and engineering graduates, the famous commitment à la André Laurent to giving precise (= industry specific) answers to subordinates' questions, and so on. Also the personalism noted in an earlier section will, in a diffuse way, act against mobility.

Finally, there is the much vaunted Italian attachment to locality and region, which will disincline people to engage in geographic moves in pursuit of their careers. On the subject of regionalism Tim Parks quotes a survey that shows higher divorce rates for couples where the partners come from different regions rather than having married 'in state' (Parks, 1996). Incidentally the explanation given in the source quoted by Parks is that with the cross-region marriages the husband will be exposed to dishes which his wife cooks to different recipes from those of his mother. There is no arguing with this.

Seniority

As a footnote to the discussion of mobility it should be mentioned that seniority has traditionally been of importance in Italian management, as it has also been in France. There is evidence at least from the 1980s that seniority plays a significant part in contractual pay. According to Santini, seniority directly or indirectly constitutes about 20 per cent of pay after 10 years of service and 38–40 per cent after 20 years (Santini, 1986).

Virtuosity rather than efficiency

Also running through the literature on Italian management is the idea that the strengths are creative rather than stabilizing, adaptive and responsive rather than forward looking and contingency controlling. As Edwards puts it:

> The predominance of interpersonal relationships is said to militate against the effective implementation of formal organizational structures. Italian managers, moreover, appear more effective at responding to situations than in planning for them (Edwards, 1996:2923).

Intimations of order

Probably the strongest impression created by the survey evidence on Italian management is its preoccupation with order and definition, variously manifested. In André Laurent's study the majority of the Italian managers believed in detailed job descriptions (90 per cent) and in the individual's functions being well-defined (94 per cent). In a consistency checking questionnaire item asserting that managers would achieve more if their roles were less clearly defined 69 per cent of the Italians disagreed. The Italian managers led the field on all of these.

Or again in response to one of Laurent's propositions that organizations would be better if conflict could be eliminated for ever (a strongly worded proposition for sure) 41 per cent of Italians agreed, the highest level of agreement for any of the national groups (at the other end of the scale, the corresponding figure for Swedish managers was 4 per cent). The Italians also had a high score (81 per cent) agreeing that an organizational structure where an individual has two bosses, that is a matrix structure, should be avoided at all costs (the French and Belgian managers scored a little higher). And the Italian managers had the highest score (75 per cent) disagreeing with the proposition that it is often necessary to bypass the chain of command.

This same concern with order and definition emerges from the Nene study, over 10 years later and based on different samples. First of all the concern with role precision is replicated by the Nene study where the proposition:

> Organizational success comes from maintaining a stable organization structure where everyone knows their role and position and works within it

was accepted by the Italians but rejected by the British. Or again the Nene study yielded the same anti-conflict orientation identified by André Laurent. The Nene proposition:

> Conflict over scarce resources is inevitable in most organizations

was accepted by the British, but rejected by the Italians. Likewise the proposition:

> Conflict is necessary in organizations as an antidote to complacency

was accepted by the British but not by the Italians.

So there is a reasonable spread of evidence on this aspect of Italian management, and it is consistent. All we have to do now is to interpret it!

The first possibility is that Italian managers simply do take a positive view of order and discipline out of professional conviction. A second view, which one can certainly infer from Hofstede's study, is that for the Italians who are high on power distance (accept inequalities of power), high on individualism and achievement, and also high on uncertainty avoidance, these three characteristics are mutually reinforcing. In particular they will tend to be opposed to conflict, by-passing the chain of command, and matrix structures, and in favour of precisely defined roles and duties because all this tends to reduce uncertainty.

A third possibility is that in their response to such questionnaire items there is an element of normative answering, where respondents give the answers that they think the researcher expects or the answers they feel will bring credit to themselves, their profession or even their country. The totality of Italian responses in the studies cited do have about them something of the quality of a management textbook, a rather old-fashioned one in the classical management tradition. Finally it is also possible that these responses are an odd expression of Italian individualism, tending to the disorderly. That is to say they are recognizing a tendency towards expressive disorder and acknowledging that it needs to be controlled by strong hierarchies and clear cut roles and rules.

Strengths, weaknesses and prospects

It may be helpful to round off with a summary restatement of some of the issues discussed in the chapter.

Strengths

Italy's strengths would include an established industrial tradition, and a strong industrial structure. And there is a high level of technology in manufacturing processes (remember the dominance of science and engineering graduates). One would also note the amazing development that Italy achieved from the late 1950s to the early 1970s, its arrival in the G7 group of nations, and its 5 per cent share of world exports, equal to that of France. In addition there are:

- functioning networks à la Porter, and vibrant industrial districts,
- high levels of formal qualifications among Italian managers,
- the ability to operate in these personalized organization structures,
- flair, and especially design flair (though 'made in Italy' may well mean conceived in Italy these days),
- flexibility; Italy is often described as entrepreneurial rather than managerial.

Weaknesses

Weaknesses would include:

- the financial system, though in recent months (time of writing July 1998) there have been a wave of bank mergers,
- the North versus South divide, and more generally regionalism as a brake on management mobility and then on professional development; there is an interesting comparison with Spain here (see Chapter 5),
- labour market rigidity, high non-wage costs, and need to reduce cost structure; note recent expansion into Central and Eastern Europe to reduce

costs; on the subject of non-wage costs the present ratio of pensions spending to GDP is likely to remain at 14–15 per cent for the next 50 years unless some change is made (*Financial Times*, 1998),

- low R&D (research & development) spending,
- a certain cultural limitation in the form of poor international competence; English speaking ability is not as widespread as in say neighbouring Switzerland.

Trends

The authors are conscious that by the time this book manuscript goes to the publisher the first stage of EMU (European Monetary Union) will be a fact not a prospect, and goodness knows what else may have changed. Against this backdrop of uncertainty present trends in Italy seem to us to include:

- Privatization and deregulation are the order of the day, as in other European countries; the current government (as of July 1998) have made some progress in the deregulation of retail (*Financial Times*, 1998).
- There is some amalgamation among smaller firms, serving to enlarge the *Mittelstand* (see Chapter 7 on Germany) – the level of company that is above the small, family firm but below that of the sizeable PLC.
- The Italian market is being opened up by companies in other countries; there is considerable cross-border merger and acquisition activity, indeed at the time of writing an Italian company acquires foreign owners every three days.

A further interesting trend is identified by an Italian business writer. Pier Luigi Celli speaks of Italian managers losing their panache and becoming number crunchers and system builders (Celli, 1997). Indeed Celli apostrophizes this new generation of Italian managers as *masterizzati*, or 'masterized' in the sense of having MBAs and all that implies. This is a particularly interesting critique since in many countries such a trend would be regarded as an unqualified professional development. Yet against the background of Italian flair it becomes more problematic.

Finally Italy showed great enthusiasm to become one of the first wave of countries to enter EMU at the start of 1999. This enthusiasm is similar to that displayed in its day by France wanting to be a founder member of the Common Market in 1957–58 (see previous chapter on France). A lot of this enthusiasm, in both cases, comes from the conviction that such European integration will be a catalyst that will transform companies and management in desirable ways. Also for Italy first entry to EMU seemed to put the European seal of approval on Italy's status as a major industrial country.

Yet acceptance for EMU was not won without effort, and on top of what the Italian government had already done to meet the Maastricht criteria it also had to promise the Dutch and German governments that it would institute further public debt reductions for another three years. This will not be easy, but here Italians may take heart from their proverb:

Ogni bambino ha il suo cestino*

References

Barzini, Luigi (1964) *The Italians*, London: Hamish Hamilton.
Brierley, William (1993) 'The Business Culture in Italy' in Colin Randlesome *et al. Business Cultures in Europe*, Oxford: Butterworth-Heinemann.
Bull, Anna; Martyn Pitt and Joseph Szarka (1993) *Entrepreneurial Textile Communities*, London: Chapman & Hall.
Celli, Pier Luigi (1997) *L'illusione manageriale*, Roma-Bari: Laterza.
Cornelisen, Ann (1969) *Torregreca: a World in Southern Italy*, London: Macmillan.
Economist (1997) 'Italy' *The Economist*, 8 November 1997.
Edwards, Vincent (1996) 'Management in Italy' in Malcolm Warner (ed.) *International Encyclopaedia of Business & Management*, Vol. III, pp. 2918–26; London: Routledge.
Financial Times (1998) 'Financial Times Survey Italy' *Financial Times*, 15 June, pp. I–VI.
Haycraft, John (1985) *Italian Labyrinth*, London: Secker & Warburg Ltd.
Hofstede, Geert (1980) *Culture's Consequences*, Beverley Hills, Los Angeles: Sage.
Laurent, André (1986) 'The Cross Cultural Puzzle of International Human Resource Management' *Human Resource Management*, Vol. 25, No.1, pp. 91–102, Spring.
Lawrence, Peter (1998) *Issues in European Business*, Basingstoke and London: Macmillan.
Levi, Carlo (1947) *Christ Stopped at Eboli*, New York: Farrar Straus & Co.
Magrino, F. (1989) 'La svolta dei mille' *Il mondo*, 1 May, pp. 92–5.
Parks, Tim (1996) *An Italian Education*, London: Secker & Warburg.
Pellegrini, Claudio (1989) 'Italy' in Myron J. Roomkin (ed.) *Managers as Employees*, Oxford: Oxford University Press.
Porter, M. E. (1990) *The Competitive Advantage of Nations*, Glencoe, Illinois: The Free Press.
Santini, F. and C. Conti (1986) 'Come si paga il manager' *Class*, 1(7).
Silone, Ignazio (1946) *Fontamara*, London: Jonathan Cape.
Vidal, Florence (1990) *Le Management à L'Italienne*, Paris: Inter-Editions.

---

* Literally, every baby has his own basket, but the meaning Italians attach to it is that everyone has what they need in order to survive in a hostile environment.

CHAPTER 5

Spain

Spain has had remarkable experiences in the last quarter of the twentieth century. In this time it has made a transition from dictatorship to parliamentary democracy; it has experienced considerable economic development, albeit with ups and downs, and has been undergoing modernization in almost every sphere from the media to the army, from the police to the privatization of formerly state-owned industry (Hooper, 1995).

At the same time all this has happened against a background of underdevelopment, economic dependence, and relative isolation from a wider European community. With Spain more than most countries there is a greater need to delve into the past, and if possible to try to understand why as well as what.

Burden of the past

One of the odd things about Spain is that outsiders know more about where it is coming from than where it has got to. This is perhaps particularly true of the British in whose school history 'the Decline of Spain' as a theme comes second only to 'the causes of the French Revolution'. The fact remains that both Spain's long-term past and its twentieth-century past are marked by certain disjunctions.

The first of these of is of course the Golden Age and the subsequent decline. The Golden Age is the fifteenth and sixteenth centuries in which Spain variously:

- united Aragon and Castille (and therefore most of Spain) via a dynastic marriage,
- Columbus discovered America,
- the *reconquista* (the driving out of the Moors from Southern Spain) was completed,

- and the *conquistadores* conquered and colonized the whole of South and Central America apart from Brazil which went to Portugal.

For an encore Spain became the powerhouse of the Counter-Reformation (opposed the spread of Protestantism), set up the Inquisition (to torture heretics and make them confess) and Ignatius Loyola founded the Jesuits. Then Spain lost it all.

Spain failed to stop the spread and indeed the permanent establishment of Protestantism in northern Europe and the New World. All the Latin American colonies rebelled against Spanish overlordship and won their independence in the nineteenth century. Texas became independent of Spain/Mexico after winning the Battle of San Jacinto in 1836 and later joined the USA, and the area that today comprises the American states of New Mexico, Arizona, California and Nevada were also lost to the USA in a war in the 1840s. The last bits of the Spanish empire – Cuba, Puerto Rico, the Philippines and so on – were also lost to the USA in a war in 1898. All that was left were a few anti-American jokes along the lines of America stole half our roads – the ones with surfaces, and the famous quip:

> *Pobre Mexico*
> *Tan lejos de Dios*
> *Tan cerca de los Estados Unidos*
> (Poor Mexico
> So far from God
> So close to the USA!)

Yet there is nothing remarkable about losing your colonies. Every European country lost its colonies, sooner or later. What is remarkable is how little Spain profited from theirs, and here the comparison with Britain is particularly interesting. Spain's empire was won in the fifteenth and sixteenth centuries, and these victories were based on forcefulness, courage, endeavour, horsemanship, and religious conviction. But these conquests were driven by notions of glory rather than greed. The colonies were exploited only in the most simple way, by shipping out heaps of precious metal, especially after the opening of the Potosi silver mountain in Peru in 1545 – though Boisot dryly notes that these shiploads of gold and silver barely 'touched base' in Spain before being sent on to bankers in Italy and Germany to repay the Spanish crown's borrowing to finance wars in Europe (Boisot, 1993).

But the British, to develop a comparison with Spain, got most of their colonies in the eighteenth and nineteenth centuries, and commercial motivation was paramount. Consider William Pitt who in the eighteenth century presided over the acquisition of India and British success in the Seven Years War (1756–63) by which Britain seized Canada from France. The Cambridge historian J. H. Plumb wrote:

Pitt had spent much time studying the statistics of French commerce and industry, which had bred the conviction that France was the greatest danger England had to face, and the only rival worth considering in the race for overseas trade (Plumb, 1950:109).

This is a far cry from the mind set of the *conquistadores.*

In fact it is easy to be misled in the British case by the association between empire and social elitism. While the empire doubtless fuelled the British class system, it remains the case that all those upper-class expats (or would-be upper class) from the tobacco farmers of the White Highlands of Kenya to the rubber planters of Somerset Maughan's Malaya were contributing to British prosperity. It is much more questionable whether this claim can be made for the relationship between Spain and its colonies. It is perhaps revealing that when Spain joined what is now the EU (European Union) in 1986 the Spanish did not complain about the end of colonial trade preference for Latin America as the British had done in the same circumstances in the previous decade regarding trade with the Commonwealth, but the Latin American countries themselves complained that Spain had dumped them in favour of Europe and that the South American citizens had lost the right of settlement and employment in Spain.

These contrasted colonial experiences tell us something about the rather late emergence in Spain of attitudes conducive to wealth creation.

There is another moral and this brings us to the second disjunction. Most European states managed a significant level of industrialization in the nineteenth century, earlier in the case of Britain, a little later in the case of some other countries such as Sweden. But the Spanish achievement is below par. Again citing Max Boisot (1993) there are three (historic) phases of industrialization in Spain:

- 1856–1886 when the basic railway network is being constructed,
- 1874–1884 seeing the development of coal-mining, more railway construction, and the start of a steel industry in the Basque Country,
- a phase at the start of the twentieth century with further development of the mines and some activity in new manufacturing sectors.

But in total it does not amount to much by European standards, a state of affairs indicated by a poignant statistic: by 1923 Spain had 7150 miles of railway track, whereas Britain, less than half the size of Spain, had 24000 miles (Boisot, 1993). In fact Spain's railway construction was not even sufficient to give the country a unified national market for consumer goods.

If in turn one asks why industrialization in Spain is relatively slight in this period a conventional answer is that the necessary investment capital was lacking. And a standard source of such capital is the profit from overseas trade and colonial exploitation, very relevant in the British case, but insufficient in the Spanish. The other classic source of investment capital for industrialization is the surpluses generated by agriculture, but these too seemed to have failed

Spain, where much of such income was siphoned off by the Church, and more consumed by landowners in the support of their lordly lifestyle. One looks unsuccessfully in Spain for the agricultural reformers of eighteenth-century England, for a Spanish 'Turnip Townsend' or a Duke of Bridgewater.

If the first discontinuity concerns the failure of Empire, and the second the limits of industrialization, then the third relates to Spain's experience of fascist government and the way this regime interacted with the world beyond Spain.

A number of European countries had the misfortune to succumb to fascist regimes in the 1920s and 1930s but Spain is in a certain sense the *cause célèbre*. Here a fascist regime came to power not as a result of a *putsch* or a *coup* or a mere 'march on Rome' but as the result of a bloody civil war (1936–39) that left half a million dead and another half a million in exile. The victor Franco was to stay in power until his death from natural causes in December 1975.

But now we come to the disjunction. Within months of Franco's victory in the Spanish Civil War the Second World War (1939–45) began, but Franco did not join in on the side of Nazi Germany and Mussolini's Italy, in spite of the fact that he had been substantially aided by Hitler and Mussolini in the Civil War. This of course earned him the resentment of his former backers without endearing him to the British and eventually the Americans fighting against Nazi Germany. And Spain was even too backward industrially to profit from war contracts for supplying Germany as did some other neutral countries including Sweden and Switzerland.

In short the Second World War precipitated Spain's international isolation, and tended to perpetuate her economic backwardness. Both became more acute with the victory of the Allies in 1945 when paradoxically Spain which had been neutral but a presumptive Nazi sympathizer was arguably treated more harshly than Germany and Italy, the actual foes. Unlike the defeated enemies, Spain did not get Marshall Aid, or more properly was not a beneficiary of the US funded European Recovery Programme launched in 1948. There was, after all, no fear that Spain with a fascist dictator would 'go communist', though the Americans in the early post-war period did harbour such fears about Italy, France to a lesser extent, and Greece. Nor did Spain benefit from the Cold War. Whether or not communist Russia ever contemplated a war against capitalist western Europe their armies would certainly not be coming via the Pyrenees, so there was no geopolitical reason to bolster the Spanish economy to enable it to resist communist aggression. Indeed Spain was viewed distinctly as a pariah country after the War. Spanish agriculture had been damaged by the Civil War, the 1940s in Spain were known as *los anos de hambre* (the years of hunger) and Spain was kept going by handouts from Juan Peron's Argentina. In 1946 the United Nations placed a trade embargo on Spain adding thereby to Spain's isolation.

All this prompted an attempted policy of economic autarky or self-sufficiency. In the 1940s Franco established the INI (Instituto Nacional de Industria) a state holding company modelled on Italy's IRI discussed in the previous chapter, which came to include most of the staple industries together with the national airline.

The thaw came gradually and there were some positive economic developments for Spain in the latter part of the Franco period. The 1960s, known in Spain as *los anos de desarrollo* (years of development) constituted an economic boom. In part it was the result of government policy, in that Franco had appointed some technocratic ministers actually devoted to the goal of economic progress who enunciated a French-style industrial policy favouring particular industries as priority sectors. Second, it was a period when there was some drawing in of foreign capital, driven largely by the recognition of Spain's low labour costs. Third, it was due in part to the take-off of the tourist industry: Spain went from having 3 million tourists in 1959 to having 30 million in 1975. But most of all it seemed to be the unprogrammed result of a world-wide economic growth that just took Spain along with it.

Certainly Spain was poised to respond. The country had for once a government committed to economic growth rather than to disciplined isolation, there was a backlog of consumer demand, and vast reserves of underemployed labour in the countryside only too eager to migrate to the towns and engage in industrial employment. John Hooper notes that in this period men in rural areas intending to stay on the land had difficulty in finding wives: to get engaged you had at least to promise that you would go to a town and look for a factory job (Hooper, 1995).

This pretty much is where Spain had got to nearly a quarter of a century ago when Franco died, viz:

- isolation reduced but not ended,
- considerable economic growth,
- with attendant urbanization and population shift,
- which in turn increased the economic inequalities between the regions,
- with much of the impetus coming from developments and initiatives outside Spain.

It is this composite legacy of the past that gives us many of the distinctive features of the Spanish economy and business life.

Business and economy

Late industrialization, inadequate indigenous capital, and a domestic market that is poorly integrated until the latter end of the twentieth century all contribute to that key feature of the Spanish business scene – small firm size. There are indeed several planks to the proposition that average company size in Spain is small, viz:

- Spain has a lot of small firms engagingly known in Spanish as PYMES (*pequenas y medianas empresas*), especially of course, family firms.

- A lot of the companies are subsidiaries of foreign multinationals, and these also tend to be of only moderate size (established late and in some cases only there to service the Spanish domestic market).
- Spain's indigenous PLCs (SA or *sociedad anonima* in Spanish) are also fairly modest.

In fact Boisot (1993) notes that of the 100 largest non-financial companies in Western Europe only three are Spanish (the corresponding figure for Britain is 42). Indeed it is usually averred that Spain's largest non-INI, private sector company is El Corte Inglès, a chain of departmental stores (it is like having Marks & Spencer as Britain's largest company or Hertie as the biggest in Germany).

Implications of small firm size

This small company size is generally regarded as 'a bad thing!' First of all the case made in the previous chapter for small firms in Italy – that they are often fast, flexible, creative, innovative, and sometimes grouped in mutually fructifying industrial districts – is not generally thought to apply to Spain. While the ranks of the Spanish PYMES do contain some shining exceptions, examples of which are offered by Mowatt (1998), the general view is that they are rather hidebound and offer only limited prospects to non-family members. It is suggested by one authority that some 1500 of them went out of business in the first two years after Spain's accession to the EU in 1986 (Bruton, 1993) unable to cope with competition from rivals in other EU countries.

Second and perhaps more important is the widely held conviction that substantial R&D (research and development) activity is the prerogative of large companies. This piece of business folk wisdom finds ample support in comparative data on the R&D spend for different countries – in such league tables Spain is invariably near the bottom. The same picture emerges for patent applications, where Spain again does rather badly. According to data quoted by Boisot (1993) the OECD average is 47 patent applications per 100 000 inhabitants and the number for Spain is four (in Europe according to this source Switzerland is top with Sweden and Germany in joint second place). In fairness it should be said that the Spanish government has taken initiatives in recent years (time of writing July 1998) to enhance scientific research and has created more Ph.D. studentships in sciences and engineering (Mowatt, 1998); also Boisot is using 1980s data, though this is acknowledged to be an area of national endeavour where it takes a long time for government policy to have an impact.

Third, small company size tends to mean that personnel departments are skimpy, that they are generally about personnel administration rather than personnel policy. Or to put it another way the debate of the 1990s concerning personnel versus human resource management, where the latter is held by its advocates to be proactive and strategic, is largely irrelevant to Spain.

Finally, it is sometimes commented that Spanish companies tend to be weak on strategy; or perhaps one should say that strategy is more of a novel concept to them than in some of the northern European countries. Certainly one of the present authors has had the opportunity to read a heap of unpublished transcripts of interviews with senior managers of Spanish companies, and these certainly tended to confuse aspirations and objectives with strategy; that is to say they knew what they wanted but had not necessarily elaborated measures for its achievement. Now there is a loose association between company size and the propensity to 'strategize', since concern with strategy implies a company large enough to have a destiny independent of its present executive incumbents (that is, not a family firm), having a cadre of general managers as well as functional managers, and the ability to distance itself some of the time from operational exigencies.

A rather different explanation is advanced by Max Boisot who attributes the same phenomenon to Spanish fatalism. Now while one might hesitate to accept the attribution of fatalism, so heavily locked into the national stereotype, Boisot goes on to cite a socio-psychological study that grades countries or groups of countries on a continuum from fatalistic to belief in self-determination (Boisot, 1993). The USA of course emerges as having the strongest commitment to the belief in self-determination, and Spain is the most fatalistic of the countries cited in the study.

Foreign involvement in Spanish business

A result of the burden of the past explored in the first few pages is that Spain is a country that in economic matters has things done to it. This is nowhere more obvious than in the high level of foreign investment in Spain, and one can even identify some complete industries that are in foreign ownership. Indeed it is noted by Kevin Bruton that Spain is in fourth position world-wide for volume of inward foreign investment, after the USA, Britain and France (Bruton, 1994).

There is of course a number of factors that have led to this situation, including:

- liberalization of foreign investments in the 1970s,
- further reduction of control on the transfer of profits and dividends around 1986 at the time of Spain's entry to the EU,
- companies being attracted into Spain, as we have noted in discussing the 1960s boom, because of Spain's low labour costs,

- a scramble by foreign companies to get in before the completion of the EU's Single European Market (1992) discussed by one of the present writers elsewhere (Calori and Lawrence, 1991).

But in addition to these the acquisition of companies in Spain is of course facilitated by the small average size of Spanish companies discussed in the previous section. Cross border take-over is heavily conditioned by size relativities: Deutsche Bank can buy Morgan Grenfell, but Morgan Grenfell cannot buy Deutsche Bank.

Kevin Bruton again notes that the chemical, cement and insurance industries in Spain have particularly attracted foreign buyers. He continues:

> While the Arabs bought into food companies, stationery, finance and real estate, British companies have led the field with, for example, the acquisition of Alhambra Publishing by the Pearson Group, the olive oil giant José Gain by Unilever, and the Petromed refinery by BP (Bruton, 1994:25).

Foreign domination of the food and drinks industry in Spain is remarkable. The Spanish bread-making companies are largely foreign owned, and while there are 'Spanish breweries', at least Spanish brands and entities with Spanish names, most of these turn out to be wholly or partly owned by the likes of Guinness, Heineken, Carlsberg, and San Miguel of the Philippines. Indeed some 90 per cent of the Spanish beer industry is said to be in foreign ownership.

Retail in Spain is also heavily dominated by foreign chains, including Alcompo and Carrefour, notwithstanding the pre-eminence of Spain's own El Corte Inglés. Indeed it has been noted that French chains in particular are dominant in Spain (Diaz and Miller, 1994). Even El Corte Inglés has done its bit in that it originally sourced in Spain all its electrical domestic appliances, but later signed contracts with Italian manufacturers after Spain's accession to the EU.

Domestic real estate in Spain may also be purchased by foreigners, and according to Kevin Bruton (1994) foreigners were spending 300 000 million pesetas a year in the late 1990s doing so. Indeed in the early 1990s one British bank was moved to set up a chain of English style estate agencies in Spain.

Finally there is the little matter of the motor car industry in Spain. As industry analysts never fail to point out Spain has become Europe's fourth largest car producer – after Germany, France, and Italy and *ahead of Britain*. And indeed Volkswagen, GM, Ford, Renault, Suzuki, Iveco, Nissan and Peugeot all manufacture in Spain, but none of them are Spanish (SEAT that was owned by the Spanish government was bought by Volkswagen in 1986).

Instituto Nacional de Industria (INI)

INI was founded in the 1940s in the Franco period. As suggested earlier it was modelled on the IRI in Italy (see previous chapter) set up by Mussolini in the

1930s, and more generally it was introduced as an initiative in economic autarky, the stock in trade of fascist dictators in this period. Indeed as suggested in the first part of the chapter the international isolation brought on Spain by the Second World War and its aftermath left Spain few options. So Franco established the INI, put heavy industry and some other strategic industries under its umbrella, and was more concerned with matters of control than with competitive advantage.

INI was largely restructured during the course of the 1990s, but before that restructuring took place INI was in the world's top fifty trading groups. It accounted for 30 per cent of production in heavy industry and transport, and for 10 per cent of all industrial production in Spain. This in turn provokes the question: What was it like? And probably the most obvious answer is that it constituted a set of overly bureaucratic companies, with a significant but not exclusive concentration in what a later age was to term 'rust belt' industries.

Senior positions in INI companies were of course government appointments. And many of the people actually appointed were army officers. It should be remembered here that Franco was not like Hitler, a corporal turned head of state, but a talented general turned head of state. The army was his natural constituency, army officers the people he could most obviously trust. But what were they like as managers of nationalized industry?

While a plausible answer can be inferred from their background, we can in a sense do better than that, in that Simon Mowatt's Ph.D. is based in the first instance on company visits and interviews with practising managers in Spain in the late 1990s. Some of Mowatt's interviewees had worked or were working for INI companies. As one of Mowatt's interviewees put it, the ex-army INI executives:

> ... brought their experiences and hierarchy with them. They brought a law and order culture. (Mowatt, 1998:59)

And again:

> The managers were appointed from Madrid. They had no experience in the sector, and no business knowledge. They had no interest in the business. However every manager that was rotated in tried to make important changes to show how *his* administration was different from that of the previous appointees. These were not business decisions. The managers were very authoritarian, so you needed their permission to implement decisions. Communication was very difficult – especially as they mostly used to spend at least three days a week in Madrid! (Mowatt, 1998:59)

The authority of these INI managers was based on their external status and acceptability to central government in the person of Franco. This did not, however, stop them from using information control to buttress that authority, as another of Mowatt's interviewees testifies:

Information was very difficult to get. Senior managers saw information as a source of power. My boss kept company policy directives, and even training manuals, in a locked cabinet in his office to ensure that we were dependent upon him. (Mowatt, 1998:60)

Mowatt goes on to refer to an article in the Spanish newspaper *La Vanguardia* (14 October 1996) which printed a set of sayings about the INI sector taken from its employees. A representative excerpt was:

A nados nos acostumbramos tan rapidamente como a trabaja despacio. (There is nothing one can learn so fast as to work slow.) (Mowatt, 1998:60)

In 1983 INI chalked up record losses and the government responded by launching its industrial reconversion policy (1984), aiming to focus the INI group on industries with a plausible future, and to restructure companies into units large enough to compete in the international arena. These endeavours of course were made more urgent by Spain's accession to the EU in 1986 and consequent enhanced exposure to competition from other Western European countries.

By 1987, 85% of the envisaged cuts had been effected amounting to about 71 000 job losses in the INI staple industries of steel and shipbuilding. Some 30 companies were closed down, and of the remaining 58 firms some were sold in part to foreign investors, of which the most famous is SEAT sold to VAG (Volkswagen). In 1988 INI recorded its first profits for 13 years.

By the late 1990s INI had been carved up to yield three blocks of companies, viz:

- AIE, a group of large scale heavy industry companies comprising 42 859 employees (as of end 1997),
- Téneo Group, supplemented by the SEPI Group from the start of 1998, jointly including the more profitable companies being run with eventual privatization in view, and consisting of a further 76 202 employees,
- Patrimonio, a group of companies deemed strategic to the existence of the state, with a further 145 446 employees, with the intention of selling off the controlling state interest.

So Franco's INI has been transformed, and its years (if not its days) are numbered. But INI has left a legacy in the sense of a mindset and an image of management in Spain.

Management in Spain

It is more difficult in the case of Spain than for most other countries to generalize about the character of management. The most obvious reason, that has been amply canvassed in the foregoing pages, is that managers are in different institutional sectors, viz:

- PYMES, the smaller mostly family firms,
- INI, the government owned sector discussed in the previous section, and its successors,
- Spanish subsidiaries of foreign MNCs (multinational companies),
- indigenous Spanish companies of reasonable size having PLC equivalent status.

The second consideration that inhibits generalization is quite simply change, and again change in Spain is more dynamic than for most of the other countries discussed in this book and comprehends the notion of change between the institutional sectors outlined above, in that:

- the PYMES sector is (mildly) under pressure because of the putative short-comings and the difficulties experienced world-wide by small firms faced with larger rivals,
- the INI sector as we have seen has been scaled down and its contraction and transformation is ongoing,
- the MNC sector is at time of writing stable, with no obvious force for a further proliferation of subsidiaries,
- the indigenous Spanish company sector is increasing gently as the state sector is scaled down, and some industries, banking for example, are experiencing concentration via domestic merger.

What we are tending to do in this chapter is to concentrate implicitly on the last group, indigenous Spanish companies, partly because they are likely to be 'the shape of things to come' and in fact because these are generally felt to represent what is distinctive in a country's management style and practice. It has to be conceded, however, that the boundaries between these four institutional types are not clear cut, being most obviously clouded by the issue of foreign ownership. How, for example, should one regard SEAT: as Italian (Fiat of Italy was the original inventor), Spanish, ex INI, or as German?

The image of management

It is probably fair to say that Spanish management has a bit of an image problem, and also probably fair to say that it does not deserve to. In any case, it is worth trying to unpick the reasons.

First of all there appears to be an element of bureaucratized inefficiency in Spanish national life. In the revised version of his widely read book published in the mid 1990s John Hooper pays tribute to Spanish officials coming to work late, leaving early, going out to the cafe for meals (including breakfast) in between, and for an encore being rude to members of the general public (Hooper, 1995). The same source documents the crippling slowness of the Spanish judicial system, such that the phrase 'why don't you sue me' has become a provocative taunt. In the same spirit one can park anywhere with impunity because the authorities will never be able to track you down let alone prosecute you. This may lead people to believe by association that Spanish management may be a little like this.

Then there is the question of INI, where management undoubtedly 'was like that', though as we have seen INI was a survival from the Franco era, now much reduced and significantly reformed. Nonetheless the INI companies may appear to offer an answer to the question, what is Spanish management like. Whatever else may be said in criticism of INI, it was one hundred per cent Spanish in the sense of the absence of foreign influence.

Third, all the FDI (foreign direct investment) and MNC subsidiaries in Spain has meant a lot of foreigners (non-Spaniards) having some experience of Spanish business life, and judging it by their own cultural standards. It is rather difficult to tell, say, an American business consultant that a Spanish manager is late, not because he does not care, but because he has decided in this instance to give priority to a relationship/interaction rather than to a schedule.

Finally, there is what we might call the torch bearer syndrome, where relatively young Spanish managers, typically in the employ of a foreign MNC, come to internalize the MNC corporate culture to the extent that they then criticize (a stereotype of) their own culture. A nice example of this phenomenon is offered in a paper by Contreras and his colleagues typically produced while on a post experience management course at a foreign business school (Contreras *et al.*, 1993). It may be instructive to look at their formulation.

Their starting point, of course, is to say that Spain is somewhat like France, except that the rules and procedures are there to prevent chaos, not as an end in themselves. Spain shares with France a similar rating on two of Hofstede's famous dimensions (Hofstede, 1980); that is to say Spain has high power distance (tolerates big differences in power in formal organizations) and high uncertainty avoidance. The hierarchy in the Spanish case, however, is based more on social roles in business, than on functional ones. What is being suggested here by Luis Contreras and his co-authors is that those who have standing in Spanish society will ipso facto have standing in formal organizations, and their standing will legitimize their position in the hierarchy – a nice inversion, and we intend to argue that it is true in a certain way. At the same time human needs are seen as more important than organizational or procedural requirements, something which in our view is probably true but not necessarily a criticism.

Again Contreras and his colleagues see fatalism as the enemy of strategy, it is considered unrealistic to make long-term plans because of the unpredictability of future events, so planning systems, both strategic and financial, are underdeveloped. Rather revealingly it is argued that Spanish managers have no taste for incorporating systematic quantitative studies into the planning and strategy developing exercise, as do the Americans *par excellence.*

Similarly Contreras regrets the characteristic lack of American style openness in Spanish companies arguing that:

- communication channels are limited,
- one-to-one interactions with the boss behind closed doors are typical,
- and interdepartmental communications may be resented as interference,

while at the same time it is noted that most communication is oral, in contrast to France.

When it comes to meetings, the boss talks and gives instructions to subordinates, while each of the latter defends his or her proposal with resolve (displays of courage and fortitude are mandatory in Spain). So-called collaboration is a chance to voice your own opinion, while consensus is best achieved by the intervention of a strong leader, with whom individuals reach separate agreements.

We have reproduced a number of the arguments from the Contreras paper for two reasons. First because in our view these writers are right to emphasize the personal nature of Spanish management. But also because their depiction has a phenomenonological interest. A group of Spaniards achieve some distance from their own culture by working in foreign MNC subsidiaries, then criticize indigenous Spanish management, implicitly with reference to the private sector, yet any condemnation could always be substantiated with reference to (the remains of) the public sector (INI). This could only happen in Spain.

Survey evidence and the critical view

In the previous chapter on Italy we used data from the Nene study of managers' values and views in different countries to support a characterization of Italian managers and to point up some ways in which they differed from their British colleagues. Unfortunately the Nene study does not (yet) include a sample of Spanish managers, but again one of the present authors with two of his colleagues (Peter Lawrence, with John Whittaker and Heidi Winklhofer) conducted a similar study at Loughborough University that does include a sample of Spanish managers. This Loughborough study is in the same form as the Nene study, it offers managers a variety of propositions concerning various aspects of management and they are invited to respond on a five-point scale from strongly agree to strongly disagree. This Loughborough study does offer some support for the characterization of Spanish management derived from Contreras and his co-authors in the previous section.

This is not the only theme to emerge from the Loughborough study but certainly there is some suggestion of a rather formalistic, power-centred management. To start with, the Spanish managers in the study evince a rather formalistic view of structure. The proposition:

> Structure is important in showing the relationship between the posts/ functions/departments or the organization

gave the Spanish the highest mean score out of all the national groups in the study and one where the contrast with the British group is statistically significant. It may of course be a case of normative answering with the Spanish respondents thinking that this was the right answer. Perhaps more authentic is the Spanish response to the related proposition:

> Structure is important for fixing the authority relations between organizational members

where again they have the highest mean score for the various national groups, and there is a statistically significant contrast with the British managers.

Similarly the Spanish score highly on the importance they attach to leadership. In response to the proposition:

> Above all the manager needs powers of leadership

the Spanish again had the highest mean score out of all the national groups, and the contrast with the British managers is highly significant in the statistical sense. Indeed there are 87 propositions tested in the Loughborough study, and there are only three other items on which the Spanish have a higher mean score, that is to say, a score closer to the strongly agree end of the spectrum (and two of the remaining three are bland statements that everyone agreed with).

The rather formalistic, old-fashioned view put forward by Contreras and his colleagues finds some support in the Spanish response to the proposition concerning the role of hierarchy. The proposition:

> The hierarchy is necessary to achieve coordination

gets the highest mean score from the Spanish and there is a significant contrast with the British. The cross-checking proposition:

> Hierarchies will become increasingly less relevant as a result of increasing improvement

drew forth the lowest mean score from the Spanish and another contrast with the British. But the proposition that yielded the strongest contrast between the Spanish and British managers was:

> The hierarchy rightly denotes rank and status

where once again the Spanish have the highest mean score.

When it comes to decision making the picture is consistent. The Spanish score highly, second only to the French, on a proposition asserting how important it is to aim at rational decisions, and a further proposition:

Decision making is the central managerial act

gets its highest mean score from the Spanish and again there is a contrast with the British managers.

Running through a lot of the Spanish responses is the idea of the manager as a strong person, who will be hard on himself, but will be respected. All the national groups, for example, disagreed with a proposition asserting that one cannot question a senior manager's decision on ethical grounds, but clearly the Spanish found it hardest (most unnatural, say) to do so with a mean score just to the disagree side of the mid point on the scale, while the other national groups rejected the proposition more emphatically.

On the basis of some of the data produced by the Loughborough study it would be fair to say that there is some support for the Contreras view, and in our experience the quite widespread body of opinion that this represents, though we would put the emphasis on the Spanish manager's concern to be and be perceived as strong and decisive rather than in an old-fashioned bureaucratic hierarchialism. This of course is a matter of interpretation rather than of fact, and the data we have cited so far do not in any case tell the whole story.

Personal qualities

We would like to suggest that Spanish management is perhaps best apprehended in terms of a configuration of personal qualities, and a loose consensus about them on the part of Spanish managers we have met, and the quite large sample interviewed by Mowatt (1998). The tendency to macho-courage-decisiveness explored in the previous section is only part of the picture (and it is fair to add that the Spanish sample in the Loughborough study rather over-represents managers from one large company that used to be in the government sector).

First of all a note on the training and education of Spanish managers may be helpful. In our experience the education level is high, and at the end of the 1990s one is speaking of a graduate profession. The older generation are most likely to have first degrees in engineering or science (Spain like Germany has technical universities) and will probably have post experience management education and sometimes MBAs. Those in their 50s are now typically in general management posts to which they have risen from posts as production managers or positions in charge of manufacturing plants or groups of plants. The younger generation may have exactly the same qualification set, but are more likely than their elders to have studied economics or business administration as a first degree subject. They are also more likely to have had (some of their) education outside Spain, and to put more emphasis on internationalism generally than did those whose education and early career experiences were during the Franco period.

But the point to emphasize is that while today such qualifications are expected, and their possession facilitates inter-company mobility, it is personal qualities rather than educational achievement that is emphasized. Spain is not France! Again there is a hint of this in the Loughborough study proposition:

> In management work common sense is a greater virtue than impressive qualifications.

All the national groups accepted this proposition, but the Spanish managers as a group had the highest mean score, and one that was significantly higher than that of their British counterparts. In our view the Spanish are not registering a vote against higher education, it is after all a Latin country with a formalized respect for learning, but a vote for other things, where 'common sense' does proxy for certain qualities that are not necessarily entailed by educational achievement.

The personal qualities believed to be crucial for managers in Spain are a mix of:

- seriousness,
- trust,
- ability to work with others,
- honour and courage,

and these are mentioned, specifically and recurrently, by Spanish managers whether you interview them in English or Spanish (Mowatt, 1998).

The Spanish manager is expected to be serious, in the sense of having character, resolve, and considered intentions. Behaviour and deportment should reflect this seriousness, but it is not simply an impression to be managed. One way in which the seriousness will show is in the acceptance of work as an obligation that may be at odds on occasion with one's personal inclinations. In the Loughborough study in response to the proposition:

> Managers owe it to themselves and their families to strike a sensible balance between the demands of work and home

all the national groups broadly agreed, that it is accepted that work must be kept in perspective, that it must be recognized that there are other claims on a manager. But it is the British and Americans who have the highest mean scores, that is agree most strongly with the proposition. The Spanish mean score is lower, and represents a highly significant contrast with that of the British managers. This sense of seriousness is perhaps caught in the Jesuit expression *puro y duro* (pure and hard) as an exhortatory definition of character and intent.

The trustworthiness has a number of dimensions. The manager must inspire trust because of his character. He must be seen to be serious. It must be clear that he can be trusted to do the job, not so much in the sense of professional proficiency but rather in the sense of engagement, in the internalization of commitment. And the manager should exhibit a certain balance, between the demands of the situation and an understandable desire for personal distinction, an idea captured in the Spanish expression *ambicion sano*, literally 'sane ambition'. *Ambicion sano* is the mid-point between supine directionlessness and a yearning for 'tunes of glory!' This trustworthiness may also have a literal dimension. In the Loughborough study the proposition:

> Unofficial private use of a company's resources by managers is basically acceptable

evoked a negative response from almost all the national groups, but the Spanish managers had the lowest mean score (that is, felt that this was *not* acceptable) and the contrast with the British managers was statistically significant.

It is an old paradox that although the Spanish are famous in their own view for individualism, caught in the expression 'every man his own king', in their testimonies concerning management work and the required human qualities, working with others figures largely (Mowatt, 1998). The emphasis on *ambicion sano* is of course part of this inclination. This conviction shows up clearly in conventional terms in the Loughborough study where the proposition:

> A manager's ability to work in a team is the most highly valued part of his/her individual performance

evoked from the Spanish managers the highest mean score (that is, expressing the highest level of agreement) of all the national groups – the contrast with the British managers was highly significant. So much for cricket versus bull-fighting.

In the Spanish scheme of things honour is an intrinsic quality but it will be reflected in deportment. Managers in Simon Mowatt's study when asked how they recruited or how they would choose a successor for themselves spoke of looking for a serious, resolute, dignified manner, the emphasis being on (the reflection of) these deeper qualities rather than on the Anglo-Saxon notion of confidence and social skills. Courage in the view of Spanish managers is manifest in the act of standing by actions and decisions, and those of trusted subordinates.

If we ask how Spanish management fosters the recruitment and retention of people with these human qualities the answer is that the process is consistent with the intention. In the authors' experience and in Simon Mowatt's account there is little recourse to assessment centres, psychological testing, or formalized indicators, with the exception of foreign owned MNCs operating in Spain. Indeed the emphasis is on personal contact and a personal evaluation of applicants in human terms rather than in terms of specific competencies. Managers always say they want to know about the applicant's family, which in turn is more feasible in view of the relative lack of regional mobility discussed in the next section. In their appraisal of the applicant's family they are looking for the same qualities – stability, seriousness, family integration, a certain conformity to Spanish norms of human decency. There are lots of references to knowing the family, getting to know the applicant, taking him out to dinner, and so on. And of course nobody ever recruits for anyone else, even if the personnel department do some preliminary staff work. It is invariably the manager who is going to be the immediate employer who is central to the selection process.

All this in practice probably promotes a certain middle-class management endogamy. Those applicants coming from good middle-class homes are more likely to be seen as having the right family and indeed their members are more likely to be socially prominent and therefore easier to identify as stable and decent. At the same time it does not seem to be about social class as such. A manager from a humble social background measured by say, father's job, who succeeds in business is likely to enjoy more rather than less success. The kind of applicant likely to suffer from these personalized selection processes is one from a disintegrated family, with members scattered regionally. Far worse that your father left your mother than that he is a dustman.

Mobility

There are unusual patterns of mobility among Spanish managers, and the phenomenon is quite complicated. First of all Spain is a heavily regionalized country in an economic and demographic sense, and the regions vary from each other in a number of basic ways:

- rich versus poor,
- industrialized versus unindustrialized,
- non-agricultural employment available (at least in good times) versus declining agricultural work only,
- urbanized versus rural,
- population rising versus population declining.

These regional differences effectively structure the geographical location of most management jobs, in the sense that industrialization tends to be concentrated in Catalonia, the Basque Country, and Valencia, and there is a massive concentration of economic activity in the two principal cities of Madrid and Barcelona.

Second, regions of Spain have an affective importance. People are attached to them, believe them to have different characters, believe their own to be the best, though the phenomenon is probably not as strong as in Italy. But it is reinforced by another phenomenon, the Spanish attachment to the family. And if you are attached to the family, you want its members to be close together, geographically as well as emotionally. The last Spanish person to speak to the authors before the writing of this chapter said with manifest satisfaction:

All my family live within 5 kilometres of where I live. I could not conceive of leaving Barcelona.

The economic structuring of regions together with their affective pull and family involvement have a number of implications for the mobility of managers. First and most important of all the attachment to family and region means that Spanish managers do not want to move, or be moved, geographically. Indeed some companies actually have a policy of non-mobility, of guaranteeing to employees that they will not have to go more than x kilometres from Head Office or whatever (Mowatt, 1998). Second, this being the case having (untypical for a Spaniard) experienced mobility is more of a selling point than it would be in say Britain or the USA. It is noticeable in Mowatt's interview sample that geographic mobility is a feature of the more senior managers (Mowatt, 1998). Third, postings overseas are more acceptable than postings to a different part of Spain, in part because they are more glamorous and more career enhancing but also because they are time bounded, 2–4 years, at the end of which the manager will be returned to his home region and family.

But there are always twists and quirks to mobility among Spanish managers. One of these is that people from the more deprived regions of Spain are probably going to have to make a one way trip out, either to go to university or to get a professional managerial job. But if thereafter they ever have a chance to return, return they will. Again in Mowatt's sample of Spanish managers there are various instances of senior people, typically production people, who had some choice about where to have their 'command post', whether at company headquarters or at one of the plants; in such cases the manager would pick a plant in his home region, and draw up a managerial rationalization later! (Mowatt, 1998).

A further point is that the reluctance to engage in geographic mobility deriving from attachment to family and region is reinforced by the importance of personal networks. While such networks have some importance for managers in any country or culture, they are more than averagely important in Spain. Recognizing this is easier than saying why, but it is something along the lines of there being less 'buying in' to abstractions such as the state, the organization, or even the profession in both Spain and Italy than in northern European countries: in this relative identificational vacuum, the people you know become a more insistent reality. Or to put it in terms of the previous section on personal qualities, if a culture places the emphasis on such qualities their presence is only guaranteed among the group of which one is already a member – hence the network's importance.

Finally, while there are some management cultures in which mobility is seen as largely superfluous (Sweden) or 'a bad thing' in itself (Holland), Spain is not one of these. If mobility did not disrupt networks, family, and attachment to region, it would be fine. Hence inter-company mobility that does not entail geographic mobility is acceptable, and again Mowatt's sample has many instances of managers, mostly the younger generation, who made career enhancing moves between various employing organizations without having to move home, typically in Barcelona and Madrid.

Creativity

In this brief discussion of creativity the reference is not to creativity in the cultural sphere, although Spain would of course 'score high' here particularly in painting and architecture. Indeed John Hooper describes Spain in 1936 on the eve of the Civil War as being a cultural superpower (Hooper, 1995). Nor is the reference primarily to design flair, a quality claimed for the Italians in the previous chapter, even though this may also apply to the Spanish.

Instead the reference is rather to what Simon Mowatt calls 'interpretational creativity' (Mowatt, 1998). This seems to derive from the admixture of honour-trust-loyalty on the one hand and the independence and autonomy of 'every-man his own king' on the other. As Mowatt puts it:

> Spanish managers often related how they felt empowered by the confidence placed in them by their supervisors, *and* by their innate sense of self-worth. This gave them the freedom and confidence to take quick decisions without consultation with their superiors, especially in the interpretation of orders and company directives (Mowatt, 1998:243).

Or again:

> Managers gave achievement greater priority than conforming to regulations ... Spanish managers are often willing to take responsibility for their decisions when they feel empowered by their superiors (Mowatt, 1998:243).

It is also interesting that many of these Spanish manager testimonies run counter to the high uncertainty avoidance attributed to the Spanish by Hofstede (1980) and mentioned earlier in the chapter. Again Mowatt quotes a Spanish manager as saying:

> I do not like routine, I like to solve each problem in a new way (Mowatt, 1998:243).

and lots of Mowatt's interviewees claim flexibility, speed of implementation, and adaptability as management strengths in Spain, with the Spanish variously contrasting themselves with the British, Germans, and Americans. There is also a bit of this in the Loughborough study where the proposition:

> When it comes to decision-making the viability of implementation is the key consideration

yielded a mean score from the Spanish managers (denoting a stronger level of agreement) that is higher than that for any of the national groups, and represents a significant contrast with the British.

Looking back over this chapter we are conscious of having changed the focus. Beginning with some discussion of what might be termed 'the downside of Spanish history' and some problematic elements of the Spanish economy, we move through traditional, Hofstede-driven views of Spanish management to a discussion of personal qualities and creativity.

This variance of course is partly the result of the different classes of companies in Spain:

- small family firms,
- Spanish mid-corporate's in the private sector,
- foreign owned MNC subsidiaries,
- state sector (INI) firms, and more recently privatized state firms,

which has already been explored. In a certain way the answer to the question, what is Spanish management like, depends on which of these four you take, while at the same time the relationships between these sectors are changing and so is their relative importance.

But it is more than this. More than any other country discussed in this book Spain has changed in the last quarter of the twentieth century. Some of that change finds expression in the structure of the present chapter.

References

Boisot, Max H. (1993) 'The Revolution from Outside: Spanish Management and the Challenge of Modernisation' in David J. Hickson (ed.) *Management in Western Europe*, Berlin: Waller de Gruyer.

Bruton, Kevin (1993) 'The Business Culture in Spain' in Colin Randlesome *et al. Business Culture in Europe*, 2nd edn. Oxford: Butterworth Heinemann.

Bruton, Kevin (1994) *Business Culture in Spain*, Oxford: Butterworth Heinemann.

Calori, Roland and Peter Lawrence (1991) *The Business of Europe*, London: Sage.

Contreras, Luis; Thierry Capell, Alessandro Katemi, Naoya Nakata, and Nikolay Tess (1993) 'Doing Business in Spain' unpublished course paper, Paris: INSEAD.

Diaz, Angel and Paddy Miller (1994) 'Managing people in Spain' in Terry Garrison and David Rees (eds) *Managing People Across Europe*, Oxford: Butterworth Heinemann.

Hofstede, Geert (1980) *Culture's Consequences*, Beverley Hills: Sage.

Hooper, John (1995) *The New Spaniards*, Harmondsworth, Middlesex: Penguin.

Mowatt, Simon (1998) 'The Development and Character of Management in Spain' Loughborough University unpublished Ph.D. thesis, Loughborough, England.

Plumb, J. H. (1950) *England in the Eighteenth Century (1714–1815)*, Harmondsworth, Middlesex: Penguin.

CHAPTER 6

Turkey

With Turkey Europe shades into Asia. Both modern Turkey and its predecessor the Ottoman Empire have been geographically and aspirationally attracted to the European continent. Turkey has been a member of NATO since 1952, an associate member of the European Common Market since 1963 and has applied for full membership of the European Union (EU). In January 1996 Turkey joined the EU's Customs Union.

Turkey has a population of about 65 million, 70 per cent of whom are aged under 35. In Europe it shares borders with Bulgaria and Greece. In the east Turkey has borders with Iran and the former Soviet republics of Georgia and Armenia (only Turkey and Norway of NATO members shared land borders with the former Soviet Union). To the South lie Syria and Iraq. Since 1974 Turkey has supported, economically and militarily, the so-called Turkish Republic of Northern Cyprus.

Historically the Ottoman Empire occupied substantial portions of South-Eastern Europe. It was one of the European continent's great imperial powers. At its peak the Ottoman Empire controlled the Balkan peninsula and Hungary as well as northern areas of the Black Sea shore and threatened to advance further northward and westward. The Empire's decline began after the failed siege of Vienna in 1683 and by the nineteenth century it was considered the 'sick man of Europe'. Attempts were made in the nineteenth century to modernize the state through reforms of the military and government in line with European models. There was also partial secularization. However, the Ottoman Empire was corroded by internal inefficiency and dissent, nationalist movements and the enmity of the other Great Powers. It was not, however, till just before the First World War (1914–18) that European Turkey was reduced to its current dimensions. The historical legacy of Ottoman rule has been particularly strong in the Balkans where Islam is as present as Catholicism and Orthodoxy. Albania and Bosnia-Herzegovina are predominantly Muslim, while Bulgaria and the independent state of Macedonia have substantial Muslim minorities.

Western Europe, too, has a Turkish and Muslim presence that cannot be ignored. Turkish 'guest workers' (*Gastarbeiter*) have made a substantial contribution to the German economy as they provided part of the labour force required to fuel the one time West German economic miracle. Cities such as Berlin have sizeable Turkish communities and the Turkish community in Germany overall numbers around 1.5 million individuals.

Other West European countries (for example, France and Great Britain) also have sizeable communities which adhere to Islam, having originated predominantly in the case of France from North Africa and in the case of Britain from the Indian sub-continent. Representatives of these communities are active in a range of business activities. An exposition and discussion of Turkish management may therefore be far more than a peripheral issue to Europeans and can help to provide insights not only into Turkey but also into broader issues involving cultures professing Islam in general.

Modern Turkey

The modern Turkish Republic was officially proclaimed in 1923 and its foundation is attributed largely to the efforts of Mustapha Kemal (Atatürk) and his successes in the Turkish War of Independence (1918–23). The new Turkish Republic is secular, nationalist and westernizing. Turkey became a secular state in 1928, even though the population is overwhelmingly Muslim. Compared to the Ottoman Empire, Turkey is also a predominantly Turkish state. Around 85 per cent of the population are Turks, with the most sizeable minority, the Kurds, living in the east of the country. In general, western Turkey is more economically developed and more 'Europeanized' culturally than the rest of Turkey.

One aspect of Atatürk's reforms was the emancipation of women. Although Turkish society was traditionally characterized by male domination, it does not follow that women were totally without influence. Emancipation brought women more into public life: around one third of today's university students are female and women are well represented in professional careers.

The military, moreover, have continued to play a significant and generally respected role because of their contribution to freeing Turkish territory from foreign occupation in the early 1920s and establishing the Republic. But apart from two brief interludes, in 1960–61 and 1980–83, the military has not been overtly involved in running the country.

Atatürk also encouraged the development of Turkish industry. Up to 1920 there had been only limited industrial development. Foreign investments ('concessions') were concentrated in the rail, road and ports infrastructure and were generally regarded negatively by the Turks. Atatürk's government abolished the concessions and foreign assets were nationalized by bilateral agreements. Turkey developed a closed economy which strove for economic self-sufficiency, as did Spain during the (early) Franco period. From the 1950s the growth of manufacturing activities was particularly encouraged. State-owned companies played a major role in this policy, while foreign investment and private enterprise were relegated to subsidiary positions. Imports were restricted and domestic production encouraged (a policy of import substitution).

The situation changed fundamentally in 1980 with the decision to open up the Turkish economy in order to facilitate structural reforms and develop the market economy. The previous policy of import substitution was replaced by a manifest export orientation. Foreign investment was encouraged and grew both in manufacturing and services.

Up to 1980 the state had determined the modes of operation of private companies as the state controlled economic policy making and was itself a major investor in economic activity. Within this context private enterprises related to the state on a personal and selective basis.

Within the private sector itself, which consisted predominantly of family-owned small and medium enterprises, a small group of holding companies played a particularly significant role (Selekler, 1998). These holding companies were family-owned, with centralized decision-making and a low level of professionalization. Personal authority was a key factor. In general these holding companies were highly diversified and lacked focus. One holding company, for example, is today primarily involved in brewing and soft drinks, with further activities in office supplies, consumer finance, production of passenger cars, commercial vehicles and motorcycles, import and sale in the CIS (Commonwealth of Independent States, the collective name of the countries that formerly made up the Soviet Union) of Russian and Korean cars and marketing of automotive products in Central Asia and the Caucasus (the supplementary activities all in conjunction with a range of foreign partners). Integration of such diverse activities has been achieved through majority ownership, interlocking directorships and cross-shareholdings. The holding companies have in general been risk-averse: out of a fear of losing control they generated investment funds internally or from their own banking subsidiaries, though in recent years there has been increasing use of equity funding (Guide to Turkey, 1996). Competition between holding companies has generally been low and predominantly directed at obtaining the resources made available by the state with which the companies shared the risk of economic activity. The government's attitude to companies could be either beneficial or detrimental, and there are instances of political discrimination against particular holding companies (Erçek, 1998).

Recent developments

The change in economic policy in 1980 represented a potential threat to the holding companies, especially in the form of foreign competition. The holding companies have responded to this threat by becoming more professional, reducing the role played by personal relationships. At the same time they have remained in family ownership and largely centralized. Up to now the holding companies have to a great degree averted the threat of foreign competition by entering into joint ventures with foreign investors. For example, another holding company has developed a diverse portfolio of joint ventures with global companies of American, Belgian, German and Japanese provenance. The aim has been to develop and exploit the Turkish market 'cooperatively' and benefit from shared learning. At the same time the joint ventures have assisted the holding companies in gaining access to foreign markets.

Evidence for the opening up of the Turkish economy can be seen in the inflows of foreign direct investment (FDI). In 1985 around $200 million of FDI entered the country; in the 1990s this has increased to something in the region of £1000 million a year (Guide to Turkey, 1997). Furthermore, the EU has become a substantial trading partner, accounting for approximately one half of Turkey's imports and exports.

Connected to the opening up of the economy have been the attempts to encourage a more entrepreneurial business culture. Traditionally entrepreneurial activities were the preserve of minority communities such as the Armenians, Greeks and Jews. Since 1985 a privatization programme has sought to reduce the role of the state in economic activity and develop the private sector. The results of the privatization programme, however, have been slow and disappointing. State-owned companies, especially the banks, have been sources of political patronage which many politicians have been reluctant to lose. In addition the programme has met with opposition from a number of other groups including the managers and employees of state-owned companies, responsible ministries, trades unions and social democratic politicians (Culpan, 1998).

Turkish culture

Turkish culture embodies a number of conflicting and interacting influences (Aldemir, 1998). These influences comprise Eastern and Western points of view as well as the relationship between rural and urban modes of life. The inhabitants of Anatolia (today's mainland Turkey) were originally nomadic warriors. From the eleventh century onward they began to settle and adopt Islam. Under the Ottomans there was considerable contact with Arabic and Byzantine (centred on Constantinople – renamed Istanbul after its capture in 1453) cultures.

Aldemir (1998) identifies three major cultural influences in contemporary Turkey:

- Nomadic: this bears the characteristics of a traditional Central Asian culture; it has a strong military component; freedom, obedience and respect for one's elders are key values. Although less than one per cent of the population is now nomadic, the values underlying this culture are still widespread.
- Rural: key values include patience and respect for elders. The rural culture is characterized by continuity and a sense of fatalism.
- Urban: in contrast the culture of, in particular, the coastal cities is marked by a sense of impatience, fluidity and openness to change. The coastal cities have historically been heavily involved in trade with the Black Sea and Mediterranean regions.

Modern Turkey has experienced not only a virtual disappearance of the nomadic lifestyle but also a substantial process of urbanization. For example, around 20 per cent of the Turkish population now live in Greater Istanbul. Over the last 50 years the proportion of the population living in urban areas has more or less doubled; nowadays around half the population lives in towns and cities. The rural population has tended to migrate to inland towns while the nomadic population has migrated both to inland and coastal urban settlements. The culture of the inland towns is thus based on the practices of rural life and tends to be autocratic, religious, militaristic and largely traditionalist. In contrast the culture of the coastal towns is more free and open, democratic and rational, consensus-oriented and conciliatory. One of the implications resulting from the internal migrations is that these differing value systems have engendered paradoxes and conflicts.

Clearly such differences in value systems also have an impact on business organizations where cultural heterogeneity can be problematical. An example of a cultural value-conflict relates to the role of Islam in economic affairs (Kuran, 1998). Religious interpretations of business activity and practices can present difficulties for certain practicing Muslims who find 'unjustified enrichment' (for example, as embodied in bank interest) unacceptable. Islamic economic and social institutions do exist, for instance, banks, grocery and fashion shores, bookshops as well as theatres, clinics and dormitories. There are also Islamic conglomerates. Moreover, there have been proposals to establish gated Islamic communities which would be built around a mosque and comprise a range of business units.

Interest in Islamic businesses has been fostered at least in part by the perceived spread of bribery and corruption as a result of the expansion of government activities and increasing urbanization. Islamic businesses are regarded by some as exhibiting greater honesty and fairness than secular businesses, although certain critics maintain that Islamic banks merely employ ruses to circumvent the charging of interest on loans. Even within Islamic groups there is controversy between traditionalists and a growing minority of modernists. Historically, commerce and trade were an integral part of the pilgrimage to Mecca.

Secularization has also had an impact on Islamic groups (apart from the ultra fundamentalists) and in general these groups strive to respond flexibly to new situations. At the very least Islamic business organizations provide devout Muslims with an opportunity to put their religious beliefs into practice as employees and/or as customers. In the case of employees Islamic business organizations expect them to be practicing Muslims and the structure of the working day is dictated by the requisite religious rituals such as the times for prayer.

Management culture

Turkish management culture has to be understood both in the context of the overall national culture but also in terms of Turkey's economic situation. Turkey today is still primarily an agricultural economy. In 1994, 45 per cent of the population were employed in agriculture and only 22 per cent in industry; the remainder were employed in the services sector, although the respective contributions to GDP were 16 per cent (agriculture), 33 per cent (industry) and 51 per cent (services) (OECD, 1997).

With regard to work-related values (Hofstede, 1980) Turkish management culture is characterized by high power distance, high uncertainty avoidance, collectivism and femininity (Ascigil and Ryan, 1998). These work-related values manifest themselves in a variety of ways in the workplace. Turkish organizations tend to be strongly hierarchical and the predominant leadership pattern autocratic (Fikret-Pasa and Kabasakal, 1998). Management style is largely directive (Zhuplev and Gray, 1998). This aspect of organizations reflects in part the military traditions of Turkish society as well as prescriptive elements of Islam. Hierarchy and authoritarianism also mitigate uncertainty (people know where they stand and what they should do). In general there are clear-cut guidelines indicating what you should do under particular circumstances.

The excesses of authoritarianism are counterbalanced by the role played by collectivism and 'feminine' (that is, caring) values. Bosses are likely to be in this context paternalistic; paternalism 'personalizes' the hierarchical relationship between superiors and subordinates and is viewed as the leadership style preferred by subordinates (Fikret-Pasa and Kabasakal, 1998). This concern for others, which extends beyond workplace relationships, also applies to one's fellow workers. Individuals owe allegiance to the group within which they work. Meeting the expectations and needs of the groups is regarded as more important than fulfilling one's own individual ambitions, although this does not mean that individual ambitions do not exist and may on occasions frustrate effective group working. The corollary of this mutually supportive relationship is that the group is in turn expected to assist individual members. According to Kaynak (Zhuplev and Gray, 1998), while money is the prime motivator of

Turkish employees, this was closely followed by social relations, security and achievement. Furthermore, Kepir-Sinangil and Aycan (1998) found that HRM practices in Turkish companies in Istanbul were marked by high degrees of paternalism and loyalty towards the community. A further consequence of the people orientation of Turkish culture is that considerations of time play a secondary role to personal relationships. Concern for people (and giving one's time to people) is therefore regarded as more important than mere punctuality (Gannon *et al.*, 1994).

Kepir-Sinangil and Aycan (1998) also found evidence of a shift in work-related values since the 1980s, in particular a move from high to medium levels of collectivism and power distance. Such shifts have a number of possible explanations. Firstly, industrialization and, possibly more significantly, urbanization have weakened traditional values such as collectivism and respect for authority. Secondly, the opening up of the Turkish economy and the general impact of global trends have worked in a similar direction. Thirdly, Turkish management and Turkish managers are strongly influenced by American perspectives. The management taught in Turkish universities reflects strongly American viewpoints and practices. Furthermore, many Turkish academics and senior business practitioners have studied in the USA and speak the language of American management. Presumably they also seek to implement in their companies what they have learned.

There is thus evidence of some evolution of Turkish management towards a synthesis of traditional Turkish and imported American values and practices. This does not signify, however, a simple adoption of American managerial values. While the agenda for companies may be largely determined by global forces, the way in which the agenda is interpreted and implemented is also influenced by the respective national culture (Edwards and Lawrence, 1996). A study of quality management in American and Turkish companies (Yavas, Janda and Marcoulides, 1998) found no difference in the way American and Turkish managers conceptualized quality. Turkish managers, however, placed greater emphasis on communicating and achieving a shared definition of quality, reflecting the group orientation of the Turkish business culture. Furthermore, Turkish managers stressed more than American managers issues relating to quality implementation and control (reflecting the greater degree of power distance).

Conclusion

Turkish managers display a number of strengths. They demonstrate an ability to manage in a volatile political, economic and social environment. The Turkish economy is characterized by high growth rates, high inflation and a widening prosperity divide. At the same time the opening up of the economy with accession to the EU Customs Union and expanding volumes of FDI has subjected Turkish managers to increasing competition from foreign companies.

A key strength of Turkish managers is their ability to use traditional dimensions of Turkish culture, in particular its people-orientation, to adapt to changes in the Turkish economy and transform work practices (for example, in the area of quality management) and to build bridges with foreign partners. This willingness to respond positively to evolving circumstances seems in turn to be influencing the very nature of Turkish management and business cultures, lessening the attachment to collectivism and acceptance of autocratic leadership styles.

The Turkish economy is likely to continue to experience numerous changes as privatization and liberalization intensify. Increasing foreign direct investment has been matched by Turkey's approaches to the European Union, but also to Eastern Europe and nearby former Soviet republics in Central Asia. In essence, this outward expansion encapsulates the Turkish position, with one foot in Europe and one foot in Asia. Accession to the European Union remains a delicate issue. If Turkey's application continues to be rejected, this stance could push Turkey into becoming a more Asian-oriented, possibly more Islamic-influenced, and consequently less European state.

References

Aldemir, C. (1998) 'The Impact of Historical, Political, Economic and Social Factors on the Organizational Context of Turkey', Western Academy of Management 5th International Conference, Istanbul, 29 June–2 July.

Ascigil, S. and M. Ryan (1998) 'Micro-politics in Participative Decision Making: a Cross-cultural Comparison', Western Academy of Management 5th International Conference, Istanbul, 29 June–2 July.

Culpan, R. (1998) 'A Critical Assessment of Turkish Privatization Program', Western Academy of Management 5th International Conference, Istanbul, 29 June–2 July.

Edwards, V. and P. Lawrence (1996) 'Country versus Industry: The Dynamics of Strategic Differentiation', Proceedings of the Twenty-Fifth Annual Meeting of the Western Decision Sciences Institute, pp. 136–43.

Erçek, M. (1998) 'Evolutionary Dynamics of Interorganizational Exchange Relationships: The Case of Turkish IT Suppliers', Western Academy of Management 5th International Conference, Istanbul, 29 June–2 July.

Fikret-Pasa, S. and H. Kabasakal (1998) 'The Impact of Historical, Political, Economic and Social Factors on the Organizational Context of Turkey', Western Academy of Management 5th International Conference, Istanbul, 29 June–2 July.

Gannon, M. and Associates (1994) 'The Turkish Coffeehouse', in Gannon, M. and Associates, *Understanding Global Cultures*, pp. 195–213, Thousand Oaks: Sage.

Guide to Turkey 1996, Euromoney.

Guide to Turkey 1997, Euromoney.

Hofstede, G. (1980) *Culture's Consequences*, Beverly Hills: Sage.

Kepir-Sinangil, H. and Z. Aycan (1998) 'Organizations and HRM Practices Contextualized: Case of Turkey', Western Academy of Management 5th International Conference, Istanbul, 29 June–2 July.

Kuran, T. (1998) 'Making Sense of the Ongoing Attempts to give Middle Eastern Economies an Islamic Character', Western Academy of Management 5th International Conference, Istanbul, 29 June–2 July.

OECD (1997), *OECD in Figures*, OECD.

Selekler, N. (1998) 'Continuity and Change in the Strategy and Structure of Turkish Holding Companies', Western Academy of Management 5th International Conference, Istanbul, 29 June–2 July.

Yavas, B.; S. Janda and G. Marcoulides (1998) 'Quality Management: A Comparison of Managerial Attitudes in the USA and Turkey', Western Academy of Management 5th International Conference, Istanbul, 29 June–2 July.

Zhuplev, A. and E. Gray (1998) 'Turkey: The Evolving Business Scene, An Interview With Erdener Kaynak' *Journal of Management Inquiry*, 7,1, pp. 55–9.

CHAPTER 7

Germany

There is quite a good case for arguing that for more than half a century Germany has been economically successful in spite of defying the laws of business and management. It may be helpful to set the scene with a story – true of course!

Once upon a time one of the authors was a guest at a firm in Germany that had two product lines, one of which was flexible metal tubes. A rival company, also German, had begun to manufacture some of these tubes in a light-weight alloy. The director of the tubes division of the visited company called a meeting of all his principal subordinates to decide how the company should respond to the competitor's challenge. The interesting thing was that the only option that was considered was developing a rival product in the same alloy that would be better than that of the competitor – and would recapture any lost market. Possibilities that were *not* considered included:

- trying to acquire or merge with the competitor,
- making the competitor's product under licence,
- withdrawing from that segment 'in order to concentrate on core business',
- trying to beat the competitor by means of price reductions on standard material products,
- any promotional expenditure to try to reinforce the loyalty of existing customers.

In other words this company was narrow, stupid, and blinkered. An undergraduate strategy seminar would have made mincemeat of them. Indeed it is even worse than may seem to be the case from the abbreviated account offered so far. That is to say, the meeting was relatively unconcerned with costs – with the cost of developing this new product. Indeed costs were not mentioned until the meeting had been going on for an hour. The competitor's alloy products were on display throughout the meeting, and attracted much interest from the delegates. They were examined, touched, even fondled. At one point in the discussion a delegate to the meeting suggested more or less copying the competitor's product with a few modifications for the sake of appearances. This drew a sharp rebuke from the division director running the meeting:

You are here to produce a better product not find loopholes in the patent law.

American standards

This tendency for German management to be strong on *Technik* and weak on business thinking was documented several decades ago when the West German (as it then was) *Wirtschaftsministerium* (approximately equivalent to the British Department of Trade and Industry) decided to commission a general evaluation of German management by the American consulting firm Booz Allen and Hamilton. The German ministry got more than it bargained for in that the ensuing report (Booz Allen and Hamilton, 1973) roundly condemned German management – for being old-fashioned, unprofessional, weak on business thinking.

Particular charges in the report included:

- German companies are person-oriented rather than system-oriented; that is they lack, in the American view, management systems – the essence of professionalism.
- Top managers are poor at formulating objectives; some companies lack a written statement of objectives; mission statements are rare; corporate planning is not very professional, and there is inadequate commitment to the idea that company performance must be measured against a plan including specified objectives.
- German managers tend to be 'operators' first and foremost; those at the top have this mentality and a penchant for (inappropriate) detail; few top managers in Germany have advanced to their position from staff functions, and this in turn vitiates their ability to engage in dispassionate strategic thinking.
- German thinking on diversification and expansion is also a weakness; Germany companies are held to be slow to diversify; they do not see merger and acquisition on the one hand and R&D (research and development) on the other as alternatives; are weak on merger activity.
- German firms are weak on delegation, German managers often have large spans of control.
- German management is criticized as being weak on the management techniques and specialisms of the time, for instance, OR, management information systems, decision theory, and so on.
- German companies are weak on marketing, as opposed to sales; do not appreciate that there is a series of interrelated decisions/activities con-

cerning pricing policy, choice of distribution channel, advertising and promotion; they concentrate (narrowly) on sales.

Finally the Booz Allen and Hamilton report concedes, a little grudgingly, that
German management is well-educated, but note that this is not the same as
being *trained* in management.

This evaluation of German management is of course somewhat partial. Its
implicit assumption is that American management practice is the best and other
countries can and should be measured against American standards. So we might
not want to accept the judgements, we might wish to interpret, point to some
corresponding strengths, perhaps even re-define some weaknesses as strengths.
But the Booz Allen and Hamilton report is helpful in characterizing German
management. In our view it makes the important points:

- German management is not Americanised.
- Systems, strategy and techniques are not in the foreground.

The report also inspires the question: What else is there, what did they miss?

German differences

Industrial democracies

One feature that differentiates public companies in Germany (those with AG
after the company name corresponding to PLC in Britain) from their Anglo-
Saxon counterparts is that they have what are usually called two-tier boards.
That is to say, instead of having a single board of directors, the AG has two: a
non-executive supervisory board or *Aufsichtsrat*, and an executive committee
or *Vorstand* staffed by full-time, salaried senior managers in the company. The
Aufsichtsrat appoints the *Vorstand*, and the *Vorstand* runs the company. To be
fair the report discussed in the previous section does mention these arrangements but only to criticize the Germans for practising management by committee: the rationale for this criticism is that in theory the *Vorstand* is a collegial
body taking collective decisions, having a chairman rather than a chief executive. In practice, however, there is probably little real difference.

Omitted entirely, however, from the report is any mention of codetermination or industrial democracy. Germany can probably claim the oldest and best
established system of codetermination in the world, having experimented with
advisory bodies representing both sides of industry as early as the First World
War (1914–18) and with a version of works councils operating in the 1920s.
All this was swept away when Hitler and the Nazis came to power in 1933,
but after the Second World War (1939–45) there was strong pressure from

German trade unions to (re-)establish a system of industrial democracy, a desire that was supported by the 1945–51 Labour government in Britain.

As early as 1950 the newly established Federal Republic of Germany (West Germany) introduced a law making one half of the membership of the *Aufsichtsrat* trade union/employee representatives (the other half, of course, together with the chairman, are representatives of the shareholders) in the iron, steel and coal industry. The 1950 Act also required the appointment of a Labour Director for the *Vorstand*, this member of course having a particular responsibility for personnel issues. Subsequent legislation, culminating in the 1976 Codetermination Act, spread a variously modified version of this system to all branches of industry. And arguably more important than these various representatives of labour in the *Aufsichtsrat* and *Vorstand* was the law of 1952 establishing Works Councils, bodies composed of elected worker representatives. These Works Councils had the right to decide, or give their consent to, all sorts of day-to-day issues in the workplace from job changes for blue collar employees to canteen prices. The Councils also have to be consulted by management on a variety of issues, and have the statutory right to receive information on the company's performance. All this has obliged a degree of cooperation between management and workers unequalled in say Britain or France.

Industrial democracy is no longer a topical issue in the hard-pressed 1990s, and as the twentieth century draws to a close the system is somewhat under strain in Germany itself. The fact remains that in Western Europe Germany has led the way, and the institutions of codetermination in that country have contributed to decades of relative industrial peace.

Technik

Moving to a new theme, in the mid twentieth century it used to be said that the only German words known to non-German speakers were ones having to do with war, such as *Blitzkreig*, *Panzer*, and *Stuka*. Then in the 1970s Britain acquired the word *Technik*. Lots of British children played with jolly construction kits from *Fischer Technik*, and then no less an institution than VAG launched the Audi advertisement with the punch line *Vorsprung durch Technik*. A word was born.

Although the English language in categorizing subjects and bodies of knowledge simply distinguishes between Arts & Science (slotting in engineering as 'applied science') German has three key terms. First there is *Wissenschaft* which denotes those subjects whose output is codified knowledge, all formal knowledge subjects that is, whether they are humanities, social science, or natural science; then there is *Kunst* which is art but the reference is to the output of the arts – the poetry, paintings and symphonies – rather than to the subjects; and thirdly there is *Technik*. It denotes engineering knowledge and craft skill; it is about the coming into being of three dimensional artefacts – something that Germans find more absorbing than anyone else.

Manufacturing industry in Germany is suffused, even dominated by *Technik*, and it shows in a variety of ways, of which the most striking is the importance attached to the products, their design, their fashioning, their quality, their reliability, and this is in the German scheme of things the essence of competitive advantage. When representatives of German companies are asked about sources of pride and success they talk products – not finance, not marketing, not strategy.

People qualified in engineering are very numerous in German industry. Engineering may not (anymore) be the best route to the top, but there are a lot of engineers and they exert an influence by weight of numbers, in the sense of being a standing lobby for products, design, and technical investment.

A further reflection of the *Technik* ethos is that managers on the technical side of the company tend to have higher qualification levels than managers on the commercial side. And managers qualified in engineering have tended to over-spill into non-technical functions – sales, purchasing, personnel, and occasionally strategy 'think tanks' and significant personal assistantships to senior executives – although the reverse is not true (non-engineers do not overspill into the technical functions). Again in German companies the technical departments or functions – R&D, design, production, engineering, quality assurance – tend to enjoy higher standing than has traditionally been the case in Britain.

Underpinning all this is a valorization of skill – its acquisition and deployment – at blue-collar level. The term *Facharbeiter* (skilled worker) is a legally protected status in Germany. And one can only call oneself a skilled worker if one has done a recognized apprenticeship, and passed the craft and theoretical tests at the end of it. Being a *Facharbeiter* in Germany means something; it is more consequential than the claim to being a skilled worker in the English speaking world. Correspondingly apprenticeship is a national institution. There are getting on for 500 occupations for which a recognized apprenticeship exists. Over 60 per cent of the age group do an apprenticeship in Germany. In contrast to Britain apprenticeship in Germany is not limited to the 'first generation' industrial revolution trades – welder, boilermaker, fitter, and so on. Apprenticeship has consistently embraced later industries – electrical engineering, chemicals, telecommunications – and spread to jobs in the service sector as well, for example to banking. A job for which an apprenticeship exists is known as a *Lernberuf*, a learning occupation, an expression with a very positive ring to it.

To complete the picture the traditional foreman in German industry, the *Meister*, is someone who has completed an apprenticeship and become a skilled worker *and* a further $3^{1}/_{2}$ year part-time foreman training course eventuating in another examination and formal qualification. A German foreman is in the first instance one who understands the work processes and the jobs, not a gang boss.

Hidden champions

Much of the strategic and market impact of *Technik* is captured in a mid 1990s study of a group of medium-sized German companies which the author, an American consultant Hermann Simon, calls Hidden Champions (Simon, 1996).

The companies reviewed by Simon are leaders in the sense of being the number one or number two in their industry, and having a high market share, absolute or relative.

Consider one or two examples*: Hauni Werke Koerber, a company a little way outside Hamburg, makes cigarette making machinery. It is the world's only supplier of complete systems for processing tobacco. All the filter cigarettes in the world are made with Hauni machines, and they have a 90 per cent market share of high-speed cigarette making machines. Or again Maschinenfabrik Rudolf Baader, on the edge of the city of Lübeck close to the Baltic Coast, makes fish processing equipment. Simon gives their world market share as 90 per cent. Or Stihl, the chain-saw manufacturer located in a small town in Baden Würtemberg in the south has a world market share of 30 per cent, twice that of the nearest competitor.

These Hidden Champion companies are not for the most part small: they belong rather to the German *Mittelstand* (medium sized companies) numbering their employees in hundreds rather than tens. They tend to be family owned, they are often located in small towns or villages rather than in big manufacturing centres. They are marked by steady rather than spectacular growth and they tend to be in specialist areas of product or service rather than in high profile areas (whoever would have thought about making machines to take the bones out of fish). The companies are innovative, and in some cases have created a market, for instance Brite which invented point of use water filters and has a world market share of 85 per cent.

In Simon's view *Technik* is in the foreground:

> Technology is the single most important factor behind the competitive advantages and global market leadership of the hidden champions (Simon, 1996:124)

They are innovative and inventive (incidentally Simon produces data to show that Germany applies for more international patents per head of population than any other country on earth). Their products are superior, discriminating as to customer need and application, and are often in specialist or niche areas that are not sufficiently obvious to attract big competition – Sachtler makes not cameras but tripods for cameras, Putzmeister makes pumps that pump concrete (they were involved in neutralizing the Chernobyl reactor), Glasbau Hahn

---

* The authors have tended to take companies they have researched or visited themselves from Simon's sample of over a hundred.

makes glass showcases for museums, Biotech makes hygiene test devices, and so on; all this is a far cry from motor cars and colour TVs.

The hidden champions take the manufacturing seriously, to put it mildly. They employ skilled labour forces, have low employee turnover, and sickness rates well below the German national average. They do as much of the manufacturing as is possible in house; Simon expresses it by saying they have 'deep manufacture' being loath to sub-contract, outsource, or buy-in manufactured parts. Some of them make (some of) the machines on which their products are made; some developed their own test equipment. Both these trends – building own machines and devising testing equipment – are quite common in the authors' experience, and not restricted to the 'hidden champion' category of companies.

Again the hidden champions avoided both product and business diversification. They specialized in servicing niche markets. Thus their expansion comes from internationalization, from servicing these niches world-wide, whether by export or by having manufacturing subsidies located abroad (but not by allowing anyone else abroad to manufacture the products under licence).

Indeed the inclination to do everything themselves, to be personally responsible, was a general characteristic of the hidden champions, which we have already noted in connection with the manufacturing process. When it comes to exporting the hidden champions again wanted to do it themselves, and have direct contact with customers abroad as well as at home. They did not like to rely on agents in foreign countries, or be represented by indigenous companies abroad.

The same 'go it alone mentality' can be seen in a wider strategic context where the hidden champions did not seek to expand, or to diversify, by means of merger or acquisition (a few had been acquired by larger companies, but largely left to their own devices). The hidden champions had no enthusiasm for strategic alliances with other companies either.

Simon's research is fascinating precisely because of the paradox it poses. Here we have a group of companies whose behaviour is really quite old fashioned: no subcontracting, no outsourcing, no make or buy decisions, no diversification, no export agents, and no strategic alliances (is this the 'failure to delegate' criticized in the Booz Allen and Hamilton report?). At the same time these companies are market leaders, successful exporters, and show considerable powers of corporate endurance.

Termintreue

There is a general presumption that Germans take punctuality seriously and that German companies can be depended upon to deliver the goods they have promised on time. We have introduced this bit of folk-wisdom for two reasons, albeit briefly. First because it is interesting to unpack it in cultural-linguistic terms, and second because there is a bit of hard evidence!

First, language. In English there is not really any set phrase for the reliability with which manufacturing companies deliver consignments of goods to customers. Delivery punctuality and delivery performance are comprehensible, in context, but are not really standard expressions. But German has a standard expression for just this manufacturing contingency and it is *Termintreue*, literally deadline faithfulness. The derivation of *Termin* is also interesting. If one were summoned for some presumptive infraction of the law the time and date on which one had to appear in court was the *Termin*: so the term is redolent with the majesty of the Wilhelminan State! In industry too *Termin* is used in all sorts of variations and compound nouns. In addition to *Termin* and *Termintreue*, *terminlich* means of or pertaining to deadlines, *Terminsachen* are deadline contingencies, and a *Termingespräch* is a production scheduling meeting – these are very grave affairs in a German company.

The hard evidence comes from a study of buying and selling of industrial goods between companies in different countries, unfortunately not a recent study (Turnbull & Cunningham, 1981). The countries in the study were Britain, France, Germany, Italy, and Sweden, and a number of aspects of their buying and selling behaviour were investigated, including *Termintreue*. The country which came top, that is had the best record for delivering goods at the time promised, was Sweden – with Germany as a close second. Britain sorry to say was bottom, by a sizeable margin.

Specialism

German management is suffused by specialism as opposed to generalism, an idea that has surfaced several times already in this chapter. To step back for a moment it might be helpful to say that management may be depicted in generalist or in specialist terms. One may take the generalist view believing that all management tasks will have much in common, that ability to perform them rests on the possession of certain personal skills and character traits and trained competencies. This tends to be for example the American view, where one needs drive, energy and ambition together with a mastery of the management systems in any company. The American manager will be inclined to the view that he or she can 'manage' anything and this is reflected in the high mobility between companies and functions noted in the chapter on the USA. Or again the British view is that managers need leadership qualities and a variety of personal skills, and that this applies generally to management jobs. The British manager is often pleased to be described as 'a good all rounder'.

Now the contrast we are making here is not a black and white one but Germans are inclined to a more specialist view of management. For them the particular job function, the specific nature of the activity, the industry, the products and processes involved all tend to matter more than management generalities. If one looks at German job advertisements, for example, there is more emphasis on the specifics – of the job, of the skills and qualifications needed, of the industry in which the company operates. If one talks to personnel managers in German companies who are charged with management recruitment they will of course mention some of the general qualities that will figure in Anglo-Saxon accounts, but they will be more specific about the knowledge and experience bases demanded of suitable applicants.

This penchant for specialism informs German patterns of manager mobility, especially mobility between companies. First, mobility is not regarded as 'a good thing' *per se*, whereas the Anglo-Saxon view tends to be to treat mobility as evidence of ambition and as an important contribution to the development of generalist capabilities. Second, mobility between companies in different industries makes no sense to Germans: in this contingency when you moved to the second company you would be discarding all the knowledge and skill you had acquired in the first company, a manoeuvre best left to flighty Anglo-Saxons!

A German view of management

There is something else that differentiates management in Germany from management in the Anglo-Saxon countries, though it is not easy to put into words. The more specific focus of the Germans explored in the previous section tends to displace the generalities of management. This focus tends to be on products, industry specifics, and what Booz Allen and Hamilton dismiss as 'operations!'. These specifics are more real for Germans than American-style questions along the lines of: 'What business are we in?'; 'What is the mission of this company?'

One might put it another way and say that Germans have a weaker view of management. Germans are purposeful, they will work hard, they will take their task seriously, but they come less readily than their Anglo-Saxon counterparts to the view that there is something separable called 'management', that one may extrapolate it, analyse it, and generalize about it. They are more inclined to the view that there is a management element in many jobs rather than that management is a discrete job with its own independent dynamics.

Similarly Germans may find American-style strategic analysis a little remote, and are more inclined to the view, rightly or wrongly, that if your company makes the best forklift trucks there is not anything else to worry about. This disposition is also evident in the German view of organizational structure. Germans see it as less salient than Anglo-Saxons, are less likely to seek to change something or get a desired outcome by re-arranging the organizational structure. The authors recall once asking a German manager about the need to change structure in line with emergent strategy, and received this dismissive reply

> *Schliesslich geht es nur um Leute die zusammenarbeiten müssen.*
> (At the end of the day the organization is just a set of people who have to work together.)

The differences we have been arguing in this section are not black and white contrasts with the Anglo-Saxon world, but differences of relative emphasis.

Tradition and change in Germany

So far we have tended to offer a traditional view of German management both via the critical testimony of the Booz Allen and Hamilton report and more sympathetically from Hermann Simon and from the authors' own research experience. But none of this is to suggest that German management is changeless.

First, there has been a change in the mix and popularity of the various qualifications. All through the 1950s, 1960s, and 1970s every survey of German managers showed that the majority who were university educated were qualified in law, engineering, and economics – both business economics (*Betriebswirtschaftslehre*) and political economy (*Volkswirtschaftslehre*). The engineers were always the most numerous, and tended to dominate by sheer weight of numbers, while law was regarded as probably the best way to the very top – people with law degrees are over-represented in top jobs particularly in the financial services sector, and on the *Aufsichtsrat* (supervisory board) of all sorts of companies, especially in the position of chairman. Economics, or rather the business economics variant, tended to be a bit of a poor cousin. It should be added that this subject *Betriebswirtschaftslehre*, is the nearest approach that Germany offers to an Anglo-Saxon style business administration degree. In the 1980s the 'poor cousin' status changed, and enrolments on business economics courses increased dramatically and their graduates began to impact on German business life.

Second, in the 1980s and 1990s there has been some restructuring of the German economy. Some household names disappeared, such as Grundig and AEG-Telefunken. Merger and acquisition activity became not uncommon among larger companies though not as common as in the USA or in Britain. Cross-border take-overs started to appear. German banks began to buy British merchant banks, and one of the big three German banks, the Dresdener Bank actually has a cross-border strategic alliance with BNP of France. At the time of writing (early 1998) three out of the four contenders to buy Rolls Royce from Vickers are German – Mercedes Benz, BMW, and VAG (Volkswagen and Audi). Or again some traditionally rather dispersed industries, for instance brewing (at the start of the 1990s it was estimated that there were between 1200 and 1500 breweries in Germany) are showing signs of concentration, as in other Western European countries (Lawrence, 1998).

Third, German industry has become more cost conscious in the last twenty years of the century. It is not that German producers have come to 'sell on price' as opposed to design-quality-reliability, but rather that both direct and indirect labour costs in Germany are very high, such as to raise in acute form the case for 'off-shore' manufacturing even though this goes against German instincts. This problem of remaining competitive in the face of high labour costs is captured in the expression *Standort Deutschland* (not easy to translate but it carries the sense of 'based in Germany' with an interrogative overtone). The same challenge is faced by Germany's neighbour Switzerland and the analogous term *Standort Schweiz* is used to signal the debate. In both countries the question in essence is why should any manufacturing operation be based in these countries in view of their cost disadvantage: there are of course answers to this question but posing the question is itself legitimate. An obvious manifestation of the *Standort Deutschland* issue is the fairly recent move by German companies to establish manufacturing subsidiaries in other countries. High profile examples of this trend in the 1990s are the Mercedes factory in Alabama and the BMW plant in South Carolina. Now while it is very reasonable to seek to service the American market in this way, the fact remains that American labour costs are significantly lower than German ones.

Fourth, though it is clearly related to the issue of costs and *Standort Deutschland* the 1990s have seen a change in the tenor of wage bargaining in Germany. The well established German system is that the relevant trade union would reach a wage agreement with the relevant branch of the employers' federation which would be binding on companies (the majority) affiliated to the employers federation (and companies not affiliated would also often accept the deal). Note that under this system wage bargaining is not at plant level, nor at company level, but at *industry* level. Also until well into the 1980s individual companies would pay more than the agreement specified. In contrast what we have in the late 1990s is employers clamouring for plant level bargaining, American style, and individual companies paying less than the trade union–employers' federation agreements.

Notwithstanding these changes the lack of strategic awareness castigated a quarter of a century ago by the Booz Allen and Hamilton report is still perceptible. In the mid 1990s one of the authors took part in a European Union (EU) funded research project that sought to probe the determinants of corporate strategy in selected industries in seven of the EU countries including Germany (Lawrence, 1998). The study proceeded in terms of interviews with senior executives in representative companies in the chosen industries in each country. Reading the transcripts of the German interviews we were struck by the unease with which many of the Germans responded to admittedly general and open-ended questions about strategy and competitive advantage. Time and again the Germans would ask the interviewer to define terms, be more specific, frame the questions in more concrete way. These German executives also showed a tendency to give answers that are straight and simple rather than strategically elaborate. Several replied to a question about international strategy by saying their purpose was to offer products that would satisfy demanding German customers such that these products would *ipso facto* find favour on world markets. This is arguably another example of the specifics dominating managerial perception, alluded to earlier.

Reunification

In the course of the twentieth century Germany has faced two quite exceptional challenges. The first was reconstruction after the Second World War (1939–45), the (very successful) story of which has been told many times, one of these accounts being by one of the present writers in an earlier book (Lawrence, 1980). The second exceptional challenge is of course reunification of the two separate German states – the German Federal Republic (West Germany) and the German Democratic Republic (East Germany) which occurred in 1990, one of the many consequences of the collapse of European communism in the 1989–91 period.*

Much less has been written about the consequences of reunification for business and management, reunification is too recent to allow for a proper evaluation, and the situation is in any case evolving. Nevertheless we can go some way to mapping the changes. It may be helpful to start with an outline of the old system of industrial organization that existed in East Germany until the latter part of 1989.

The old regime

East Germany was communist, and had a command economy or centrally planned economy, where nearly all the commercial and manufacturing entities were state owned enterprises (SOEs). The system was driven by the Plan Commission at the top which developed an overall plan for the productive economy. This plan was disaggregated via the various industry ministries and eventually reached the SOEs in the form of output quotas for the year. Meeting

---

* We intend to use the popular rather than the official names for these two states, namely West Germany and East Germany.

quotas was the primary objective of the *Betriebsdirektor* (works director) who would head up each manufacturing SOE. If you met the quota you were fine, if you exceeded the quota you would get a bonus, if you failed to meet the quota you would try to fake it and to fabricate acceptable excuses. In the attempt to meet the quota the works director and other staff would do all sorts of things ranging from those that lay within their discretion officially on the one hand to operating the informal system and occasionally engaging in criminal acts on the other. This ethos is caught in a piece of folk wisdom of the communist period:

> *Der Betriebsdirektor steht immer mit einem Fuss im Gefängnis.*
> (The works director already has one foot in jail.)

The SOEs were big. Bigger that is to say than the equivalent works in West Germany and in the West. Generally the communists believed that big equalled efficient. There was also considerable vertical tiering of institutions in communist East Germany, where several SOEs making similar or complementary products would report to a *Kombinat* (combine) and several of these combines would report to the appropriate industry ministry which would in turn be coordinated by the Plan Commission. The research and development (R&D) function was often taken out of the individual SOEs, and 'bulked' at the *Kombinat* level; sometimes the R&D function was exercised on behalf of the *Kombinat* by a university linked research institute. Most of the nation's foreign trade was with other COMECON countries, that is the group of central and eastern European communist countries orchestrated by the former USSR (communist Russia). These COMECON countries traded primarily with each other in non-convertible (soft) currencies. While they sold to the West to acquire hard currency whenever they could, they would avoid buying from the West as much as possible, both on ideological grounds and to preserve scarce supplies of hard currencies.

The *Betriebsdirektor* lacked the managerial discretion and strategic responsibilities of his Western counterpart. He (they were usually men) would normally be qualified in some branch of engineering and would rise through the production management hierarchy. Production would be his prime concern, and a higher proportion of all employees would work in production compared with a Western company. There was no sales or marketing function, but the purchasing function was critical – if you could get all the materials you were well placed to meet the production quota – and purchasing also employed relatively more people.

Finally because the whole system was bureaucratic, inflexible, and inefficient, individuals strove to insulate themselves against the inefficiencies of the system in various ways:

- by massively over-staffing, especially with production workers,
- by making 'in house' everything they could (no outsourcing or sub-contracting),

- by 'internalizing' their sources of supply wherever possible, for example, a civil engineering SOE might well make its own bricks,
- by having elaborate 'in-house' maintenance capability; note the equipment tended to be junky and unreliable,
- by stockpiling anything you could get your hands on; even if you did not need it, you might be able to trade it with another SOE for something you did need.

These tendencies were summed up in a standard expression from the communist period, *Autarkiestreben* – striving for autarky or independence.

Die Wende

The change, *die Wende*, was rapid when it came. Since the building of the Berlin Wall in 1961 the East German state was pretty effectively sealed off from the West. But East Germany was tied to other communist European countries. In the summer of 1989 communist Hungary opened its border with capitalist Austria – East Germans started to escape to West Germany via Czechoslovakia – Hungary – Austria. When the East German government managed to close the border between Czechoslovakia and Hungary would-be escaping East Germans camped *en masse* at the West German Embassy in Prague, and eventually had to be let out. Throughout the summer and autumn anti-communist demonstrations gathered momentum in East Germany. Then on the evening of Thursday 9th November 1989, after a rather ambiguous TV announcement to the effect that East Germans would be allowed to visit West Berlin the communist authorities actually opened the crossing points into West Berlin and thousands of East Germans streamed across for the night of their lives.

The opening of the Berlin Wall signalled the end of communism in East Germany. A provisional government was appointed, and eventually accepted West German political leadership and the inevitability of reunification. In preparation for this, currency union was implemented in July 1990, that is to say the West German Deutschmark became the currency for East Germany as well, on a one-for-one basis, and unification itself took place on 3rd October 1990, thus ending 45 years of separation.

Immediate consequences

Reunification added about 17 million people to the population of West Germany, making Germany by far and away the largest state in the European Union (EU) as well as the largest economy. Our focus here, however, is on the implications of reunification for the SOEs of the former state of East Germany.

First of all the former SOEs were affected by currency union, which as we have seen was in place before reunification. Currency union made East Germany a hard currency country thus disrupting its foreign trade with its former COMECON partners whose currencies were still inconvertible. Second, the combined effect of currency union and reunification was to open up the East German market to West German competition. In the early days of reunification a lot of former East German SOEs lost control of their (East) German domestic market; since West German companies typically offered goods of higher quality, the companies had better productivity, and there was among the former communist citizens of East Germany a fashionable preference for western and West German goods. Third, because the communist regimes in the other communist countries were also destabilized and then swept away trade relations between them were further disrupted. Remember that under communism an SOE always sold to a public authority of some kind, whether at home or elsewhere in the communist world, not to a private corporation or to members of the general public. At the time of the fall of communism in these central and eastern European states confusion reigned, it was difficult to determine who or what were 'the public authorities'. In short the former East German SOEs were hit pretty badly, especially in the first year after currency union.

In a sense reunification is a misnomer. What happened is that communist East Germany was assimilated to the capitalist West German state. That is to say former East Germany acquired at the time of reunification West German companies' legislation, labour courts, trade unions, commercial law, political parties and the West German codetermination system. East Germany also became part of the EU with reunification, not that this helped former East German SOEs much since they lacked the quality, and credibility, to sell to other EU countries.

The key development regarding the East German SOEs, however, was the decision taken to privatize them. The decision was taken in the interim period between the fall of communism and the act of reunification. In 1990 an organization known as the *Treuhand* was set up, charged with finding buyers for several thousand SOEs, but for many SOEs there was a significant lapse of time between the crumbling of the communist system in the last months of 1989 and acquiring new owners. In this interim a lot of the SOEs had to 'look out for themselves', the communist state having ceased to do it for them. It is to these changes in this period that we now turn.

The run-up to privatization

With the coming of reunification a few of these SOEs promptly collapsed – ones for whom the government was not only the order placer but the end user were particularly vulnerable; some others in consumer goods areas fell to West

German competition; some failed because they were so large, unwieldly, and over-manned that they would never receive another order for their products.

But most of them survived. A few of them continued to be run by *exactly* the same set of managers that had directed them in the later stages of the communist period, but in most cases the top managers from the old regime 'deserted ship' or were pushed out by popular demand with authority passing to some existing manager in the SOE, someone who enjoyed the confidence of the staff, someone less identified with the communist regime.

Those surviving SOEs were quick to recognize their problems with reference to markets and currency referred to above. They made efforts to maintain or recover their 'East German' domestic market and diligently sought out the appropriate authorities in other former communist states in the hope of continuing export sales. Initiatives of this kind were aided by the German government introducing in the Spring of 1991 a kind of export guarantee scheme for former East German companies selling into the former COMECON countries.

Those in charge of the SOEs also tended to review the range of products, and typically reduced it, concentrating on the things they did best. They also slimmed down their companies in terms of manpower and range of operations, selling off inessential bits, closing ancillary sites, out-sourcing, slimming the workforce, reducing the size of the purchasing section (see above) and enjoying more choice in the purchasing of materials and parts on the open market.

But what managers running the SOEs awaiting privatization did above all else was to compare themselves with their West German counterparts in terms of manufacturing efficiency, productivity, and product quality.

They found, of course, their own firms to be seriously wanting in these respects, and most of the SOEs saw this as the principal challenge. So they struggled to improve manufacturing efficiency, to achieve the good manufacturing practice norms of the West, and strove for West German product quality. These endeavours were fuelled by upgrading the technical process of production, that is by the purchase of modern machinery and equipment – a very German emphasis. These purchases were variously paid for out of retained earnings, by selling off unwanted sites or assets, and by loans from banks and from the *Treuhand*.

Now these manufacturing efficiency and quality goals which the SOEs set themselves were of course very challenging, and the SOEs became absorbed in them. The SOEs' managers also fell readily into the trap of assuming that when they had carried out these manufacturing improvements they would have solved their problems, 'the phone would ring', and orders would flow in. For the most part this did not happen. However much the German SOEs spent on new manufacturing they had a bad image in the Western market place, no corporate record, and faced the uncertainties of privatization. The SOEs awaiting privatization often made heroic efforts but circumstances were against them, and they tended to lack an overall strategy for success, putting their faith in technical improvement alone.

Privatization

As we have seen a few of the SOEs went bankrupt in the early stages of *die Wende* and were not available to be sold by the *Treuhand*. At the other end of the spectrum there were a hard-core of ultimately unsaleable companies – typically large, old-fashioned engineering companies, often with poor equipment and inflated work forces. In between these extremes were the majority of companies that the *Treuhand* did indeed sell. Some but not very many were management buyouts (MBOs), but the majority were bought by other companies – some by foreign companies (British, American, Japanese and so on) but most of all by West German companies and investors. The generalizations which follow refer largely to the majority of SOEs acquired by other companies not to the MBOs, but first a note of caution is in order. This is that the privatization period in which the *Treuhand* was selling these companies lasted well into the 1990s so that at time of writing (1998), the companies have not been privatized very long. So there is not much research on the consequences, especially the consequences for the individual SOEs as opposed to the macro-economic consequences for Germany. With this qualification it is possible to identify a number of trends.

First, the acquiring company would usually eliminate the top level of management in the former SOE if it had not already been eliminated at the time of the *die Wende*. And they would put in their own appointees, in the case of West German firms typically transferring a few key executives to the acquired SOE (though being moved to East Germany in the mid 1990s was viewed as being a bit of 'a hardship posting' by West Germans).

Second, they would continue to break-up and slim down the companies they acquired, often continuing the moves made in the interim period when the SOE was awaiting privatization. Third, they would invariably engage in investment in capital equipment; that is to say they would up-grade the company's manufacturing capability, putting in new plant and machinery. Sometimes they would build a completely new plant on an existing site, perhaps merely enlarging productive output such that the new site could replace several existing ones. Fourth, acquiring companies would impose their own financial reporting systems and budgetary controls, and of course their own information technology (IT) systems on the former SOE.

Fifth, the acquiring company would also tend to review the range of products produced by the former SOE, typically reducing or simplifying the product range. Similarly the acquiring company would tend to deconstruct the apparatus of autarky, referred to earlier, that the SOEs had tended to build up in the communist period. That is to say acquiring companies would tend to sub-contract, out-source, close down ancillary operations, and make genuine 'make or buy' decisions rather than doing everything 'in house!'

Privatization also often led to a change in the relative distribution of employees between different departments or functions. So production would be slimmed down, this being facilitated both by better workplace discipline and by more capital intensive production (new plant and machinery). R&D would usually be closed down, since the acquiring company would have its own research capability in West Germany or other country of ownership. The bloated purchasing departments of the communist period would also be trimmed. And on the plus side there might be moves to set up a sales force, at least a sales force for East Germany as a region and sometimes for export sales to Central and Eastern Europe. In some instances a marketing department would also be established, drawing of course on western know-how and typically presided over by a West German.

But probably the most important point to make is that when a western company buys a former SOE it does so for a purpose. The purpose may vary, but it will be the acquiring company's purpose, and the acquired company will have to fit in. There are few cases where an SOE is acquired with the buyer intending that it will carry on exactly as before – making the same things in the same way for the same market and with the same plant and workforce. The SOEs were not for the most part seen as good investment opportunities: they were not acquired in the spirit that for example Rolls Royce was acquired in the course of 1998. Sometimes the acquiring company wanted to have additional productive capacity; sometimes they would service the former East German market from within, sometimes they wanted an establishment in East Germany as a jumping-off ground for Eastern Europe. Sometimes the acquiring company wanted the SOE to make the new owner's products rather than the products it used to make; sometimes it wanted some of the SOE's products but not all of them; on other occasions the acquired company would be integrated into the new owners' global manufacturing system and its plant dedicated to producing say a single product for the whole group. But whatever the intentions of the new owner the SOEs were invariably subject to change and their position was subordinate. And in some cases the acquired company was changed 'out of all recognition' (Edwards and Lawrence, 1994).

Retrospect

As said in the last section it is too soon to evaluate the consequences of reunification for East Germany, but we can attempt a quick look 'in the rear view mirror'.

For the most part East Germany has become a branch office economy. The bulk of its productive enterprises are owned and directed from West Germany or from abroad. Strategic and managerial control has largely passed out of the region: what is more East Germany has become a region, for the most part, without large enterprises. The result of the breaking up of the often enormous communist SOEs, de-manning, and simplifying product ranges and dedicating plants to particular products has all resulted in seriously reducing the average size of the manufacturing establishments in East Germany.

While there has indeed been some entrepreneurial initiative in East Germany, particularly marked in the early post-reunification period, this has not (so far) resulted in much in the way of sizeable industrial operations. The entrepreneurial explosion of the early 1990s was rather in the service sector – domestic services (plumbers, electricians, jobbing builders, repairmen of all kinds), garages, hotels, cafes, and sausage stalls – all of which had been noticeably lacking in the communist period.

Side by side with the development of the branch office economy, East Germany has been 'West Germanized' in the sense of the prevalence of West German brands, products, fashions, and retail chains. Even before reunification one saw the opening of West German retail chains and branches of West German banks across the region. Then East German beer brands were systematically displaced by West German brands. Then West German second hand cars appeared, and then new West German cars, displacing the Wartburgs and Trabants, and so on.

Side by side with this commercial domination of East Germany by West Germany there has also been a transformation of the East German infrastructure – largely paid for by the West German tax-payer of course. To put this observation into context it might be said that anyone who ever wondered what Germany looked like during the Third Reich would have got a pretty good idea by visiting East Germany in 1990. Everything seemed old and shabby. The East German Autobahns dated from the 1930s and looked as though they had not been touched since then. Roads generally were awful, signposting dreadful, street lighting inadequate; outside of Berlin and a few big towns most houses in East Germany did not have main drainage; the public transport system in Berlin in particular was totally messed up by the Berlin Wall; there were hardly any public telephones, and even at 10 p.m. you would see queues in the street to use them; the telephones never had an international dialling facility; whenever you arrived anywhere there was nowhere to get anything to eat, and when you found the cafe it was just about to close; whatever it was you wanted you could not have it (and you certainly could not pay for it with a credit card!). This is what East Germany was like in the communist period, and it was still like it at the time of reunification. In these respects it has been largely transformed, and has much of the choice, facilities, and range of services that one associates with West Germany.

But probably the most obvious way in which the region of the former East Germany is differentiated from West Germany is in its persistently high unemployment rate. In the communist period full employment had been contrived by means of low wage over-manning. After reunification high unemployment resulted from a variety of causes, some of which have been canvassed in the last few pages:

- de-manning; workforce reductions of between 20 per cent and 80 per cent were normal in manufacturing establishments in the SOEs of East Germany after reunification,
- bankruptcies at the time of *die Wende*, and later,
- shrinkage of the (communist) government sector (think how many people worked for the Stasi – they could not all have joined the CIA!),
- some rationalization of institutions and facilities resulting from reunification (for example, both West Berlin and East Berlin had a central library – guess which one was closed),
- the absence so far of any *Aufschwung Ost*, the much hoped for take off of the regional economy of the former East Germany.

The only thing that can be said in mitigation of East German unemployment is that the rate is higher among the over 50s than among the young. However tragic this may be for the individuals concerned at least the later-middle-aged unemployed seldom turn to crime, violence, and 'anti-social behaviour'.

Germany in comparison

Finally, we would like to consider the views and values of German managers, using comparative survey data from the late 1990s, pointing particularly to differences between the Germans and the British. The sources we are using here are the Nene study, described in the discussion of Italian management in Chapter 4, and the Loughborough study referred to in Chapter 5 in characterising Spanish management. Both these surveys include a decent example of German managers.

One finding from the Nene study is that it tends to dispel the myth that the Germans are more authoritarian and more inclined to display an 'orders are orders' mentality than are the British. The myth, no doubt, is the legacy of a thousand and one war films. The proposition:

Everyone, whatever their status, should have the right to say what they think

was accepted by both British and German managers, but was accepted more strongly by the Germans, this difference being statistically significant, as are all the contrasts cited in this section. The Germans also agreed more strongly than the British with the statement:

Employees at all levels should be consulted on matters of company policy and operation

this finding being consistent, of course, with the German record on industrial democracy discussed earlier. And in similar vein the Germans accepted more strongly than the British the proposition:

Conflict is necessary in organizations as an antidote to complacency

where one might view conflict as hostile to authority.

The Nene study also highlights in a small way the German commitment to *Technik* which has been a central issue in this chapter. The proposition:

Today well made products for which there is a known demand are likely to ensure a company's profitability

was accepted more enthusiastically by the Germans than by the British, as was the proposition:

Organizations with quality products and a motivated workforce will prosper whichever political party is in office

Clearly these are not propositions that anyone is likely to refute, but the higher degree of acceptance by the German managers is indicative.

The second source, another multi-country survey using a (different) scalar questionnaire, developed by John Whittaker, Heidi Winklhofer and Peter Lawrence at the University of Loughborough, which we call the Loughborough study, confirms the anti-authoritarian leanings of the Germans highlighted in the Nene study. The Loughborough study contains a whole battery of propositions asserting the importance of hierarchy, along the lines of:

The hierarchy rightly denotes rank and status

and:

The hierarchy is necessary to achieve coordination

All but one of these seven propositions found less acceptance among the German managers than among their British counterparts. The Germans also reject more strongly than the British a proposition to the effect that managers who challenge authority do not get promoted.

Again the Loughborough study offers some confirmation of the idea that German managers have a more specialist orientation to their work. The proposition:

Above all the manager needs specialist knowledge and relevant experience

was accepted much more enthusiastically by the Germans than by the British. Another proposition read:

In management work common sense is a greater virtue than impressive qualifications

was strongly accepted by the British managers, but found much less favour with the Germans. Indeed this Anglo-German contrast was one of the *leitmotivs* in the whole study that contained 78 of these propositions. The Germans are clearly voting for qualifications because these denote specialist knowledge.

Another indication of German specialism comes from a proposition regarding the line manager's responsibility for staff development:

Staff development is primarily the responsibility of a firm's human resource specialists

The British managers disagreed with this proposition, that is they accepted a line manager's responsibility for developing subordinates. The German managers, however, accepted this proposition, as well as the following one:

Staff development is specialist work, *ipso facto* it should be done by specialists

The Loughborough study also highlights the German enthusiasm for training. The proposition:

The main benefit of company training sessions is the opportunity they offer for getting to know people in other parts of the organization

is enthusiastically accepted by the British, and for that matter by samples of French, Spanish and Americans. Only the Germans have serious doubts about networking being more important than training, and the Anglo-German contrast here is very sharp. Training, of course, is a means to acquire the specialist competence that the Germans prize.

The German managers in the Loughborough study were also distinguished by having a longer-term orientation. The proposition:

Meeting short-term financial targets is the main criterion for promotion

was accepted by the British but rejected by the Germans, indeed the German managers were more hostile to this proposition than any of the national groups in the survey. The proposition:

Negotiations with third parties should focus on getting the 'best deal' for one's company not on building long-term relations

was rejected by all the national groups, but with the German rejection being more emphatic than the British (the British were the most sympathetic to the idea of 'best deal' among the national groups in the survey).

Cynicism

In the authors' view the German managers represented in the Loughborough study were also rather less cynical about business and management than their British counterparts. We have already seen in the Nene study that the German managers have a more democratic orientation, and are less daunted by authority. We have also noted their view that challenging prevailing ideas in the company does not bar an individual from promotion. There are further items in the Loughborough survey on which the Germans seem less cynical. The proposition for example:

> Managers avoid introducing innovations unless the financial reward systems formally recognize them

was accepted by the British but rejected by the Germans. Similarly the proposition:

> Innovation by managers is stifled because mistakes are punished, rather than being viewed as part of an individual's learning experience

was also accepted by the British but rejected by the Germans. Or again the proposition:

> Management is primarily about the setting of objectives and the monitoring of plans for their achievement

was accepted by all the national groups, but with least enthusiasm by the Germans, the Anglo-German contrast again being statistically significant. Now while this last proposition might quite fairly be held to be about the degree to which the different national groups of managers have a professional model of management in their minds, when the British response is put in a wider context – of over pressurized short-termism – the linkage with cynicism becomes clear.

Pressure

The Germans also on the evidence of the Loughborough study seem to experience less pressure, and are less alienated by an ethos of competition and control. For example the proposition:

> Downsizing and de-layering have put increasing pressure on middle management

is accepted much more strongly by the British than by the Germans, indeed the British have the highest mean score, that is are furthest towards the 'strongly agree' end of the spectrum of all the national groups: the Germans have the lowest mean score. Similarly the proposition:

> The key change in the last 10 years is the greater emphasis on results, performance and accountability

is accepted much more readily by the British than by the Germans. Indeed the British have the highest mean score ('agree') of all the national groups, and the Germans have the lowest. Finally, the proposition:

Management jobs today involve less judgement and discretion than formerly is accepted by the British and rejected by the Germans. And once again the British have the highest mean score and the Germans the lowest.

In this last section we have relied exclusively on survey data from the second half of the 1990s, and have only introduced items where the contrast between managers from Germany and managers from Britain passes tests of statistical significance. This data does support in a mild way at least the contention with which the chapter began: that the Germans have to some extent exempted themselves from the rules of business and management, and still won.

References

Booz Allen and Hamilton Report (1973) English translation 'German Management' in *International Studies of Management and Organisation*, Arts & Science Press Inc., Spring/Summer 1973.

Edwards, Vincent and Peter Lawrence (1994) *Management Change in East Germany*, London and New York: Routledge.

Lawrence, Peter (1980) *Managers and Management in West Germany*, London: Croom Helm.

Lawrence, Peter (1998) *Issues in European Business*, London and Basingstoke: Macmillan.

Simon, Hermann (1996) *Hidden Champions*, Boston: Harvard Business School.

CHAPTER 8

Switzerland

Running through a discussion of business and management in Switzerland is a certain danger. This is that one may attribute to Switzerland propensities that it does not have because they seem to go with ones that it does have. Let us start with order.

Order in Switzerland

Everyone is agreed that Switzerland is characterized by order and decency and a desire for security. And this order is collective and self-imposed. Anyone who has lived in Switzerland knows that you will be told where you can and cannot park, that passers-by will remind you if you forget to turn off the ignition while waiting at a level crossing, reprimand you if you cross a road before the little green man appears on the traffic light, and call your attention to the derelictions of your children in public (including ones they have not actually committed). As one writer on Swiss business life observes.

> *En effect, s'il est difficile d'échapper à la vigilance de la police . . . il est tout à fait impossible d'échapper à celle de ses voisins* (Bergmann, 1994:56)
> (If it is difficult to escape from the vigilance of the police, it is impossible to evade that of your neighbours.)

Again Switzerland is an over-insured society. Citizens like to be insured against a variety of contingencies: insurance policies, policy up-dates, renewal certifications are treated with the loving care that in Britain might be devoted to ones golf trophies. In a doctoral thesis devoted to the characterization of management in Switzerland, Karen Pemberton notes that as of 1996 Switzerland had 146 insurance companies, 21 of which were devoted to re-insurance, in which activity the Swiss are world leaders (Pemberton, 1999). The Swiss like to boast about having the highest per capita insurance spend in the world (so do the Canadians!): it is the spirit rather than the statistic which is revealing.

It is also noticeable that the Swiss as citizens submit to the regulation of aspects of communal living that are unregulated in other countries, or they are subject to more far reaching regulation. Take dogs for example; dogs of course have to be licensed, registered, and carry ID. And the last is not any old ID; the dog owner cannot lovingly craft a disc with the legend 'Fido our Beloved Pet' in a material of his own choosing; dogs must wear Cantonal tags, standardized ones issued by each of the 26 Cantons and Half Cantons. Then there is the far from little matter of dog death. When your dog dies you cannot chuck it in the dustbin or tenderly bury it in the back garden according to your temperament; the death must be reported to the proper authority who will arrange collection and disposal (and charge for it). This system applies to all household pets, and charges are graduated. So while the death of a family hamster may be no big deal financially, if you happened to have a Great Dane it would be prudent to make some middle-term arrangement.

Waste disposal is a related heavily-regulated area where Switzerland rivals Germany for comprehensive provision. There are in Switzerland endless separate collections and public depositories for different kinds of waste or refuse – newspapers (every 6 weeks, must be tightly bundled, no pornography), shoes (but no ski boots or wellingtons), glass of course, tins (must be washed first and beaten flat), and so on. Basic household garbage is collected in bags: you buy the bags from your local supermarket, and then buy a separate sticker to say you have paid (SFr.2.50 for a 35-litre sack, SFr.4.00 for a 60-litre sack) from a separate shop in your own Canton. The dustmen will check bags for tagging. All untagged bags will be opened and searched for owner ID (maybe you were careless enough to throw away an envelope bearing an insurance renewal notice) and if the perpetrator can be identified a SFr.60 fine will be levied.

But the interesting thing is that all this regulation is accepted without demur; only foreigners are struck by it, and sometimes try to find ways round it (for example, 'garbage tourists' dumping untagged waste bags under railway arches). This desire for order and cleanliness is very evident in the workplace. Facilities are not always new, but are invariably neat and clean. The Swiss blue-collar worker does not show his manliness by messiness. Things will be neatly stowed away, machines cleaned, repairs done promptly, defective parts replaced.

As with the work place, so with companies. They are obliged by law to have reserves, expressed as a proportion of the previous year's outgoings. Companies undervalue their stock and their assets, they have unreasonably fast depreciation rates for assets. Manufacturing companies in non-food industries are required to hold stocks of materials and bought-out parts that would enable them to withstand an industrial siege – a disposition that may owe something to Switzerland's neutrality in the two world wars of 1914–18, and 1939–45. Whatever the origin of these requirements they serve the ends of order, predictability, security.

At the end of the 1980s the Swiss were saving more than 7 per cent of household receipts. Switzerland has of course the highest GDP per capita in the world excluding some oil producing states (though if you relativise for purchasing power parities the USA comes out top). One may add to this that the Swiss have the highest gold reserves per capita and the highest bank deposits per capita. All part of an inclination to avoid nasty surprises, eliminate misfortune, and do away with exceptions. As Frochaux remarks in a book engagingly entitled *Heidi ou le défit Suisse* (Heidi or the challenge of Switzerland):

> *En Suisse, pas de grèves, pas de prostitution, pas de jeux, pas de nègres, pas de bas fonds, pas d'invalides de guerre, pas de chômeurs, pas de bidonvilles, pas de mendiants, pas de clochards. Partout la propreté, la décence.*
> (Frochaux, 1969:64)
> (In Switzerland, no strikes, no prostitution, no gambling, no blacks, no dropouts, no war-wounded, no unemployed, no shanty towns, no beggars, no drunks. Propriety and decency everywhere.)

As might be expected, in Hofstede's famous study the Swiss emerge as having a fairly low tolerance for ambiguity or to use Hofstede's own expression rather strong uncertainty avoidance (Hofstede, 1980).

At the same time all this compulsion concerning order does not appear to lead them into a desire for centralization, hierarchy, the glorification of formal authority or for bureaucracy generally. This is the first of these possible misapprehensions of Swiss culture alluded to at the start of the chapter.

Centralization in Switzerland

Whatever else it may be, Switzerland is emphatically not centralized. While our concern here is not primarily with Swiss politics or the constitution, and their complexities in any case demand a sustained and painstaking exegesis (Steinberg, 1976) it might be simply noted that much of the theoretical power of central government is:

- devolved to the 26 Cantons or Half Cantons,
- devolved in turn to the *Gemeinde* or local unit level (there are some 3000 of these *Gemeinden*),
- and also devolved to the citizenry in the form of some direct participation in national decision-making going beyond participation in elections at various levels.

To unpick this last point a little there are referenda and citizen initiatives (partitions), unusual in other European countries. Nor are these 'once in a lifetime' events like the one or two British referenda on Common Market membership or separate parliamentary assemblies for Scotland and Wales. Again Karen Pemberton notes that in the last 20 years of the twentieth century there have been referenda on UN, European Economic Area, and EU membership; on nationalization procedures for foreign residents; on the rights of Swiss citizens married to foreign nationals; on environmental concerns; and on the voting age – not lightweight issues (Pemberton, 1999). Conjoining the referendum with the issue of self-regulation, however, it might be noted *en passant* that in 1993 the Swiss voted to raise the price of petrol: who else could one imagine doing this?

The same decentralisation is observable in corporate organizations. While it is the big companies such as Nestlé and Ciba Geigy that always come to the mind of the foreigners in fact:

- Swiss companies are mostly smaller,
- ditto operating units,
- the holding company, loosely federating various businesses tends to be a preferred organizational form,
- all the evidence suggests a rather high level of operational flexibility.

While Swiss companies may well take the results seriously they do not seem to be heavy on controls or on the American-style institution of systems. Indeed the criticism is sometimes made that Swiss companies tend to be strong on operations but weak on strategy (Bergmann, 1994) where the posited neglect of strategy tends to imply a lack of centralized authority.

Hierarchy in Swiss companies

As Geert Hofstede himself notes, reliance on a strong hierarchy may assuage concerns about uncertainty (1980), and this interpretation has been run for one or two countries in particular in the present book. The association, however, does not seem to hold for Switzerland.

In Karen Pemberton's numerous interviews with Swiss managers there is very little in the way of hierarchical thinking or managerial self-importance. Perhaps indicatively one of her interviewees notes that where managers have a doctorate this is usually omitted from the organization chart (though kept for visiting cards as a courtesy) (Pemberton, 1999). This view is strongly supported by the Loughborough study, referred to in the earlier chapters on Spain and Germany. The Swiss managers in that survey were less inclined to accept the proposition:

A clear cut hierarchy is essential to the proper functioning of any organization

than were the British and American managers, and the contrast with the British is statistically significant. Again the Swiss responses were on the disagree side of the midscale for the proposition:

The hierarchy rightly denotes rank and status

whereas the British and even more the American mean scores were on the agree side, and the contrast with the Swiss statistically significant in both cases. Exactly the same pattern of results appears in the response to the proposition:

The hierarchy is necessary to achieve coordination

and the Swiss similarly reject the proposition:

Hierarchy is the formalized expression of merit

which is accepted by both the British and the Americans.

The Loughborough study also suggests that as with hierarchy in particular, so with organizational structure in general. The survey included the proposition to test the attachment to structure, the belief in the efficiency of structure among the various national groups, viz:

Too much importance should not be attached to the notion of organizational structure: at the end of the day companies are made up of people who have to work with each other.

Now all the national groups had mean scores on the agree side of the scale. But the Swiss managers led this rejection of structure in favour of cooperation, and the contrast between them and both the British and Americans is statistically significant.

Authority in Swiss companies

Both Pemberton's doctoral research and the Loughborough study give some sense of the matter-of-factness of authority and its acceptance in Swiss companies yet it should be said here that a key source illuminating this issue is Alexander Bergmann's study, in the form of multiple interviews at 39 Swiss companies, spread across the three main language areas, and ably supported with references to a general literature on Swiss life and culture (Bergmann, 1994), though as far as we know this work in French is not available in English or in German (nearly 70 per cent of the indigenous Swiss population speak *Schwyzerdütsch* or Swiss German, and all of this majority group are able to read *Hoch Deutsch* or 'proper German').

First of all the Swiss have little sense of class, and no sense of class war, and have a long-term anti-communist orientation. So they have no sense of the factory as a place where capitalist oppression occurs. Rather the Swiss style is pragmatic, down to earth, unpretentious, anything but flamboyant. So those who are 'in authority' in Swiss companies are not going to parade the fact, will not give themselves airs and graces, not demand deference or subservience. In this climate authority can only be justified by what German speakers will call *Fachkompetenz,* by knowing what you are about, by gaining relevant knowledge, experience that may in part be authenticated by seniority, by knowing more about the operational dynamics inside and outside the company than others with a different place in the, as we have seen, weakly perceived hierarchy.

One may add to this the conflict-avoiding strands in Swiss culture and organization. Most obviously there is the freedom from industrial relations conflict that has its origin in the *paix du travail* agreement between employers and trade unions dating originally from 1937 and repeatedly revised. Then in 1941 it became obligatory to have collective agreements to regulate labour relations between employers and workers (Pemberton, 1999). There is though no formal codetermination or worker democracy system in Switzerland, and it would in any case be largely redundant. I recall the emphasis with which a personnel manager interviewed at a Swiss company responded to an inquiry about co-determination with the remark: 'We are not Germans! There is no radicalism here.' This testimony is rather ironic if you happen to be British.

Within companies there is a corresponding inclination at executive level to collective decisions. Agreement among the senior management team, if necessary developed over time, will have a higher value to the Swiss than decisiveness. There is no American-style tradition of the larger-than-life, legend-in-his-lifetime executive mover and shaker (Lawrence, 1996).

Similarly, there will be an attempt to 'take people with you', not by means of formal codetermination nor by a slavish response to the wishes of the organizational rank and file – at the end of the day the senior management will decide – but they will consult first. Management will not want to 'ride roughshod' over people, violate their expectations, or get them on board by means of heavy propaganda or pep talks. Management will want instead to be associated with reasonable proposals with which a reasonable work force can agree.

In Bergmann's view this is both their strength and their weakness (Bergmann, 1994).

Competence and professionalism

In the earlier discussion of management in Germany we suggested, perhaps over-dramatizing the issue, that the Germans seem to have broken the rules and still come out on top. There is also some suggestion of this in Switzerland, where the emphasis tends to be on specialized competence rather than on *managerial* professionalism.

First of all the Swiss take their training seriously. In the Loughborough study the proposition:

> The main benefit of company training sessions is the opportunity they offer for getting to know people in other parts of the organization

evoked a half-hearted response from the Swiss. Only the Germans had a lower mean score (one more to the disagree end of the scale) and the contrast between the Swiss and the British was highly significant in a statistical sense. The Swiss are not indifferent to networking, but training is important to them.

Second, it is also clear that there is abundant training provision in Switzerland. While having adequate university provision, and two separate technical universities in Lausanne and Zürich respectively, Switzerland like Germany has a second tier in the higher education system, below the university level, and having a strong vocational emphasis. Also like Germany, Switzerland has a strong apprenticeship system. It would seem that some 55 per cent of the age group have some form of post-secondary school education, not including those who go to university.

At the other end of the scale there is nothing in Switzerland that equates with the *grandes écoles* in France, that is to say, no highly selective institutions nurturing a self-conscious elite. This of course would be at odds with the Swiss preference for the modest and unpretentious. One of Bergmann's interviewees, a director of an electronics company observes:

> *Je préfère de loins les gens qui font très bien et parlent très mal aux gens qui parlent très bien et sont très mal.* (Bergmann, 1994:66)
> (I prefer by far people who do things well and are poor talkers to people who talk well but are not any good.)

In other words there is no point in Switzerland in being able to talk a better game than you play! In similar vein Bergmann quotes a retiring Swiss professor as saying:

> *Le livre que j'ai le plus lu était celui de pratique.* (Bergmann, 1994:67)
> (The book I would most like to have read was about practice.)

This testimony is all the more persuasive coming from a professor: no theory, no flights of fancy, but feet on the ground and practice.

Third, in practice there seems to be a remarkable spread of qualifications among Swiss managers, where everybody has something and many have several qualifications. Pemberton has recorded the education and qualification sets for a portion of her substantial interviewee sample, where degrees are common but not invariable, second tier qualifications are frequent, and sometimes found with degrees. And apprenticeships are very common, again often combined with higher level qualifications, and double and multiple apprenticeships are not uncommon either, again after the manner of Germany (Pemberton, 1999). In this sample if there is one institution that seems to come up more often, it is the ETH, the Technical University of Zürich. This is likely to be a tribute to technical specialism rather than to elitism. The *leitmotiv* is an educational preparation which is sober and relevant.

Now in all the sources we have been able to access, together with a little personal experience, the accounts of their work given by Swiss managers are correspondingly pragmatic. When asked by Pemberton to give an overview of their jobs, pick out priorities and so on, they give straightforward, readily comprehensible answers. Their understanding of their jobs is not especially driven by visions of change or remarkable achievement, but of getting on with things and doing what needs to be done. Perseverance triumphs over virtuosity. There is a marked contrast here with managers in the USA whose disposition we tried to outline in an earlier chapter.

Internationalism and protectionism

Switzerland is clearly, and rightly, recognized by the rest of the world for its internationalism. In political terms it is, of course, distinguished by a long tradition of neutrality and internationalism, as we have seen in the brief listing of plebiscites questioning involvement in Pan European and other Western collectivities after the Second World War. The Red Cross of course was founded by a Swiss, and has been headquartered in Switzerland ever since. When the League of Nations was set up at the end of the First World War it too was sited in Switzerland, indeed the country has played host to a variety of international organizations.

Turning to business then, with regard to its size it is striking that Switzerland has world class companies in several industries, and it has strong exports. There are a number of companies which have come to dominate luxury or up-market niches on a world-wide basis, for instance Rolex watches and Bally shoes. Certainly in the 1990s a stratum of Swiss industry seems to have followed western trends of concentration and merger and acquisition activity, for instance in pharmaceuticals and in banking.

All this is rather well known; much less well known outside Switzerland is the various restrictions on competition and on the free play of market forces. Like Germany at an earlier time in its history Switzerland is a country where cartels have been not uncommon (where a cartel is an agreement between independent producers or suppliers to harmonize prices). There may also be agencies which have the franchise for the importation and distribution of goods not domestically produced. Cars are a good example. Unlike its neighbours France, Italy, and Germany, Switzerland has no indigenous motor car manufacturer, nor like Spain or Belgium, does it have subsidiary plants of other European or

American motor manufacturers. So all cars sold in Switzerland are imported and the Swiss will tell you the prices are artificially high.

Or again when one peers into some particular industry it often emerges that there is less competition than one might have expected. Consider banking. One of the things that strikes foreigners coming to Switzerland is the plethora of private banks (banks that manage the fortunes and investments of rich people); on inspection most of these turn out to be owned by what were the Big Three and are now the Big Two Swiss banks. There are lots of Cantonal banks, but there again all their international operations are handled by a single organization. Or as a more homely example I visited a Swiss brewery and tried to get an overview of its operations. It emerged that the brewery supplied the region in which it was located, did not expect to sell into other parts of Switzerland, and did not expect breweries in these other parts to try to sell on its patch. When the question of export sales was raised (Switzerland is after all next to Germany with its population of 80 million and the highest per capita beer consumption in the world) this was treated as a wild impossibility. It should be added that the move to deregulation and privatization that was strongly in evidence in Britain in the 1980s is in Switzerland an (incomplete) phenomenon of the late 1990s.

While Switzerland's success as an exporting country is well recognized, rather less obvious is the fact that the domestic market is in practice protected. First of all, however rich the Swiss may be there are only 7 million of them, so it is not attractive to exporters in other countries in scale terms. Second, Switzerland is a fragmented market, both culturally and politically: it is culturally differentiated by language – German, French, and Italian speaking areas, plus some 70 000 Romansh speakers – and politically differentiated by decentralization down to the Cantons. All this serves to make Switzerland too much like hard work for would-be foreign exporters. Finally, one should remember that Switzerland is not a member of the EU, and this has become rather more significant since the implementation of the Single European Market (1992–93) measures for the elimination of non-tariff-barriers (Lawrence, 1998). In short Switzerland's internationalism is not unqualified.

Work and proactivity

There is little doubt concerning the strength of the work ethic in Switzerland. Survey data shows that the Swiss get up early and go to work early. OECD data shows that only the Japanese work more days per year. As Fabien Dunand (1987) points out 81 per cent of the Swiss taking part in a survey rejected the proposition:

Il faut chercher à travailler le moins possible
(The best thing is to try to work as little as possible.)

Bergmann's interviewees are similarly work conscious. They speak variously of doing what you have to do, of doing not what you can but all you can. One of Bergmann's interviewees, a middle manager in a construction company, says of his work:

Ce n'est pas un job, mais une partie de ma vie (Bergmann, 1994:31)
(It isn't a job, but a part of my life.)

And one of his foremen says proudly that 'apprentices learn to work when they are with me!'

The Loughborough study includes the proposition:

For the senior manager work will inevitably invade leisure time

in the response to which the Swiss managers had the highest mean score, that is they agreed most strongly out of eight countries, and the contrast with the British managers is statistically significant. In response to the checking proposition:

Managers owe it to themselves and their families to strike a sensible balance between the demands of work and home

all the national groups agreed, but the Swiss agreement was significantly weaker than that of the British managers.

No doubt there is popular agreement on this point but we have documented it a little as a preliminary to suggesting that an undoubted devotion to work is not necessarily accompanied by proactivity in the Swiss case, although the two often do go together. To unpick this a little, proactivity tends to imply striving and achievement, yet these are not always welcome in Switzerland, where it is felt to be 'not the done thing' to push yourself forward, set yourself apart from others, unless it is by diligence and what the German speakers call *Fachkompetenz*, being good at your job/specialism. In Karen Pemberton's interviews with Swiss managers one looks in vain for the formulation of either expansive corporate objectives or personal success targets. The 'In Search of Excellence' movement that energized the Anglo-Saxon world in the 1980s did not enthuse the Swiss. It is not that they do not attain excellence but that it is vulgar to proclaim it.

Proactivity also implies change, and change is, for the Swiss, perhaps the worst of all six letter words. Alexander Bergmann (1994) waxes lyrical (and is perhaps a little unfair) on the Swiss aversion to change. The essence of his testimony is:

- They don't like it!
- Technical change is more acceptable than other forms of change.
- It can only come from the top (it will not be popularly demanded) or from 'experts' being thereby de-personalized.

- You must consult first.
- Do it bit by bit.
- If change is inevitable, don't be the first.

In Karen Pemberton's interviews which post-date those of Bergmann, a bit of a shift of opinion is perceptible. There are more references to things that may have to be done, to the need for leaders, and for a broader strategic view. Yet the impression is that they are acknowledging deficits rather than recording achievements.

Efficiency and teamwork

Efficiency in organizations is usually thought to imply good teamwork, yet it is doubtful whether the Swiss have a natural inclination to 'teamliness!'

No one has ever questioned the operational efficiency of the Swiss. The Loughborough study includes the proposition:

> Management work is essentially about 'fire-fighting' and removing 'road blocks'

The highest mean scores, and ones that placed them on the agree side of the response scale, were registered by the managers from Britain, Spain and the USA. But revealingly the Swiss (and the Dutch) had low mean scores placing them on the disagree side of the scale – the contrast between the Swiss on the one side and the British, Spanish, and Americans is statistically significant. In other words fire-fighting and improvization are in the Swiss mind the hallmarks of the bungler.

Now while managers in Switzerland extol the virtues of teamwork as do their counterparts around the world the Swiss inclination is probably to get on with tasks as individuals and do a good job by their own lights. I once worked in an organization as the only British national among Swiss and Germans. The two groups were equally efficient, but in different ways. The Swiss way might be described as 'quietly efficient', and the quietness came from the inclination to work at self-prescribed tasks without interference.

The idea is readily caught by Bergmann who says that every Swiss seeks a '*domaine reservé*' where they are prepared to cooperate with colleagues but basically they want to get on with their own work and complete it to their personal satisfaction. He quotes one of his interviewees, a clerk in an insurance company, as saying:

> *J'ai mon bureau; je suis seule; ce sont des conditions quand même attrayantes.*
> (Bergmann, 1994:77)
> (I have my office; I am alone; these are the most attractive conditions.)

Or if an insurance clerk is felt to be a loaded example another of Bergmann's interviewees, this time a manager in a mechanical engineering company, observes:

> *Je ne veux pas savoir tous les problèms; nous avons les nôtres et nous devons les résoudre nous-mêmes.* (Bergmann, 1994:78)
> I don't want to know all their problems; we've got our own, and we're going to have to solve them ourselves.)

The missing link is that little operational coordination is required in Swiss companies because the organizational members, albeit individually, are all self-driven task completers, so they achieve a team-effect without actually being team-players.

Communications

In Swiss organizations communication tends to be a low-key and relaxed affair. Since companies or at least operating units tend to be fairly small, as an ethic of decentralization prevails, because there is little in the way of class tensions or industrial relations dissidence, there are few barriers to communication. Oral communication usually predominates over written communication; for most the focus is the work group rather than the company as a whole, the content of communication tends to be matter-of-fact and operational. People will talk less about themselves as individuals, you will know less about their private life; they will be less inclined to pose or to influence others, and will neither expect nor receive charismatic pep-talks from the higher-ups.

When it comes to communication between the company and the outside world a paradox exists. Swiss companies are likely to be closed to the general public, and will certainly not welcome media attention (most of them do not have PR departments or even anyone whose prime responsibility is the interface with the wider society) but will communicate more closely with relevant constituencies, be they customers, shareholders, suppliers, trade unions, or trade associations.

This paradox is caught in the matter of company performance and employees. In Swiss companies there is no German style *Wirtschaftsausschuss*, no committee of worker representatives officially entitled to information regarding company performance. And while company newsletters are common these are primarily concerned to give a mixture of personal and personnel information, to record the various milestones and anniversaries of organizational members, not to communicate performance figures or to 'cascade' down company strategy. Yet if you are a company member, they will tell you if you really want to know. One of Bergmann's interviewees speaks of a *Holschuld*, of an obligation to go and fetch information about the company's performance, which will be given if asked for but not served up on a plate.

Careers

If one raises the question, how is a successful career in management in Switzerland facilitated, there are a number of ingredients to the answer. First of all training, qualification, operational knowledge, and *Fachkompetenz* are basic. And the idea of *Fachkompetenz* has a specialist inclination in Switzerland. It is important to know about *something*. Nobody wants to be seen as 'a jack of all trades'. The idea of 'the overall view' is not essentially Swiss. But the *Fachkompetenz* is just a minimal requirement.

Next comes social or organizational integration. In practice this means being acceptable to colleagues, not 'slagging off' the employing organization, and not being too pushy. Switzerland is not run by whizz-kids. There is a seniority and/or acceptability element in much advancement. You have to go along with things as they are, not try to beat the system.

If one asks about the role of inter-company mobility in all this the answer is unclear. Bergmann tends to emphasize the conservative element in Swiss temperament, and the corresponding desire to proceed and progress in a single employing organization. In her research on Swiss management, on the other hand, Pemberton gives many examples of the managerial career paths of her interviewees, and these are very mixed. There are managers who have pursued a career in a single company; and there are others who, whatever they have done before do not expect or intend to move from their present company. Among the mobile it is noticeable that :

- some of them have made a point of not moving house while changing employers,
- a lot of those in human resource management/personnel have come to it sideways via other jobs or functions, rather as in Britain up to the 1980s,
- Pemberton's quite exhaustive sample does not offer many examples of individuals alternating between management and entrepreneurial roles, in the American style (Lawrence, 1996),
- much of the mobility may well be conditioned by a combination of the smallness of the Swiss economy and the differentiation of Swiss society.

Perhaps the Swiss are immobile by temperament, and mobile by need.

Given the right temperament and demonstrable *Fachkompetenz*, advancement in Switzerland also depends on interpersonal savoir faire. One is convivial with equals, consultative with subordinates and unpretentious with everyone.

Finally, the rule of 'the smaller the country the more important the networks' holds for Switzerland. What is more the differentiated nature of Swiss society yields a plethora of associational possibilities – political, community, and linguistic as well as recreational. An aspect of Swiss management life that has been nicely documented is the range of hobbies and recreations in which individuals are active (Pemberton, 1999). Every manager does something out of work, a lot of them a number of 'somethings', many of which are associational – network-building. And of course virtually all men do military service, and it carries a rolling, incremental obligation that continues into middle-age. This, and in particular membership of the officer corps, is a very traditional Swiss network.

Switzerland is a country that is more often stereotyped than most. In this chapter we have sought not so much to challenge the stereotype, which is mostly positive in any case, but to qualify it. And we have done so in part by gently underlining paradoxes:

- order loving but not bureaucratic,
- a cult of competence rather than of American style management professionalism,
- a mixture of internationalism-protectionism,
- a commitment to work rather than to proactivity with its potential for change and conflict,
- efficiency without teamwork,
- competence as a given, integration and a very Swiss *savoir faire* as determinants of career success.

Perhaps because of these mild paradoxes management is likely to change more in Switzerland in the next ten years than is the case for most of the countries considered in this book.

References

Bergmann, Alexander (1994) *Le Swiss Way of Management*, Paris: Editions ESKA.

Dunand, Fabien (1987) *Dessine Moi un Suisse*, Lausanne: Edition 24 Heures.

Frochaux, C. (1969) *Heidi ou le défit Suisse*, Lausanne: Edition La Cité.

Hofstede, Geert (1980) *Cultures Consequences*, Beverley Hills: Sage.

Lawrence, Peter (1996) *Management in the USA*, London: Sage.

Lawrence, Peter (1998) *Issues in European Business*, Basingstoke and London: Macmillan.

Pemberton, Karen (1999) 'Management in Switzerland' Loughborough University unpublished Ph.D. thesis (incomplete at time of going to press), Loughborough, England.

Steinberg, Jonathan (1976) *Why Switzerland*, Cambridge, England: Cambridge University Press.

CHAPTER 9

Sweden

Sweden is a remarkable country in three ways which overlap. It has a remarkable economic history, it has a remarkably diversified industrial economy for a country with so small a population (less than nine million), and its companies have a remarkable record in exporting and in internationalization.

The Past

In the eighteenth and nineteenth centuries Sweden was not of no consequence economically but its economy was based primarily on raw materials – pulp, timber, iron ore, and so on – together with some shipping and agriculture.

Then in the late nineteenth century industrialization began, and proceeded rapidly. In the thirty years or so before the First World War (1914–18) most of the big name companies that are around today were founded, many of them based on particular inventions in this period, for instance, Nobel's explosives, AGA's lighthouse, the Diesel Engine developed by the Atlas Copco Company, Ericsson's telephone, Gustav Laval's dairy separator, and so on. In short Sweden did rather quickly and certainly far reachingly what every Third World country has attempted ever since – to make the transition from being a materials supplier to full-scale industrialization.

What is more Sweden largely achieved the industrialization without the alienating effects that were experienced in France, Germany, and above all in Britain, albeit somewhat earlier. In the British case 'industry' came to signify urban squalor, alienating work, and child labour, in the national folk memory. In Sweden industry was seen much more positively as the force that transformed the country into one of the world's richest states in the space of two generations. Also in the early stages of the industrialization at the turn of the century Sweden had lost around a quarter of its population as a result of famine leading to emigration: against this backdrop it was industry that 'saved the day'. Even now blue-collar workers in Sweden will often feel a distinct personal loyalty to the companies that employ them that probably has its roots in more positive folk memory.

Institutions

Something else that is striking is how quickly the organizations and institutions that are associated with or even central to industrialization emerged in Sweden. It is recognized by students of politics that left wing political parties appealing to a mass electorate only emerge with industrialization. In Sweden this party, the Social Democratic Party, was founded in 1899 and was to dominate Swedish government for most of the twentieth century – for example the Social Democrats were in power, either alone or as the major partner in a coalition, without interruption from 1933 to 1976. And it is instructive to compare Sweden with Britain in this matter: the British Labour Party was only founded in 1900, though Britain's industrialization had begun in the 1760s.

Trade Unions also developed quickly in the early phase of Swedish industrialization, and by 1898 a national blue-collar trade union umbrella organization invariably known by its initials, LO, had been set up. LO is comparable to the TUC (Trades Union Congress) in Britain, though LO is more consequential in Sweden than is the TUC in Britain. Throughout the twentieth century Sweden has had a strong trade union organization, and high trade union membership rates. As late as the mid 1990s, the union membership rate in Sweden was over 80 per cent, among the highest in the world. And to complete the picture Sweden also created at an early stage (1902) an employers' federation, also invariably known by its initials of SAF. This body is roughly the equivalent of the CBI (Confederation of British Industry) in the UK, although again SAF has been more important in Sweden than is the CBI in Britain.

Not only is it interesting that these institutions developed at an early stage relative to the process of industrialization, they have also been of considerable importance. We have already noted that these institutions, LO and SAF, came into being at the turn of the century; it is also the case that they were complementary, 'needed each other', and indeed became bargaining partners. Pay bargaining in Sweden became highly centralized, and for blue-collar workers pay was determined largely by a national level negotiation between SAF and LO (and corresponding negotiations between SAF and two other organizations representing white-collar supervisory technical staff and graduates respectively). This high-level centralized wage bargaining lasted until 1990 when SAF withdrew, so that the wage deals are now done by SAF and LO member organizations, at industry level.

Saltsjöbaden

In fact the 1920s had been a period of labour unrest in Sweden, and the following decade saw some of the unemployment consequent on the Great Depression. But in 1938 representatives of organized labour and of the employers met in the Grand Hotel in Saltsjöbaden, a fjord-based resort a half hour's suburban train ride from downtown Stockholm to discuss their common interests. Two things emerged from these discussions. Firstly, there was agreement on various specifics – grievance procedures, negotiating procedures, and an early warning system for lay offs, the regulation of disputes, and so on (Johnston, 1981). But secondly and perhaps more important than the procedural arrangements were the model and spirit of the agreements. The implicit model was that of the state (firmly Social Democratic by 1938) as a non-interfering watchdog so long as the contracting parties kept the peace. The spirit was one of mutual accommodation, bargaining, and compromise. In short the two sides simply agreed at Saltsjöbaden to be reasonable, and to act with restraint in the future. There is an expression in Swedish, *Saltsjöbadensande*, the spirit of *Saltsjöbaden*, which expresses this spirit of forbearance and the potential for cooperation.

But this *Saltsjöbadensande* did not last for ever, at least not in the narrower sense of regulating industrial relations and pay bargaining. Even if restraint and compromise are still more generally regarded as Swedish values, cracks in the system were perceptible in the 1970s already, when LO demanded far-reaching changes in the labour law, and criticized companies for what seemed to them to be excessive profits – *övervinster* in the parlance of the day. The same decade, the 1970s, saw the high-point of the Swedish industrial democracy system with the passing of the 1976 Codetermination Act, discussed later in this chapter, which employers subsequently came to view as overly bureaucratic and somewhat restraining.

The Social Democratic party were out of office for the period 1976–82 but when returned to power they instituted the so-called *Löntagerfonder*, or wage earner funds, a controversial measure whereby money would be set aside to buy up the shares of companies, in the middle term having the effect of transferring ownership from shareholders to the public at large via state or trade union holding companies – the exact mechanism was always left rather vague in the debate about 'the funds'. This idea was strongly opposed by the right wing parties and the industralists in the run up to the 1982 election; when the Social Democrats won and it was clear that the *Löntagerfonder* would indeed become a reality industrialists in a very Swedish way announced that it was not so bad, that 'the funds' could be managed in a reasonable and Swedish way, and so on. But by the mid 1990s the climate of opinion had changed sufficiently for a now non-Social Democratic government to abolish the funds, and re-allocate the accumulated proceeds to higher education.

But let us for the moment return to the immediate post-Second World War period.

The Golden Age

Only four European countries were neutral during the Second World War (1939–45) – Spain, Portugal, Switzerland and Sweden. And it is above all Sweden that had a diversified industrial economy, whose products were in demand during the war, from both sides! But rather more significant than the fact that Sweden 'sold to both sides' during the war (and experienced a massive increase in its exports to Nazi Germany in the early part of the war) is a Swedish court ruling little known outside the country. In 1944 the courts decided in favour of equal pay for equal work, irrespective of the geographic location or the employing organization with whom the work is done.

This court ruling represented a dramatic gain for labour, in the sense that it is levelling up on grand scale! The gain for the employers is less obvious but just as substantial; the new ruling was as good as a 'no poaching' ban in a period of enhanced demand for products and a labour shortage. There is more to come.

For the deal to be implemented there had to be some way of determining what was 'equal work'. To this end it was decided to train a large number of time and motion specialists, who could analyse and classify jobs in manufacturing. First a tussle ensued between the trade unions and industry over how these time and motion people were to be trained. The trade unions wanted this training to be public, in the sense that it would be done in state institutions, publicly funded, whereas industry, in the institutional manifestation of SAF, wanted to direct this operation. Eventually (1948) LO and SAF reached an agreement (how Swedish!) that the training would be carried out by *Svenksa Management Gruppen* (Swedish management group, or SMG). SMG was an educational and training off-shoot of SAF. In the next four years some 10 000 time and motion people were trained. And these trainees were for the most part taken from the shop floor. In other words a sizeable group of workers had the fun of going on the course, experienced an occupational upgrading, and had more interesting work to perform thereafter. All this helped to popularize the 1944 deal with the body of blue-collar workers – this semi-engineered integration is also very Swedish. But there is a more important effect of the implementation of the 1944 ruling.

Since the Scientific Management movement began in the USA in the 1890s with the work study experiments and writings of Frederick Taylor it had been clear that gains in terms of output and cost savings could be made using time and motion study. The difficulty had always been 'selling' time and motion study, understandably unpopular with workers and their organized representatives. What the Swedes did in the implementation of the 1944 ruling was to sell time and motion study to themselves! They managed to overcome worker reluctance by means of the advantages of the 1944 deal to both sides, eventual SAF and LO agreement, and the involvement of workers in the training.

This was tremendously important in the post Second World War period. There was a backlog of world demand for industrial goods, Germany and Japan had been temporarily eliminated as suppliers, and most European countries had suffered bomb damage or been fought over, but Sweden had been neutral, and its industry was intact. Thus Sweden enjoyed the same advantage after the war as the USA, albeit on a smaller scale. And in a period in which investment money was in short supply Sweden managed to raise output by substituting time and motion study for capital investment.

In the Nordic Museum in Stockholm there is a display room given over to depictions of (newly prosperous) everyday life in post-war Sweden. Not for nothing is this room entitled The Golden Age.

The breadth of industry

In our view it is remarkable that Sweden, that began to industrialize late and has a population of around 8.8 million today, has come to have such a wide range of industries. Consider that Sweden:

- makes cars, trucks, buses, and aeroplanes,
- has one of the world's leading electrical consumer goods companies (Electrolux),
- and one of the world's leading telecommunications companies (L.M. Ericsson),
- has strength in power generation/power engineering,
- has an enormous range of metal and mechanical engineering and industrial products including mining equipment, rock drills, welding equipment, rolling stock, ball-bearings, instruments, lighthouses, industrial gases, turbines, diesel engines, cutting tools, process industry equipment, and guns,
- has a chemical industry,
- and a pharmaceutical industry,
- as well as a massive presence in wood, wood products, pulp and paper.

In addition one might note that unlike many countries Sweden makes its own cigarettes (and the matches to light them with), brews its own beer, and processes a lot of its own food. And it has two retailers, Mauritz & Hennes and the omnipresent Ikeå, that have been successful cross-border, something that was relatively rare until the 1990s. All of this has been achieved by a country that is demographically not much bigger than Switzerland and not much more than half the size of Holland. It is also often noted that for its small size Sweden has a lot of big companies, MNCs even, as well as a big concentration of ownership for a socialist country.

Internationalization

To pick up the third remarkable thing about Sweden, flagged up at the start of the chapter, Swedish industry shows a high level of internationalization. It is a simple syllogism: a country that has a small population (= small internal market) and a plethora of big companies, must have internationalized, and in the Swedish case this has come to mean high exports and lots of companies with manufacturing subsidiaries abroad.

One of the authors worked in Sweden in the 1980s and interviewed a range of Swedish managers. When talking about their companies' operations and markets they would commonly claim that:

We think of Scandinavia rather than Sweden as our domestic market

or:

We think of Western Europe rather than Scandinavia as our domestic market

and then go on to list other more distant territorial markets that had been penetrated (Lawrence and Spybey, 1986). This tends to be borne out by Orjan Sölvell's study (Sölvell *et al.*, 1991) which lists the top 50 industries in Sweden by share of world exports, where the top industry (paperboard) has a 41.7 per cent share and the number 50 industry (textile machinery) a 6.1 per cent share: remember these are shares of *world exports*. The same source lists Swedish companies that have more than 50 per cent of their total sales abroad (outside Sweden): there were 196 companies that could make this claim.

The second manifestation of this internationalization is the extent to which Swedish companies commonly have operations, as opposed to simple sales, in other countries. A standard measure for internationalization in this sense is the proportion of a company's workforce that are outside the country of ownership. Again Orjan Sölvell and his co-authors give this data for some 15 leading Swedish companies (their list is meant to be exemplary not exhaustive) and includes such gems as:

Company	Proportion of workforce outside Sweden (%)
Ericsson	53
Sanvik	61
Alfa-Laval	70
ABB	79
Electrolux	80
SKF	88

This internationalization of course has implications for Swedish management. There is a general requirement for 'outward lookingness', for adaptation, for cultural tolerance, for a calm restraint in dealing with the complexities of global spread. One down-to-earth reflection of the internationalization is the near universal English-speaking ability of Swedish managers and professionals generally. One of the present writers recalls overhearing an exchange between two British businessmen in the departure lounge at Arlanda, the international airport at Stockholm. The two visitors had been to a number of companies in Sweden, and were struck by the relative classlessness of Swedish society. The exchange went like this:

When you go to a factory in Sweden, how do you tell who are the workers?

and the reply was:

They're the ones who aren't so fluent in English!

The internationalization also impacts on the careers of Swedish managers. As a quick indicator, in the previous research in Sweden by one of the present writers (Lawrence and Spybey, 1986) it emerged that two-thirds of the interviewees had worked outside Sweden, not just gone on business trips abroad, and a lot of those who had this foreign experience had been at subsidiaries of Swedish MNCs, from North Africa to Latin America.

Management and society

It might be helpful to offer a few generalizations about Swedish society, and to move from these to some characterization of management. Two things that are generally recognized about Sweden are:

- It is a caring society with a high level of welfare provision.
- It is egalitarian.

Both these generally held beliefs about Sweden are in our view true, even if welfare expenditure is coming under pressure in the late 1990s. Indeed the first may be viewed as a manifestation of the second. That is to say, the effect of welfare provision in the broadest sense is to eliminate or at least ameliorate the disadvantages that afflict its recipients thereby enabling them to approach the norm of material and psychological well-being.

But Swedish egalitarianism goes further than this. It can in part be apprehended by the lower value accorded to individualism. To put it another way, differentiating behaviours are less acceptable in Swedish society. It is not done to be different, to parade your cleverness or wit or sophistication, and certainly not to set yourself apart by intimations of superiority. The Swedish language is a little treasury of phrases and proverbs asserting the basic equality of man, along the lines of *en man är lika god som en an* (a man is as good as another) kind.

This inclination to insist on fitting into the collective rather than parading individuality and difference have a number of implications for management:

- It militates against personal dynamism and outstanding individual advancement, such behaviour being seen as psychologically suspect and socially disruptive; it is OK to be a Nobel Prize winner in Sweden, but you have to be quiet and unassuming.
- It inclines the population to be 'joiners'; Sweden is corporatist; you express your citizenship through membership of collective organizations; some of this we have seen already with the high rate of trade union membership and the discipline exerted in the past by the employers' federation SAF over its corporate members.
- One cannot in Sweden presume a universal desire for promotion and personal advancement among managers, as one can for instance in the USA, nor is lip service paid to the goal of advancement in Sweden.
- Because there is less individualism and striving, relations between the various functions and departments (sales, engineering, personnel, production and so on) in Swedish companies tend to be better; there is less rivalry and more restraint.
- Greater egalitarianism reduces social distance between management and workers, and facilitates communication and cooperation.

Indeed one might take this idea of egalitarianism, reformulate it a little, and say that Swedish society in general is marked by a lack of differentiation. First of all there is a lack of class differentiation. In a sociological sense, one can point to differences in income, level of educational attainment, and job status in Sweden, as in other countries, but these differences are not as sharp, as meaningful, as keenly felt in Sweden as in the Anglo-Saxon countries; one would not readily use an expression like 'job status' when speaking Swedish. But perhaps more important than this is the fact that class is a weak behavioural construct in Sweden: the range of class related behaviours and styles that is so familiar in England, is relatively absent. There are differences in Sweden, but they are less obvious, less numerous and less significant.

Second, there is a higher level of gender equality in Sweden than in many western countries. This is partly a matter of law: women in Sweden simply have more rights and the law guarantees equality of treatment in more cases. It is also a result of welfare provision, which will tend to render women less dependent on men. Swedish women marry later; free legal abortion means that unplanned pregnancy is not likely to push them into marriage; because of welfare support Sweden is an easier country in which to be an unmarried mother than is say Britain: and it is also noticeable to a foreigner that Swedish women deport themselves differently. It is not that they are more assertive exactly (assertiveness is not a Swedish inclination) but their behaviour is more independent, and they defer less to men. As an interesting aside to this point Chris Brewster quotes a female Swedish manager working in Britain being appalled by wifely subservience among the British: 'I find here among women who work in my group that their husbands decide when they finish . . . So if their husbands say I want you home by whatever hour, they comply' (Brewster *et al.* 1993: 19). Women are also for the most part well-represented in the more desirable strata of the occupational system – in the state service, in the media, in publishing, for example, and in the (Lutheran) church. At the time of writing (June 1998) Sweden has just appointed its second female bishop.

Third, Sweden is less differentiated as to income than most western countries. Welfare provision eliminates poverty; a strong trade union movement and centralized wage bargaining has in the past kept the lower end of the wage scale up. At the other end of the scale progressive income tax and high taxes on unearned income render 'the rich' in Sweden relatively less rich than in many other western countries – though top management salaries have certainly risen in the late 1990s. There are also strong norms against ostentation and parading wealth, albeit not as strong in the late 1990s as ten years ago. Furthermore salaries are less sharply distributed across the occupational structure. In Sweden the (salary) difference between skilled and unskilled, between blue collar and white collar, between the brain surgeon and the bricklayer, is less than in most western countries. And the tax system also has a levelling effect, again not as sharp as in earlier years. If we have understood the system correctly, on a gross annual salary of about £23 000–£25 000 one would pay income tax at the rate of 55 per cent, and of course the rate will rise with higher income. Having said this it is only fair to say that Swedish income tax includes what in Britain is called Council Tax, and that there are rather more things one can off-set against income tax in Sweden.

Fourth, on the theme of lack of differentiation there is a sense in which the regions of Sweden seem to be less differentiated than in some other countries. That is to say when Swedes assess regions other than the one in which they presently live they tend to do so in a severely practical way, without a status element being built into the perception. Now clearly there is not a great deal of enthusiasm for relocating to say Kiruna in Swedish Lapland; it is well into the Arctic Circle and does not get light until after ten o'clock in the morning in the winter time; but if one excepts the far north, the different parts of the country will be assessed simply in practical terms of logistics and employment possibilities. There does not seem to be an equivalent of Britain's 'north of Watford' or the American 'out in the boondocks'.

Now all this relative equality and lack of differentiation make for a higher level of social integration than is observable in for instance Britain. At the same time it is also mildly constraining – there is something to be said for being allowed to be as different as you wish, so long as it does not harm anyone, but this is not what you get high marks for in Sweden.

Management style

These Swedish values of equality and of mildly repressed individuality impact on the style of Swedish management. As suggested earlier Swedes tend not to be overtly dynamic. This is not a polite way of saying that they are ineffective – far from it. But quite literally they do not typically espouse dynamism; their manner, deportment, body language and communication is not, and is not meant to be, 'larger than life', not redolent with intimations of personal power, persuasiveness, and pugnacity. A Swede does not seek to become 'a legend in his lifetime' but largely to conform to the expectations of other Swedes. In this connection it is interesting to note that in Hofstede's classic study Sweden has the lowest score on masculinity, that is, it is the least aggressive and assertive of the 39 countries in the study. (Hofstede, 1980).

Remuneration

Given the relatively narrow income distribution found in Swedish society, the question must be raised, are Swedish managers adequately remunerated? The answer probably has to be in several layers. First, Swedish managers are probably (still) not as well remunerated as their counterparts in many other European countries in terms of gross salary (though the cross country differential is narrowing). And second, in terms of net income they would compare unfavourably with managers in other continental countries. Third, traditionally there has been little in the way of fringe benefits in Sweden, (cf. Britain where at least until the 1980s relatively poor management pay was off-set by fringe benefits, particularly cars) though by the end of the 1990s these have to some extent made their appearance in Sweden – cars for senior executives, and golden parachutes certainly. Fourth, in the authors' experience Swedish managers enjoy moaning about their under-remuneration by comparison with other countries. Having said all this, managers as a group are not *particularly* disadvantaged, in the sense that all professional and managerial occupations in Sweden tend to be underpaid by comparison with other countries, while blue-collar and ordinary service sector jobs are relatively better paid. A quite subtle effect of the remuneration relativities is that management as a career and the nexus of material satisfactions have been uncoupled. The contrast with Britain is instructive in this matter. Just consider a *Daily Telegraph* management job advert: the biggest sized type will be used for the salary, next biggest for the job title, and any fringe benefits – car, medical insurance, and so on – will figure prominently. It has not been like this in Sweden, literally or metaphorically, though there are trends in their direction in the late 1990s.

Politicking

An interesting effect of the lesser emphasis on careerism and individualism is that there is less politicking in Swedish companies, especially in the sense of the endless manoeuvring for personal advantage and favourable resource allocation decisions. On the basis of our considerable probing of Swedish managers on this matter, and questioning of expatriate Britons working in Sweden, the only exception to the generalization about the relative absence of politics concerns the interface between management and what would be called a works council in Germany, an elected committee of worker representatives: when speaking English, Swedes usually refer to this works council body as the MBL Committee, where MBL is short for *Medbestemmendelågen*, or codetermination law, the reference being to the 1976 codetermination law referred to earlier which put the coping stone on the hitherto piecemeal system of industrial democracy in Sweden.

Other countries that have a system of legally based industrial democracy, for example Holland and Germany, usually endow the works council with specific powers, with certain things regarding which it has the right to decide, to be consulted, or to be informed. In contrast the 1976 codetermination law in Sweden gives the MBL committee the right to negotiate, to open a discussion with management on any issue that it feels is relevant to employee interests. If this negotiation, it is called a *verhandling* in Swedish, fails to reach a (compromise) agreement, then the negotiation would be pushed up to the overall corporate as opposed to works level, and then again to the level of a negotiation between the LO and the SAF – a negotiation at this august level is known in Swedish as a *Centralverhandling*! Now when all these steps have been gone through, and should agreement fail to be reached, then the company concerned can do what it wants anyway: there is a cynical employee view in Sweden that says 'before they used to run us down, and now they tell us first and then drive over us!'

Now this cynicism is on balance not justified in the Swedish case. The Swedes take disagreement seriously and will try hard to get a peaceful compromise; a Swedish company would feel dreadfully embarrassed by a *Centralverhandling*, a confession that it failed to secure in-house agreement. So the power to initiate negotiation, the prerogative of the MBL committee, is worth more in Sweden that it would be in societies that are more inclined to be competitive, that espouse a 'winner take all' inclination. At the same time it will be appreciated that this ability to initiate a negotiation, and *in extremis* to force the issue to the level of *Centralverhanding*, confers political and tactical power on the MBL committee.

There is a further effect of the codetermination or industrial democracy system upon the behaviour of management, albeit one that is implicit and invisible. This is that the existence of the MBL committee and its power to challenge management initiatives and decisions by instituting negotiations, may put up the cost of such initiatives for middle managers. In short, managers may decline to decide, initiate changes, to do things they think desirable because of the 'political costs'. So Swedish companies are not wholly denuded of politicking activity, even if there tends to be less intra-management politicking and manoeuvring.

Motivation

We have suggested in the earlier discussion of remuneration that Swedish managers have not been well-remunerated by international standards. Conventional (Anglo-American) wisdom would suggest that this ought to impact negatively on their motivation. It has to be said that there is no evidence in our own study or in anything that we have read to indicate that this is true. Indeed the relatively poor remuneration may induce a greater purity of motive: people do management jobs because they want to; if they accept promotion, take on more exposed line jobs, accept greater responsibility, all this in Sweden is rather more likely to be for intrinsic reasons – interest, involvement, the effective deployment of one's abilities, the opportunity to shape and decide, and so on, and rather less for extrinsic reasons of higher emoluments and material satisfaction. There are some things that Swedish managers appear less inclined to do than their counterparts in other Western countries but this is more readily explicable in terms of rival values, ones that compete with the work-achievement career nexus, than with the relativities of remuneration.

Rival values

These rival values include:

- equality, especially gender equality,
- commitment to the family and to the exigencies of family life,
- a value attached to leisure, particularly linked in the Swedish case to love of nature, the enjoyment of outdoor activities of the sailing, hiking, camping kind,
- this leisure-nature value is also reinforced by the tradition of second homes; a second home is a home in the country, a *stuga*; a lot of Swedes have them, sometimes in the shape of farmhouses inherited from older, rural relatives: having a *stuga* is a Swedish ideal, and when you have one, you want to spend time in it!

Furthermore this whole nature-leisure-*stuga* phenomenon is in turn reinforced by Sweden's northern latitude, which makes for long dark winters and a corresponding enjoyment of the all too short summer months. It is a standing joke in Sweden that the whole country closes down for July: this should be seen against the backdrop of the northern winter rather than as an expression of some whimsical irresponsibility. This point is engagingly made in a business report that came across the desk of one of the authors. It is a two-page monthly performance and status report furnished by a Swedish subsidiary for its British Head Office, and under the heading *Important Activities* the first paragraph reads:

> Without warning the summer suddenly hit us. Consequently we have been occupied with all sorts of 'spring activities', such as picnics, golf tournaments, beer drinking, and so on. We are in a great hurry because summer holidays start within two weeks and after that 'igloo time' is here again. The above means that there is about nothing of importance to report.

It is a reasonable assumption that the writer is engaging in a little bit of self-pastiche tinged with amusement at the effect this 'position statement' is likely to have on a British financial controller. It should be added that the subsidiary report from which this excerpt is quoted does not date from the laid-back 1970s but from May 1998.

To return to the specifics of management behaviour the equality-leisure-family set of values mean that Swedish managers will be:

- relatively disinclined to work long hours just for show, or to demonstrate putting work and the company first, or to show themselves to be promotion worthy,
- unenthusiastic about business entertaining, variously seen as an imposition on one's wife or intrusion into family leisure,
- inclined to avoid business travel that starts on Sunday or ends on Saturday, if that is possible,

- unenthusiastic about promotion that involves a geographic move.

This last point leads us into the controversial area of management mobility.

Mobility

While hard data seems to be lacking, informal opinion suggests that Swedish managers are not especially mobile between employing organizations, do not move readily from one company to another in the way that Americans do. The reasons for this are a mix of structural and perceptual. First there are a lot of big companies in Sweden, any one of which may offer the opportunity for a long and successful career. Second, while Sweden has a surprising number of big companies *for a small country*, it is still not a large economy in that mobility is sometimes restricted by the fact that there are only one or two companies in a given industry: where, so to say, would one move to from L. M. Ericsson? And third, Swedes are not inclined to do things for the sake of appearances. The Swedish view would be that it makes little sense to change around and work for four different companies by the time you are 35 just to show you have 'get up and go!', are a self starter and are 'on the way up'; the Swedish view would be that it makes better sense to show what you can contribute to the success of one company over time.

When it comes to geographic mobility between different sites or subsidiaries of the same company general reluctance to move tends to be based on the fact that most of the managers concerned are male, but with wives who are likely to be professionally employed graduates with their own career aspirations. There is nothing absolute about the reluctance to move, and moving is probably becoming more common. The reluctance and the reasons for it tend to be recognized by Swedish companies who on their side will not move people without serious reason; managers will not be asked to relocate just to demonstrate their loyalty to the company or to show that they are 'fully mobile'.

Finally in this consideration, mobility abroad, going to work in the company's overseas subsidiaries, is something of a special case. As noted earlier it is a requirement that will come up rather more often for Swedish managers because of the high level of international activity. Indeed more Swedish managers work abroad as a proportion of the occupational group, than the managers of any other country. The case against, namely the probable disruption of the spouse's work and career is often even stronger since the wife, as it usually is, may not be allowed to work in the foreign country or will be precluded from doing so for reasons of language or differing occupational structure or qualification requirements. At the same time the material inducements are much stronger than for a move within Sweden in that the manager is likely to be paid an internationally competitive salary and then have it taxed according to the rules of the host country which will often be more indulgent than that of Sweden. As it was put to one of the authors:

When it comes to foreign postings you have two problems. Getting them to go, and getting them to come back.

Or as Chris Brewster's expatriate Swedish manager bluntly concedes:

Money is a big advantage for a Swede working in the UK (Brewster *et al.* 1993:18).

Competence

We have made much play earlier in the chapter with the idea that Swedish society lacks differentiation, and that it is egalitarian and opposed to displays of wealth, power, and ostentation. But the quality that is allowed to differentiate individuals is competence, indeed Sweden engages in what might be termed 'the cult of competence!' In so far as people in Sweden meeting for the first time have 'a hidden agenda' it is to establish degrees of competence, not social antecedents or status relativities. In Sweden there is no amateur point of view. If you don't know, you keep quiet and let someone who does know, who is competent, take the lead.

Porter comes to Sweden

If we can imagine management writers at the end of the twenty-first century looking back to our period it is likely that Michael Porter, American economist turned business strategy analyst, would be identified as the dominant thinker of the last quarter of this, the twentieth century. In 1990 Porter enlarged his model of competitive advantage and applied it at the nation state level in an attempt to highlight the economic strengths achieved by industry groups within countries if not exactly by countries (Porter, 1990). Sweden was one of his illustrative country cases for this *grand oeuvre*, and this fact gave rise to a later monograph devoted to Sweden to which occasional reference has already been made (Sölvell *et al.*, 1991). It may be nice to round off the chapter with one or two ideas from this source which tend to build on our general introduction to Swedish industry at the start of the chapter.

First of all Porter and his collaborators see a strong demand in particular segments in certain countries which calls forth a corporate response and thereby confers competitive advantage on companies in that industry. One example proferred in the Sölvell book concerns provision for handicapped people:

Sweden's long-standing, highlevel of concern for handicapped persons, for example, has spawned an industry supplying products for them that is becoming a world-class industry (*ibid*. p. 33).

Or again:

Worker safety is a demand parameter that has caught the attention of Swedish producers of industrial products like rock drilling equipment and heavy trucks (*ibid*. p. 33).

the implication being that no one else, no other country, has exploited this angle to the same degree.

Again the same source traces the demand conditions which predisposed Sweden to develop competitive advantage in the development and manufacture of heavy trucks. Considerations include:

- the fact that as the Swedish road network expanded there was a marked need for trucks that could transport large amounts of stone and gravel, in other words *heavy* trucks,
- the railway system was uneven, and did not really cover northern Sweden; this made the need for heavy trucks more critical,
- the north needed big trucks to transport timber and pulp, these big trucks were more necessary to northern Sweden than to say southern Italy,
- the harsh climate in Sweden put a premium on durable trucks,
- and the relative absence of filling stations and garages outside of the main cities put a premium on big trucks that don't break down.

and so on.

But the idea that is central to Porter and his Swedish colleagues' analysis of Sweden's advantage is that of industry clusters. The essence is the idea that one industry will depend on others as suppliers or facilitators or producers of manufacturing machinery or whatever, and the book (Sölvell, 1991) gives a range of examples of such clusters, where the constituent industries are having a mutually stimulating and supporting effect on each other. Just to give one example within a basic industry in Sweden, logging, it is argued that logging fuels the paper and pulp industries, that the industry processes depend on the use of certain chemicals, that the processes require sets of specialist machinery, that the production of paper fuels the packaging and printing industries, that these in turn demand particular machines, and so on.

A related idea, running through some of the industry cluster examples, is that of a shared technology, for example:

Swedish engine know-how, such as the diesel technology, has been shared across industries like ship-building, aircraft (in earlier periods), trucks, buses, and marine engines (*ibid*. p. 37).

Or again:

Know-how in refrigeration techniques has benefited Swedish firms in an array of industries, ranging from domestic and commercial appliances to refrigerated forwarding, reefers, and cold storage (*ibid.* p. 37).

It is a tribute both to Swedish cooperativeness and to the breadth and depth of the industrial structure highlighted at the start of the chapter that Porter and his colleagues find examples so readily.

In fact we will return to Sweden in the last chapter of this book, and look at it again as a test case of late twentieth-century change.

References

Brewster, Chris; Annika Lundmark and Len Holden (1993) *A Different Tack: An Analysis of British and Swedish Management Styles*, Lund: Studentlitteratur.

Hofstede, Geert (1980) *Culture's Consequences*, Beverley Hills: Sage.

Johnston, T. L. (1981) 'Sweden' in Eric Owen-Smith (ed.) *Trade Unions in the Developed Economies*, London: Croom Helm.

Lawrence, Peter (1982) *Swedish Management: Character and Context*, London: report to the Social Science Research Council.

Lawrence, Peter and Tony Spybey (1986) *Management and Society in Sweden*, London: Routledge and Kegan Paul.

Porter, M. E. (1990) *The Competitive Advantage of Nations*, Glencoe, Illinois: The Free Press.

Sölvell, Orjan; Ivo Zander and Michael E. Porter (1991) *Advantage Sweden*, Basingstoke and London: Macmillan.

CHAPTER 10

Denmark

A possible answer to the question, what is Denmark and its management like, is to say that it is Scandinavian, that it has features common to a region rather than to a single nation state.

A Scandinavian character

This line of argument is pursued by a Danish academic, Jette Schramm-Nielsen, who has a strong sense of these regional commonalities, especially for the three core Scandinavian countries – Norway, Sweden and Denmark (1998). First of all, one might note that these three countries have existed as nation states for more than a thousand years, in contrast to, for example, Italy and Germany. What is more the destinies and identities of these three countries, and also that of Finland (Nordic but not Scandinavian) have been intertwined. This is particularly true of Norway and Denmark, these countries having been united in what is known as 'the double Monarchy' under Danish kings for more than 400 years (1380–1814). Sweden similarly ruled Finland for ages, and 'took over' Norway from Denmark in 1814 when Denmark was punished by the other European powers for having been on the wrong (losing) side in the Napoleonic Wars; Norway eventually became independent of Sweden in 1905, and promptly chose a Danish prince to be its king! All three countries have been both sovereign and separate since then.

Cooperation, however, has continued through the agency of the Nordic Council, established in 1953, of which Finland and Iceland are also members. A major effect of the Nordic Council is the establishment of a common labour market as between their participating countries.

There are further historical commonalities. All three countries were largely by-passed by the Renaissance, but affected by the Reformation. In the period 1527–37 all three became Protestant, in fact Lutheran-Evangelical, and have stayed Lutheran. While Church attendance is low in all these Scandinavian countries, Lutheranism is still important in having provided a moral and ethical basis with its emphasis on sober self-responsibility, on behaviour rather than on faith. This disposition was given a further thrust in Denmark in particular by the philosopher Søren Kirkegaard (1813–55) who laid the foundations for what came to be known as existentialism, a philosophy stressing perceptions of truth and personal responsibility for moral choices.

All three countries industrialized late; Denmark was probably the first, and was certainly the first to develop an organized labour movement – by 1914 more than half its workers were unionized. But all these countries did industrialize, all became wealthy in the twentieth century, all are both monarchies and stable parliamentary democracies, all developed strong welfare states in the period after the Second World War, all have been marked by industrial peace in the sense of a relative absence of strikes in the second half of the twentieth century, and all have high rates of trade union membership. All three also have high rates of female participation in the labour force – 60 per cent for Norway, 76 per cent for Denmark and 86 per cent for Sweden (Schramm-Nielsen, 1998).

The Scandinavian countries also tend to be 'on the same wave length' in the sense of being identified as close and similar in multi-country studies. In what is probably the first international study on managerial thinking and management practice (Haire *et al.*, 1966) the Scandinavian countries consistently come out as one country cluster. In Hofstede's famous study (1980), the three countries discussed here are again closely placed on the four dimensions used for the categorization of the various national cultures.

Egalitarianism

If one had to identify a single value as characteristic of the Scandinavian countries it would be egalitarianism, a theme explored in the previous chapter on Sweden. One thing that is certainly entailed by their espousal of equality is a rejection of organizational hierarchy. As Schramm-Nielsen notes:

A hierarchy is considered a necessary evil for the functioning of an organization, but not a goal in itself (Schramm-Nielsen, 1998:9)

It is in fact a Danish-Norwegian author Aksel Sandemose (1899–1965) who has 'philosophized' this value, and given it an anti-competitive twist. Sandemose promulgated what he called the Jante Law (Jante is the fictional name Sandemose gave his home town in Denmark, where the operation of the law was seen to be particularly dynamic!) The key values of the law are said by Sandemose to be conformity, uniformity and envy. Among 'the commandments' implied by the law the first four are:

Don't think that you are somebody
Don't think that you are worth as much as we are
Don't think that you are wiser than we are
Don't think that you are better than we are

Not exactly a charter for individual excellence, or compatible with the ethos of American success and striving outlined in the second chapter!

Management implications

As with Sweden, an idea developed in an earlier chapter, the effect of this philosophy is to de-emphasize hierarchy, status, and to some extent the striving that might be linked to their achievement. At the same time its people/employees/managers cannot be differentiated so obviously as in other societies on the basis of class and status, so skills, experience, relevant knowledge and competencies become more obvious as the things that differentiate people, make one person more suited for some tasks than others.

The egalitarianism and censure of paraded superiority (the Jante Law) also make for greater homogeneity. This does not make the Danes 'like the Japanese' where rejection of individualism is near total, but it does make them a little bit more like the Japanese than are say the French or the Germans. It is interesting in this connection that there is survey evidence indicating that the Danes rather more than the Swedes and Norwegians recognize the distinctiveness of Japanese culture and also the possibility of learning from it (Sjøborg, 1985).

This egalitarianism is also, of course, a factor in the ease of internal communication across the Scandinavian countries. And conjoined with the desire to avoid open conflict, noted already in the case of Sweden it gives us relatively peaceful industrial relations, fairly stable wage bargaining, and a negotiative approach to disagreements. The same quality of quiet cooperation rather than challenging individualism also leads to rather good relations between different departments and functions in manufacturing companies.

The egalitarianism then has a generally integrating affect. Combined with weak hierarchicalism it leads to a climate of delegation with employees having a responsible autonomy, as opposed to the more programmed and systems driven behaviour of say American employees, a phenomenon noted in Chapter 2.

Denmark compared

So far we have dealt in terms of Scandinavian generalities – of history, development, culture and behaviour – in order to get started on a characterization of management in Denmark. But it is, of course, possible to ask the question:

Within this Scandinavian consensus, is it possible to differentiate Denmark from Norway and Sweden, at least in terms of degree? One study does indeed address this issue, and it is that of Norwegian business consultant Eddie Sjøborg (1985), who has surveyed decent-sized samples of senior managers from the three main Scandinavian countries. The survey is largely in the form of propositions offered to the samples of managers rather along the lines of the Nene and Loughborough studies cited in various previous chapters. Sjøborg however, has a stronger focus on productivity – a lot of these propositions are about how important this or that is as a determinant of productivity, though this focus is not exclusive and Sjøborg does not use the classic five point scale of the Nene and Loughborough studies but tends to group responses in the form of:

Stor	*Middels*	*Liten*
(big)	(medium)	(not much)

to designate degrees of perceived importance, or:

ja, enig	*vet ikke/delvis*	*nei, venig*
(yes, agree)	(don't know/to some extent)	(no, disagree)

It should be added that while Sjøborg's book is temptingly entitled 'Riding the Tide' it is actually written in Norwegian, so perhaps to give the flavour of possible differences within Scandinavia we should start with Norway.

Norway

There are some modest patterns of Norwegian difference in Sjøborg's study, but first a word of introduction. Norway in a sense is the last of these three countries to achieve independent statehood. While the country's long association with Denmark (see above) was largely harmonious the same cannot be said for the period of Swedish rule (1814–1905). Indeed Norway's national day is 17th May, the day that Swedish overlordship was terminated (cf. Sweden whose national day is 6th June, chosen simply because it is in the summer and stays light late.) Thus Norway has been more consciously involved with state building in the twentieth century than the other two Scandinavian countries (Sweden, after all, was a major European power in the seventeenth century).

A second introductory consideration is that shipping, in the sense of ship owning and ship operating, has been an important industry in Norway. As an industry it is marked by 'dynasty' type companies, with power centralized at the top, where a small number of very important decisions are made – commissioning new ships, fleet acquisitions and the disposal of craft. This has tended to give Norway a model of big-decision leadership, only exercised by a few, but which may have passed into the sediment of national consciousness.

Combined with the later achievement of fully independent statehood Norway also industrialized late, as did Sweden, but it did not industrialize on such a wide front as Sweden (see Chapter 9). So that Norway has some industries, but in the sense of particular strengths – pharmaceuticals, fishing, fish farming, fish processing, oil exploration and refining, hydro-electricity, and so on – not the broad front industrialization of Sweden or Germany.

There are reflections of all this in Sjøborg's survey results. While all three countries strongly reject any suggestion of authoritarian leadership, the Norwegian managers in the survey attached more importance to leadership style in general than the Swedes and Danes. Similarly, Norway is top for emphasis on motivation, on the perceived importance of personal qualities (overtones of leadership), on the importance of corporate culture (shaped by leaders), top on the importance of developing people, and in viewing the human factor as more important than technology.

There is also some reflection of Norway's relative isolation, in that the Norwegian managers attached most importance to an overall market orientation, showed most enthusiasm for foreign languages, and incidentally, expressed concern for the future supply of university educated personnel; Norway is a little under-endowed with universities, a reflection no doubt of its more recent statehood as well as its small population – traditionally many Norwegian students have studied abroad, for instance at the universities of Strathclyde and Herriot-Watt in Scotland.

Sjøborg's responses for the Norwegians also show more concern with national differentiation. They led the all country sample in rejecting the idea of a pan-Scandinavian style. Perhaps even more tellingly they were very luke-warm about the idea that Pehr Gyllenhammer and Jan Carlzon were typical examples of a Scandinavian management style. It should be added that these two were high profile *Swedish* business leaders in the 1980s. Gyllenhammer had a long reign as head of Volvo, finally resigning in 1993 when the strategic alliance between Volvo and Renault foundered. Carlzon turned round SAS and was the subject of eulogizing management case studies in the 1980s; he also resigned in 1993 with the failure of the Alcazar talks, an initiative sponsored by Carlzon, aimed at instituting cooperation between several smaller airlines – KLM, Swissair, Austrian Airlines and SAS itself – to enable them to survive in a deregulated world dominated by mega-carriers, such as American Airlines and British Airways.

In short a little collection of modest differences, but differences nonetheless, that it is possible to link to features of Norway's history and economic structure.

Sweden

Eddie Sjøborg's results highlight some aspects of Sweden to which attention was drawn in the previous chapter. Perhaps the strongest thing to come through is that, of the three Scandinavian countries, it is Sweden that is in the lead for the extent of industrialization and for the importance of manufacturing, supported by an abundance of large companies. Sweden comes out top in Sjøborg's study for:

- being proud of their productivity orientation,
- regarding productivity as the key responsibility of the line manager,
- measuring productivity,
- believing top management must be productivity oriented,
- recognizing the importance of new work systems,
- seeing the importance of their wage systems.

And again, because out of the three countries Sweden is the land of large industrial companies, the Swedish managers attach most importance to access to capital. While as suggested at the start of this chapter all the Scandinavian countries are strong on socialism and welfare this is true *par excellence* of Sweden. In Sjøborg's study it is the Swedish managers who were in the lead for believing that their companies were affected by the political and economic structure. They were also the group most strongly committed to the view that management must be community oriented.

And so back to Denmark

It is clear from Sjøborg's study that there is a distinguishable Denmark as opposed to a component of Scandinavia, albeit this is not a matter of black and white contrasts but of pastel shades.

People and pragmatism

The first thing to say would be that this sample of Danish managers does not show the Norwegian concern with leadership and distinguishing human qualities. The Danish emphasis is rather on social integration. So the Danes come out top on a questionnaire item asserting the importance of choosing the right colleagues (the aim is integration not distinction). Again the Danes are top in their response to a quite subtle proposition that motivation is important in releasing 'concealed resources' (my translation of the Norwegian may be a bit stilted) among employees. The Danish managers also come top for the importance they attach to teamwork. And to give the thesis a new twist the Danish managers exhibited least enthusiasm for new organizational forms; this may be interpreted as a vote for humanist pragmatism where 'new organizational forms' is seen as a bit airy-fairy and not really about people, who matter.

The manufacturing orientation

In the case of Sweden we noted a strong commitment to the mechanics of manufacturing and to large companies. In contrast the Danish managers showed least interest in new work methods. They also attached less importance than the Swedes to access to capital, and to new uses of existing capital resources. And again, the Danes were least concerned about wage costs, and least beset by striving to raise productivity, though interestingly they were top for identifying productivity as a *competitive* advantage. The Danes were bottom on their response to the questionnaire item asserting the impact of economic and political conditions on business – the item on which the Swedes with their more all encompassing socialist governments came top.

Denmark more integrated in Western Europe

While looking at Sjøborg's results I was reminded of the fact that there is an expression in Swedish 'to go to the Continent'; it means to go to Denmark! (though by the time the book is published the Malmö–Copenhagen road bridge/tunnel, Øresundsbro, should be open giving Sweden a road link to 'the Continent').

The issue of Denmark's greater integration into Western Europe is also highlighted by the respective history of the three Scandinavian countries with regard to the EU. At one extreme Norway had a referendum on EU membership in 1972, the majority voted against, and Norway did not join; in the autumn of 1994, Norway held another referendum, got another 'thumbs down' and is still (time of writing November 1998) not a member; the cynical view is that only the collapse of oil prices will force Norway in. Sweden also held a referendum in the autumn of 1994, got a slim majority in favour, and joined in 1995. Since then Sweden has been a somewhat half-hearted member: EU membership is favoured by the business community, but not by the general public, and Sweden like Britain opted not to take part in the first wave of monetary union in 1999. Denmark on the other hand joined in 1973, at the same time as Britain and Ireland.

In Sjøborg's study the Danish managers came top on the importance they attach to internationalization. They also take the threat of inflation more seriously, which has overtones of being less influenced by Swedish socialism and more influenced by what has come to be called German 'central bankism' – a deep-rooted German fear of inflation and a readiness to adopt stern monetary policies to achieve its suppression.

Not only do the Danish managers give some sign of their country's more natural integration into Europe, they also come out top on several other propositions in the Sjøborg study about recognizing the distinctiveness of America and of Japanese culture, and on a willingness to learn from the USA and Japan.

Mainline management

In a sense it is an extension of the idea developed in the previous section, but it would be fair to say on the basis of the Sjøborg data that management in Denmark is a little more inclined to converge on what is becoming an Anglo-Saxon norm.

The Danish managers in the sample were most sympathetic to the idea that family demands would to some extent be sacrificed to those of one's career. These same Danish managers were the most outspoken on the theme of management salaries (in Denmark) being too low (a common theme in Scandinavia). Or again Danish managers were the most positive in their attitude to mobility, that is to managers moving from one company to another – an idea explored in Chapter 2 with regard to American management. The Danes also showed a higher commitment to Anglo-Saxon style management generalism, they expected managers in the 1990s to be better trained, that is, expressed this view more strongly than the Swedish or Norwegian managers. The Danes also came out top on the expectation that senior executives would be recruited externally, rather than being promoted internally; this is a distinctly American viewpoint (Lawrence, 1996).

Finally, the Danes come out top on the desirability of a Scandinavian management style. One of Eddie Sjøborg's questions reads:

Er det ønskelig å ha en egen skandinavisk lederstil?
(Is it desirable to have a real Scandinavian management style?)

In response 67 per cent of the Danish managers said yes to this, as opposed to 37 per cent of the Norwegians, and a mere 14 per cent of the Swedes. My interpretation is that the Danes are more secure in their national identity, for reasons suggested at the start of the chapter, therefore more able to applaud a regional style. An overlapping view expressed by one or two Danes with whom I have discussed this finding is that Danes have a stronger view of what is distinctively Scandinavian and subscribe to those values.

Companies at large

Denmark probably has rather less large companies than most of the countries discussed in this book with the possible exception of Spain. And outside of Copenhagen a common occurrence is a middling-sized company dominating a provincial town, sometimes even located in a village. This probably explains in part the rather strong company-community relations that seems to be a feature of Denmark. All the companies I ever visited in Denmark reported a plenitude of company-society relations, with sports and leisure clubs (with teachers and trainers in some cases), and open days for the family. Several reported networks of research activity in institutions of further education, and all referred to visits from school children, provision of work experience, taking apprentices, visits from students at design schools, architectural schools, engineering schools and in some cases allowing their premises to be used for civic occasions. There is no suggestion that this is unique to Denmark, only that these testimonies were invariable in that country.

A further twist to the community standing idea is that several companies were conscious of paying their workers well over the regional or local rate and rather priding themselves on being the premier employer in a particular area. Companies in Denmark seem to like being seen in this light. And the corollary is that they tend to be over-concerned if anything they do might tarnish their image in the community: one of the companies I visited for example, a chemical works, had experienced an on-site explosion; another had fired a small group of permanent staff blue-collar workers; both were concerned about the possible impact of such events on their reputation.

Strategy and positioning

Again it is not a black and white contrast but there is a certain conditionality and discrimination about the strategy and use of competitive advantage exhibited by some of the companies visited. To put this into context, or at least to put this on to an international continuum, there is a relative absence in Denmark of companies deploying American style economies of scale crossed with market dominance, and playing off a substantial domestic market.

One of the companies investigated in preparing to write this chapter is a brewery, not Carlsberg, and this is highly relevant, (all these research visits to companies in Denmark were made together with my friend Jette Schramm of the Copenhagen Business School). Carlsberg according to 1997 figures has 71 per cent of the Danish market, it has two of Europe's top beer brands – Carlsberg and Tuborg: in Europe it is second only to the mighty Heineken of the Netherlands, and is the ninth largest brewery in the world. So what can you do if you are in the shadow of a national champion such as Carlsberg?

Our brewery had a variety of responses:

- It largely keeps out of what the Danes call 'discount beer', own label beer, to be sold by supermarket chains at lower prices; the margins are low for own label beer and it only makes sense if you have excess brewery capacity, or you can do it on a vast scale.

- Restaurants and hotels, on the other hand, only want to sell branded beer; a lot of these are smaller entities (rather than vast chains with centralized buying like the supermarkets) so the sales links may be more personal, something which possibly favours the smaller brewery.
- Unlike the big players in the European brewery industry such as Kronenbourg, Interbrew (Stella Artois), Heineken, and Carlsberg, our brewery does not have production sites in other countries; but services foreign (non-Danish) markets with beer brewed in Denmark, thus making Danishness a strength.

All this is easy to understand when it is laid out for one's benefit, but it is marked by a certain subtlety and conditionality; it is a far cry from the production of the Model T Ford at the River Rouge plant at Michigan.

Or again another of our companies makes chewing gum. It is called Dandy, and is in fact the world's third largest manufacturer of gum – the top two, as one would expect, are American. Dandy, however, has managed to differentiate itself. Most American chewing gum is in strips, but Dandy's is mainly in tablets (and they say this is better for preserving the taste). It is also worth noting that different industries and within them sometimes even particular companies segment their market in different ways. In 'the world according to Dandy' it looks like this:

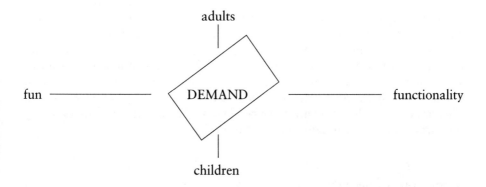

That is to say chewing gum is bought by both children and grown-ups, both for fun and because of some presumptive functional benefit such as dental hygiene or pain relief (asprin impregnated chewing gum is given to people who have had their tonsils out). There are sales on all four quadrants but the growth areas are children buying it for fun and adults using it for some quasi-medical purpose: this is where Dandy put their efforts.

Or take furniture. For the most part furniture is a fragmented industry world wide, made up of a lot of small to medium sized firms. Denmark for instance has some 600 to 900 furniture manufacturers in the late 1990s, though only ten of these have a turnover of more than 250 million Danish Kronor (*c.* 10 DK to £1). What is more, especially in Scandinavia a lot of furniture firms supply Ikeå, sometimes Ikeå is their only customer – and they have suffered as that company has progressively sourced cheaper produce in post-communist central and eastern Europe.

Against this background our Danish furniture company is a study in differentiation. It is differentiated by its:

- design philosophy (functionalist and minimalist),
- design creativity,
- product quality.

This in turn enables it to position itself in the market as high-price and high-end. And again these considerations facilitate their choice of segments, namely:

- conference furniture,
- dining area,
- reception area,
- office furniture, but not desking (desks smack of mass production!).

All this is for the contract market, that is to say it is sales to organizations; sales to the general public go through retailers, DIY chains, and discount stores, with a consequent emphasis on price competition – bad news!

But there is a further twist to the story. Designers are crucial to the Danish furniture industry, but they are not usually employees of particular furniture making companies. The relationship is rather more like that of Michelangelo to a Renaissance prince. This designer-company relationship is not programmable, but it tends to be a virtuous circle. Gifted, creative designers want to work for high-status, up-market companies. Traditionally, the consequence of this has been that while the company makes it, it is sold by the designer's name. The *démarche* of the company described here is that it is successfully branding products under its own name, not that of designers.

Intimations of decency

American anthropologist Steven Borish in an epic book on Denmark's folk high schools, makes the point that Denmark is not only a rich country by conventional economic standards but is also a fine place in which to live in terms of a number of quality of life indicators (Borish 1991). Indeed Borish notes with manifest satisfaction that in some years Denmark was ranked top by the United Nations: the rivals are usually Sweden, Norway and Canada (beating Sweden will of course have a certain piquancy for Danes!).

There are intimations of the decency in our company visits and interviews. One thing that is very obvious to visitors to Danish companies is their pleasant appearance. They are attractively laid out, the grounds and gardens are appealing, the office designs and decor invariably tasteful, the reception areas stylish, the furniture perfect and pleasing as an ensemble. The furniture company described in the previous section is of course a *par excellence* example, the company as showcase for its product, but perhaps more indicative is the fact that the shipyard and the chemical works we visited were of much the same standard. And if you comment on this the reply is usually along the lines that it is expected by the workforce, that it is something one can do for employees in a state where fringe benefits and salary increases are heavily taxed.

Or again when speaking of workforce satisfaction, managers tend to mention non-material factors: responsibility for own their work, making their own decisions, being allowed to act independently, and so on. One company described a quality bonus system that had been in operation in their works. The nature of the manufacturing process was such that it was easy to check the quality of the finished product and ascribe any defects to individual operators. For 100 per cent quality the company paid a modest hourly bonus – over the course of time standards rose so that just about everyone got the bonus because they reached 100 per cent. So the company, believing that the bonus no longer discriminated meaningfully between individual workers simply abolished it. Quality standards were unchanged. Any reader who thinks this is an unremarkable story should try to imagine the results of abolishing a quality bonus in Britain or the US.

At another company they had introduced an honour based system of travel claims. When employees travelled on company business, that is, they did not have to document their travel claim with receipts, and no-one checked the claim: they were simply paid what they claimed (anyone working in higher education in Britain in the 1990s will find this truly amazing.) At the chemical plant which had experienced the explosion much else was happening. What seemed to me a major re-organization was underway, the company was downsizing, they had closed an R&D facility in Copenhagen and dragged the research staff and their even more reluctant wives to upstate Jutland (if you live in Copenhagen Jutland is viewed as a close second to Siberia). All this moved me to ask, quite gently, if they suspected sabotage in connection with the explosion: I have never seen a more horrified expression on the faces of people to whom a question has been put.

The company visits also offered instances of restraint and conflict avoidance. One of the companies visited in 1997 had acquired another same industry company in 1989: the product range had been integrated, but a start had only recently been made on the rationalization of administrative and IT systems. When questioned on this the Administration Director admitted that this was done with some reluctance since it implied that 'one company's system was better than another's'.

All the companies visited were Danish owned, with one exception – a company taken over by a larger concern in Finland. While such takeovers often breed resentment with the victim frustrating the intentions of the acquirer (Lawrence 1998), in this case the fact of Finnish ownership only came after an hour or two of discussion and the references to foreign ownership were in the context of enhanced support and market opportunities.

Modesty and equality

It was said of the head of the shipping conglomerate A. P. Møller that 'old Mr Møller' (82 in 1997) used to drive a Ford Fiesta. In particular that he was prone to use this vehicle for visits to government ministries in Copenhagen where he would protest against unnecessary expenditures. At the A. P. Møller shipyard Odense Lindø it was claimed that promotion was invariably from within, that people of humble origins could work their way up to ship's captain and thus become partners; and on the wage front that newly appointed graduate engineers would earn less than a foreman in the first instance – and indeed less than blue-collar workers.

Relative wage equality is a theme in Danish life. Morton Strange, a Danish born author who left Denmark at the age of 20, worked abroad for 20 years, wrote a book provocatively entitled 'Culture Shock' after his return to his native country (Strange, 1996). Among other things Strange has assembled some salary data which is particularly cute in linking high status and more ordinary jobs in the same occupation or industry. Working in terms of gross monthly salaries in Danish Kronor we have, for example:

Journalist	: 25 806 DK
Editor	: 33 258 DK

And:

Flight Attendant	: 23 928 DK
Pilot	: 36 978 DK

Or:

Lawyer	: 20 910 DK
Lawyer's secretary	: 18 604 DK

But the pair I found most indicative were:

Nurse	: 18 090 DK
Doctor	: 31 098 DK

Of course it is always tricky to get proper cross-country comparisons, but I tried out the doctor-nurse one on a British doctor who suggested a junior consultant (hospital based doctor) would have double the pay of a nurse, a senior consultant three times and a general practitioner four times a nurse's pay, and this is taking a nurse specialist towards the top end of the scale as the *point de repère*.

There was ample evidence of this phenomenon in the testimonies of the companies visited. The differentials between skilled and unskilled workers seemed modest; incidentally there is no class of *semi*-skilled workers in Denmark as there is in Britain and Germany. The biggest differential volunteered in any of the companies visited was DK125 as a gross hourly rate for skilled workers as against DK100 for the unskilled.

There were also references across the companies to unskilled workers being treated as skilled if they had the appropriate experience, of post experience courses to 'upskill' unskilled workers, and so on. Foremen also had differentials that seemed modest, and incidentally there was no shortage of women foremen including some with men as subordinates.

Another instance of characteristic restraint that emerged in the interviews was the Danish response to a question concerning key or important decisions that individual managers felt they had taken in a particular post. In the Danish companies, there was a general reluctance to answer this question. This reluctance was informed by the view that these managers had not taken any decisions unilaterally, there had been consultation, it would be arrogant to claim something as 'my decision', and so on. One exception was a recently appointed general manager in a company that was being 'turned round'. He cited as most important: deciding between a functional structure and a business process structure for the organization. On asking which way this key decision had gone we received the titillating reply: 'something in between'!

Denmark and the 1990s

This account of modesty, equality, and decency should not, however, be taken to mean that companies in Denmark have been immune to the trends and pressures associated with the 1990s, even if they are not as marked as in say Britain or the USA.

Among the companies visited there were:

- instances of downsizing, de-layering, reorganization, and closure,
- a company that fired blue-collar workers for poor performance,
- a company that reduced its wage bill via a deal that introduced a performance element into the blue-collar wage, but under a restriction that it could only be paid to the best performers, not *to all* who reach a required level of performance,
- another company that downsized on the basis of performance, not LIFO (last in first out),

- the merged company discussed above was indeed integrating administrative systems (even if it had waited eight years to grasp the nettle),
- another company had implemented work force flexibility with a deal that offered employees the same money, and slightly lower hours , but with a commitment to unpaid overtime at the company's discretion.

Yet perhaps the most striking testimony encountered in the interviews was that of a production manager who spoke of a corporate intention to eliminate trade union representation altogether in the middle term. When I expressed surprise at this (according to figures from the British TUC Denmark has a higher trade union membership rate than even Sweden) the reply was: Jyllandsposten has already done it. Jyllandsposten is a national newspaper, with of course Jutland origins. It also uses a number of advertising slogans appealing to equality and solidarity. Yet this intention to abolish trade unions is not quite the Denmark immortalized by Steven Borish in his discussion of folk high schools.

References

Borish, Steven M. (1991) *The Land of the Living*, Nevada City, California: Blue Dolphin Publishing, Inc.

Haire, Mason *et al.* (1966) *Managerial Thinking: An International Study*, New York: Wiley.

Hofstede, Geert (1980) *Culture's Consequences*, Beverley Hills: Sage.

Lawrence, Peter (1996) *Management in the USA*, London: Sage.

Lawrence, Peter (1998) *Issues in European Business*, London & Basingstoke: Macmillan.

Schramm-Nielsen, Jette and Peter Lawrence (1998) 'Scandinavian Management: a cultural homogeneity beyond the nation state', *Entreprise et Histoire*, No 18, pp. 1–14.

Sjøborg, Eddie R. (1985) *Riding the Tide: Skandinavisk Management mot År 2000*, Oslo: Bedrifstøkonomens Forlag.

Strange, Morton (1996) '*Culture Shock: Denmark*', London: Kuperard.

CHAPTER 11

The Netherlands

When banks in the Netherlands introduced queuing systems this was universally welcomed by customers, not so much because of its fairness but because it reduced the likelihood of another customer standing just behind you at the counter and hearing your business. Similarly, customer satisfaction surveys conducted by Dutch banks are always very positive on the subject of personal bankers – having a named person at the branch who (alone) always deals with you and your transactions; this way a customer knows that his personal affairs will not be known to, or discussed by, a miscellany of employees at the branch!

In short privacy is a Dutch virtue. This applies not only to personal matters, but also in a sense to Dutch society. Dutch citizens in general are proud of their country; they think well of it, and they want you to think well of it, but they do not necessarily want you to unpack it, know all the details, sometimes tear the paper from over the cracks, and reach independent judgements.

These introductory remarks are not meant to be critical. But the typical Dutch stance of 'proud and private' does not make things easy for a foreign enquirer. Never in the line of duty have I been bamboozled as in The Netherlands, where they all tell you different things, no-one wants to make a 'full disclosure' and they will pick holes in any generalization you dare to profess – no matter how flattering it may be to them.

To give one little example of 'Dutch consensus' I was intrigued, when I went to work in the Netherlands, by the role of the multinational companies: after all it is unusual for a small country to have so many MNCs, of its own, not those of other countries located or headquartered there as a matter of convenience. And while these MNCs might not have a big influence in a big country, it seemed likely that they would have a big influence in a small country, and that one should try to understand how they impacted on the management standards and business practice. Deciding to start with something straightforward I asked a number of interviewees whether the MNCs paid more than other companies. Answers were in the range:

- yes,
- no,
- we have never thought about it (= you shouldn't be thinking about it either),
- it is a stupid question, that is not why people want to work for MNCs!

There is, however, a silver lining as I discovered when invited to give a public lecture on my impressions of Dutch society the day I went home after the first four-month period spent researching Dutch business and management. The pay-off was in the form of a certain grudging admiration that I had had the guile and gall to 'hang in there' and try to break the code.

Dutch society

It may be helpful to set the scene by asking whether there is anything distinctive about Dutch society. The first thing to mention would have to be some episodes in the country's past:

- The Netherlands owe their existence to a successful revolt against Spanish overlordship in the sixteenth century; the episode figures in British history books as the Revolt of the Netherlands and is known to the Dutch as the Eighty Years War (1568–1648); suffice it to say that by the early seventeenth century the seven provinces that make up the Netherlands today had achieved their independence *de facto* and have been free and independent ever since except for a period of Nazi occupation (1940–44/45) during the Second World War.
- The ten provinces which make up modern Belgium also took part in the sixteenth-century revolt but failed to achieve independence, largely because they lacked the advantage enjoyed by the Dutch of east-west rivers (Rhine, Waal, and Maas), offering a defensive line against the Spanish; the Belgian failure, however, has coloured Dutch attitudes to Belgium, which incline to the patronizing (the Dutch tell Belgian jokes after the manner of English jokes about the Irish).
- In the sixteenth century Revolt, the then predominantly Calvinist provinces of Noord Holland, Zuid Holland, and Zealand took the lead; they confirmed the supremacy of Calvinism in the new state although a part of the population is Catholic.
- After achieving independence the new state became a major trading and colonial power, and its sea power rivalled that of England in the seventeenth century.
- Dutch colonial possessions at various times included holdings in the Caribbean and mainland South America, footholds in North America

(New York City was originally New Amsterdam), the Transvaal and Orange Free State in what became South Africa, and the Dutch East Indies which became the independent state of Indonesia after the Second World War; all this reinforced the Dutch inclination for international trade, and made the country important as a commodity trading centre, which it still is, and gave it a lead in dry groceries and tobacco.

- The seventeenth century was also a Golden Age in terms of culture and science; there are literary achievements in this period, admittedly not widely known given the status of Dutch as a minority language; the philosopher Spinoza was Dutch and Descartes who was French lived in the Netherlands by choice; but the Golden Age is most renowned for its painting: there is the fame of Pieter de Hooch, Jan Vermeer, Frans Hals, and of course of Rembrandt; in the seventeenth century the Netherlands was a cultural superpower!

All this is remarkable for a fairly small country and no doubt underpins the Dutch desire to be thought well of. But there is more.

Verzuiling

The word *verzuiling* is sometimes used in the English language political science literature, and is usually translated as 'pillarization'; it signifies any major socio-political variable that transcends/cuts across socio-political strata or social classes. In the Netherlands, religion still does, and in the past did so strongly with a plenitude of institutional ramifications.

As noted in the previous section Calvinism was the historically dominant religion in the Netherlands, its ascendancy enhanced by the role of certain Calvinist provinces in the West. But there are two other provinces – Limburg and Brabant – in the South which are largely Catholic, and yet other provinces where Protestant and Catholic population elements are mixed. This Catholic v. Calvinist distinction took on a new and sharper meaning in the nineteenth century with the growth of public education and controversy over its control.

The upshot was a segregated school system, but more than this, in its heyday from the late nineteenth century to the 1960s or so, *verzuiling* meant a practical segregation of many aspects of ordinary life – one would buy one's meat from a Catholic butcher, support a Catholic football team, join a Catholic tennis club, or the Calvinist equivalents – with all such allegiances being exhorted from the pulpit. With the declining influence of religion and other social change this strong community-felt *verzuiling* is gone. Yet is has left an institutionalized legacy, for example:

- Primary schools are still confessionally segregated; when I worked in Holland my youngest daughter went to the Catholic primary school but there was a state primary school and a Calvinist primary school on the same block.

- There are two Catholic universities, Nijmegen and Tilburg, and Amsterdam has a Protestant university.
- Radio time and TV channels are allocated along confessional and political party/ideology lines.
- There are still Catholic hospitals, with different policies on for instance, abortion and euthanasia.
- There is a major political party, the CDA, which is Christian (that is what the C stands for), the amalgamation of three smaller confessional parties in 1977.
- Even employers' federations and trade union confederations are divided on a Christian versus lay dimension.

Yet perhaps more important than these institutional survivals is the fact that Calvinism, even if support for organized religion has declined, has left what one might call a characterological legacy – sober, hardworking, restrained, resolute, strong anti-corruption and anti-display norms and so on.

Regionalism

The Netherlands may be a small country but regional differences matter. The dominant one is the north versus south divide, where north means north of the rivers (Rhine, Maas and Waal) and south means south of them. The phrases *boven de rivieren* and *beneden de rivieren*, above the rivers and below the rivers, are standard expressions in Dutch, and so is the more picturesque *boven/beneden de mordijk*, where the *mordijk* is a famous bridge across the Hollands Diep on the north south road from Breda to Dordrecht. This north v. south divide loosely overlaps the Calvinist v. Catholic divide and in the Dutch mind tends to reinforce it.

Thus the north is seen as more severe, judgemental, serious minded, hardworking, and people from the north are in the Dutch view above all dependable; 'when someone from (name your favourite northern province) says he will do something, you can depend upon it' they tell you. The south on the other hand is viewed as more given to display, deference, and good living, outward appearances, gracious manners, and so on, but you can't depend on them! Readers are exhorted not to take either the geography or the ethics of this too seriously; I am simply trying to give the popular Dutch view.

A second element in Dutch regional consciousness might be expressed in the phrase 'the West outranks the Rest!' The four major towns – Rotterdam, Utrecht, Amsterdam and the Hague – are all in the west, indeed the provinces of Noord Holland, where Amsterdam is, and Zuid Holland, where Rotterdam is, constitute a near continuous conurbation, referred to by the Dutch as the *Randstad*. The West is richer, much more densely populated, has the headquarters of pretty well all the main companies apart from Philips which is in Eindhoven, has the only significant airport (Schipol at Amsterdam), the political capital (the Hague), the real capital (Amsterdam), the largest port (Rotterdam) and all the old and more prestigious universities – those of Leiden, Utrecht, Delft (technical university) and Amsterdam. The *Randstad* is conscious of being the nation's centre of gravity, and is a bit superior. If one scans the management job adverts in the weekly paper *Intermediair* one will see expressions such as 'our client's location is in the West' alongside other plus points such as the company's size or prominence in the industry. Similarly, job adverts may carry in the manner of a health warning remarks such as 'you will need to relocate to *Overijsel*' (the province in the east on the German border). While the longest train journey one can do in the Netherlands, from Amsterdam to Maastricht in the bottom right hand corner, only takes around $3^1/_2$ hours, these journeys across the country are a long way in terms of psychological distance.

Finally, in the Dutch mind different towns are thought to have different characters (and often voting patterns in the sense of fairly consistent support for a particular political party). In particular there is a kind of rivalry between Amsterdam and Rotterdam, some of which is caught in the Dutch joke:

> Rotterdam is where you make money
> Amsterdam is where you go to spend it
> And the Hague is where you talk about it

Institutional differentiation

Probably the thing which makes the Netherlands a difficult country for foreigners to understand is its differentiated nature. As we have seen it is differentiated in regional and confessional terms, as well as marked by its history. And we have noted some of the institutional results of this – different schools, hospitals, universities, TV channels and so on. There is also strong political differentiation in the sense of:

- four major political parties (instead of the British and American two),
- a larger overall number of parties,
- a strong tradition of coalition governments.

The four main parties are:

CDA: a centre-right Christian Party
VVD: a more recent centre-right, pro-business Party
PvdA: the Labour Party

D66:   a mildly reformist democratic party, the 66 referring not to the
number of deputies, but to the year (1966) of its formation

And there are a number of smaller parties that do, actually, get a few seats in
general elections. The Christian party, the CDA, is itself the result of a merger
of Catholic and Protestant parties in 1977. The present government (time of
writing autumn 1998) is a coalition of PvdA, VVD and D66. The only thing
that would strike Dutch people as a little unusual about this is the fact that the
CDA is not in government: the pattern of the last 20 years or so has been that
the CDA has been at the centre of a series of coalitions alternately aligning itself
with parties to its left and right.

In short the Netherlands is not a 'winner take all' system, as are Britain and
the USA. A general election in the Netherlands does not typically give rise to a
government, but to an often protracted period of bargaining and negotiation at
the end of which a (new) coalition emerges.

The simple message is that Dutch society is seldom simple: it is not a mono-
chrome, there are few 'blacks and whites', indeed to extend the metaphor one
would say it is a society of pastel shades. It is made complex by differentiation
and its institutional representation. This is turn feeds through into Dutch values,
though the expression is perhaps a bit clinical.

Dutch values

First, what is probably the most basic value is what has been referred to as the
legacy of Calvinism, in the sense of a commitment to a personal moral responsibility together with a kind of 'godfearing' conformity. On the whole the Dutch
tend to censure excessive individualism, rampant ambition, pride, eccentricity,
arrogance, flamboyance, and display. There is an instinctive preference for
something more sober, restrained, and quietly meritorious.

This orientation is very evident in, for example, Dutch proverbs. There is in
Dutch, as in German, an exact equivalent of 'pride comes before a fall', but it
does not end there. The Dutch also have:

Naast je schoenen lopen
(to walk beside your shoes)

meaning to be too big for your boots, and rather more picturesquely an
expression

hoog te paard sitten
(to sit too high on your horse)

meaning to be too full of yourself, giving yourself 'lord of the manor' status.
But the greater vanity which feeds on the mindless praise of others is caught in
the proverb:

over het paard getild zijn
(to be lifted *over* the horse)

suggesting that the individual's eventual surrender to sycophants means they could not even get him into the saddle! Neither does the wise man (= good Dutchman) take unnecessary risks, a thought captured in the exhortation:

steek niet je hoofd
boven het maaifeld
(don't put your head above the trench)

Yet probably the most revealing and most often cited, is the notion:

als je gewoon doet
doe je al gek genoeg
(when you act normal, that is already crazy enough)

This is a fairly powerful condemnation of any tendency to idiosyncratic exhibitionism. Better to conform, be like others and thus accepted by others.

Second, and arguably related to the differentiation discussed in earlier sections, the Dutch have an ability to deal with difference and complexity. It is compounded of restraint and adjustment, a willingness to recognize difference and work for accommodation. What happens after a general election is illustrative of this disposition.

Third, Dutch society shows a strong commitment to equality, which in turn implies a strong post-Second World War welfare provision. The egalitarian disposition tends to minimize class differences and to depress hierarchy.

This is not meant to be an exclusive list but these are the three things – conformity, restraint, equality – that as a foreigner living in the Netherlands I felt most marked that country off from Britain.

The Dutch economy

It may at this stage be helpful to note some quasi distinctive features of the Dutch economy.

The first of these features will seem relatively unremarkable at the end of the twentieth century, and this is that the manufacturing sector has never been as large in the Netherlands as in most of the other 'advanced industrial countries.' While all these countries have now moved away from manufacturing in terms of relative importance (even in Germany the services sector is now a larger part of GDP than manufacturing) and the importance of services is a theme of the late twentieth century, in the Netherlands this is nothing new. It is easier to make the case if one deliberately goes back a bit in time. Consider 1980:

Structure of exports 1980 (%)

	Netherlands	West Germany	EU
agriculture and food	22	5	11
energy	22	–	7
machinery	13	29	22
vehicles	4	16	12
other manufactured goods	35	42	43

Source: *Tweede Kamer* (Dutch House of Commons)
    Export Nota 1981–2, No. 17532, p. 51

Straight away one can see an unusual (for a rich country) strength in food and agriculture. In the Dutch case this is made up of just about everything that can be raised, grazed or grown in a country with a temperate climate, including some things the Dutch don't eat much of themselves, such as mutton, that are still produced for export. In addition the Netherlands is a major producer, exporter and also domestic consumer of cut flowers, the production of which is normally dependent on long hours of winter daylight (the advantage enjoyed by Israel in round-the year flower production) but the Dutch do it artificially.

Then there is the Dutch strength in energy. In 1958 natural gas was discovered near the northern town of Groningen, and brought on stream in the early 1960s: the Dutch were so confident of their reserves they actually closed down the coal mines in Limburg, the southern province with the now EU-famous town of Maastricht. This development has given the Dutch cheap domestic and industrial gas, and lucrative exports. The other plank to the energy advantage is petroleum refining: this is done on a huge scale on the Rijnmond (Rhine Estuary), Rotterdam is the centre of the oil spot market (real time, real price purchases, not forward buying), and Royal Dutch Shell is the country's largest company by turnover.

Then when we come to the data on vehicles, machinery, and other manufactured goods we see the relative Dutch weakness. The fair comparison in the last column of figures is with the EU average; note that this is the EU/EEC of 1980 with 9 member countries, not the end-twentieth century EU with 15).

In fact the Dutch strength in the manufacturing industry has actually declined since 1980: in the early 1990s the truck manufacturer DAF 'went to the wall'; in the mid 1990s the independent aircraft manufacturer Fokker failed and was broken up; Philips quite literally is not 'all that it used to be', having sold off its domestic appliance business to Whirlpool of the USA (making them the world number two in domestic appliance manufacture after Electrolux of Sweden). All that is left of motor car manufacture in the Netherlands is an entity called Nedcar jointly owned by Mitsubishi, Volvo and the Dutch government whose assembly line produces the Mitsubishi Galant and the Volvo S40.

In short, when it comes to manufacture the Netherlands is not a country like

Germany (note the sharp contrast with Germany on the export data) or Sweden, or to a lesser extent Switzerland, that manufactures everything, but a country with some specific manufacturing strengths. These would include oil refining and gas production as said, electrical and electronic goods (Philips), chemicals (AKZO and DSM), beer (Heineken and Grolsch), dry groceries (Douwe Egbert), food and personal care products (Unilever), and so on.

The country has, of course, a number of strengths which are not mainline manufacturing. Again these would include:

- Trucking, logistics, supply chain management, international freight forwarding.
- Shipping and dock transshipment (note that Rotterdam is the world's largest port).
- Air transportation where KLM has a disproportionately large route network: there are various measures of airline size but if one takes international ton kilometers KLM comes into the top half dozen of airlines worldwide, remarkable for a small country.
- Airport services, where Schipol airport at Amsterdam is endlessly applauded by business travellers; readers of the US *Business Traveller International*, for instance, rated Schipol second only to Changi, Singapore, at the end of 1997.
- Computer services and software, where there are some exceptionally entrepreneurial companies (Lawrence, 1991); the high cost of labour in the Netherlands and particularly the indirect cost of labour has led companies to outsource computer services long before 'core business' and 'outsourcing' became watchwords.
- Banking and other financial services, driven in the Dutch case as elsewhere by some high profile mergers, for example ABN and AMRO merged at the beginning of the 1990s, and NMB and the Postbank and the little of what was left of Barings after the Nick Leeson *debâcle* merged to form Ing Bank.

To this list one should probably add rail transportation. Everyone likes the Dutch railways, their frequency and reliability. Indeed as William Shetter has pointed out the Dutch railway timetable repeats itself every hour, and in some places every half hour (Shetter, 1987). And indeed Nederlandse Spoorwegen (NS), the Dutch railways, are actually the largest single employing organization in the Netherlands (Lawrence, 1986). What is more, in contrast to practically every other European country, the Netherlands expanded their rail network in the 1980s; the first cuts to the network were announced in April 1999.

Noting that the railways are the largest employer, the largest in the private sector is Philips of course, but the 'top twenty' list for workforce size actually includes two retailers. One of these, Vendex International, consists primarily of the Vroom and Dreesmann chain of departmental stores, a kind of John Lewis of the Netherlands. The other, Ahold, seems set to be the retail superstore of the early twenty-first century. Ahold is essentially the chain of Albert Heijn grocery stores (no shopping centre anywhere in the Netherlands is complete without an Albert Heijn, named of course after the folksy founder). Now it should be noted that Dutch retailers are not slow when it comes to cross-border expansion (C&A would be an early example), but Ahold under CEO van de Hoeven in the late 1990s has engaged in massive cross-border expansion, focusing particularly on South America and to a lesser extent on the Far East. This is in a different league from British retailers making acquisitions in Ireland!

So far we have drawn attention to the overall shape of the Dutch economy, specific strengths in manufacture, and a variety of strengths in services. To this testimony two simple points should be added. The first is to say that the Netherlands is a strongly exporting economy with a favourable trade balance. Indeed the Netherlands vies with Canada for exporting the largest proportion of GDP (and moved into first place in 1997). Second, as suggested at the start of the chapter, the Netherlands is unusual as a small country in having so many multi-national companies, including Shell, Philips, Akzo, Ahold, Heineken, KLM, Unilever, not to mention some of the less well-known financial service providers.

The final point would be to say that if the Eighty Years War was the decisive event of the sixteenth century, that the Second World War and the Nazi occupation from 1940–44/45 was for the Dutch the apocalypse of the mid twentieth century. It might be noted *en passant* that as a result of the Nuremberg War Crimes trials of 1945–46 only 16 people were hanged: they included Arthur Seyss-Inquart, the Nazi governor of the Netherlands from 1940 to his arrest by the Allies in 1945. But to 'accentuate the positive' the Second World War seems to have cemented for all time the mutual regard of the Dutch and the British. And this regard clearly has some economic substance. Whenever one scratches the surface of the Dutch economy Anglo-Dutch business connections are there. Not only are two of the Netherlands' leading MNCs – Shell and Unilever – Anglo-Dutch, but the Netherlands is the second largest recipient of British FDI, foreign direct investment, after the USA. The two countries also liberalized their air relations in the mid 1980s, long before 1992 and the Single European Market and later deregulation of air services. The impact of this 1980s agreement is that the two countries totally liberalized the market – routes, frequency, price, and access to destinations. This was at the time an unprecedented development. One anomaly that has resulted is that Schipol is connected to more destinations in the UK than is London Heathrow.

Management and society

Organizational differentiation

In the Dutch case there is a strong parallelism between management and society. To begin with something tangible, the institutional differentiation discussed earlier is present in the world of companies, business, and work relations. First of all the publicly quoted Dutch Companies, those with NV after the name, have two-tier boards, exactly like those of Germany described in Chapter 7. The supervisory board in the Dutch case is the *Raad van Commissarissen* and the executive board is the *Raad van Bestuur*, the former being part-time and non-executive and the latter being composed of senior full-time executive directors. With regard to the *Raad van Commissarissen* it would probably be fair to say that they function a little bit as a status barometer for the company: an illustrious company needs illustrious Commissarissen, and you may well find an ex-prime minister among their ranks. Also for the big companies having an international *Raad van Commissarissen*, that is one with some members who are not Dutch nationals, is common too. And it is also quite common for such supervisory boards to have meetings in English rather than Dutch.

Second, the Netherlands has a system of industrial democracy, one which has been in place for more than a quarter of a century, and whose principal institution is a workplace works council, *Ondernemingsraad* (OR) in Dutch, with elected members, rights to discussion, recommendation and information. It is very like the German *Betriebsrat* described in Chapter 7. The OR meets in private of course, but each meeting is followed up with a joint meeting with management, known as the *overlegsvergadering*. In particular these follow-up meetings are a tribute to Dutch restraint and the spirit of accommodation.

Third, when it comes to wider employer and employee representation there is again an organizational differentiation that is loosely *verzuiling* derived. That is to say there are two employers' federations, the NCW and the VNO where the C in the first one stands for *Christelijk* (Christian), and the various trade unions or industry/occupation specific divisions thereof are organized into three confederations – FNV, CNV, and Unie BLHP – where the C of the second one again stands for *Christelijk*.

These three confederations have traditionally engaged in periodic bargaining with employers regarding pay and conditions. This process is quite complicated, but the Dutch can handle complication. The outcome of such bargaining sessions is the collective works agreement or CAO. Now I have read a number of these CAOs for different companies and/or industries, and they are also very Dutch in the restraint shown and in the emphasis on welfare. To be more specific the CAOs tend to be quite modest in the pay settlements awarded, and indeed with regard to any benefit having a demonstrable cash value. Their emphasis is rather on quality of working life, welfare, and policy issues: training, retraining, apprenticeship, entitlements to time off for personal reasons, and so on.

Industrial relations in the Netherlands have been good. Time and commitment have gone with negotiation and adjustment, but the result has been a 'low days lost through strike' rate, and the relative absence of that lower level disruption and disharmony in the workplace that has been so common in the past in Britain (Lawrence, 1984). Naturally the 1990s have seen in the Netherlands, as elsewhere, the tendency for bargaining to be decentralized and for agreements (CAOs) to last for a longer time period.

Verzuiling, regionalism and mobility

Dutch management has traditionally been rather immobile, in the sense of not changing companies or employing organizations. In this, of course, they are in contrast with American managers and also with those of Britain, both in terms of 'the facts' (though internationally comparative data on inter-company mobility are difficult to come by) and perhaps more importantly in terms of attitude. Deep down inside Dutch people feel it is wrong to chop and change employers. There are a number of reasons for this orientation.

The multinational companies are of course an exception to this generalization, but the effect of the legacy of *verzuiling* is that SMEs (smaller firms) would normally be headed-up by someone with the right religion; to put it bluntly one would think twice about appointing a Calvinist to head a smaller firm in say Brabant. Indeed the matter of religious difference is more complicated than was suggested earlier in that there is not only the Catholic v. Calvinist split, but also two branches of Calvinism, the *hervormd* (the majority) and the *gereformeerd* (more radical). There was talk in the 1980s of the two merging (Shetter, 1987) but it did not happen. And there are communities in the Netherlands in which the *gereformeerde* church is dominant, and this will affect the culture and behaviour of companies in such communities. An example appeared in Henk Mulder's fascinating book 'the 49 best companies to work for in the Netherlands' (it is in Dutch) where there was no drinking or swearing at work, and everything in the community was closed on Sundays (Mulder, 1989).

The regional differences are also a brake on mobility in the Netherlands. Again it does not apply to MNCs who will deploy their staff both nationally and internationally according to company needs, but managers working at other companies may well be affected in the choice of company and loyalty to an existing employer by considerations of region. It does not matter that the distances are not very large: it is psychological distance that counts. A consultant once told me:'We are recruiting for this really fantastic company ... but it is in Venlo' (in the south, on the German border, and a long way from the Randstad).

It should be added that regionalism is also a constraint on labour mobility generally, not just for managers and professionals. Added to this is the fact that Dutch workers do not like long journeys to work (remember many of them cycle there).

But running through the Dutch loyalty to employers is the set of values we indicated as the Calvinist legacy – soberness, steadfastness, conforming to acceptable standards, and so on. In traditional Dutch thinking an American-style changing of employers would suggest:

- lack of responsibility and loyalty,
- personal instability,
- overwhelming ambition,
- greed,

and these are all bad!

There are some reasons for thinking this has changed somewhat in the course of the 1990s. First there has been some downsizing and some company failures, as already noted, which implies some involuntary mobility. Second, perusing *Intermediair*, the weekly professional job advertisements paper, there seem to be a lot of adverts requiring several years experience, (with another company), rather than seeking to hire newly qualified entrants to the professional labour market. While writing this chapter I have also asked friends who teach *Bedrijfseconomie* (business economics) in Dutch universities who say their current students expect mobile careers on the Anglo-Saxon model (though whether or not they will still think so when they are 40 is another question).

Management style

We have suggested earlier that egalitarianism and what has been termed the Calvinist legacy are key Dutch values, and they clearly influence the style and practice of Dutch management. We will take this as a starting point.

Dutch managers are unpretentious and generally 'low key'. Their manner and behaviour do not suggest that they see themselves or wish to be seen by others as 'larger than life' figures; they do not seem to aspire to be 'a legend in their lifetime'. They are opposed to display, flamboyance, expensive cars in the parking lot, and 'the privileges of office'. Titles are not used much, a lot of company telephone books are organized in terms of names only, not job titles or functions.

There is a strain towards conformity. Dutch managers do not typically engage in personality cults. They aim to be fair, decent, consistent and dependable – just like everyone else. There are limits to individualism. One does not set oneself apart. Dress is a little less formal than in Britain, France or Germany – but it does not vary much from one person to another. They nearly all speak English well, but do not give themselves 'airs and graces' as linguists (the only thing they don't like is you trying to say something in Dutch!).

Dutch management is restrained, in all sorts of ways. Speech and expression are moderate. Excessive displays of anger, persuasion or even dynamic pro-activity are uncommon.

Ambition will be modulated, not paraded. The aims and purposes of the company will be taken seriously, but they will not be deified. They are, after all, merely the work of man.

Another manifestation of this restraint is the Dutch ability to deal with the differentiation and the plethora of organizations detailed earlier. So the Dutch manage their two boards, the OR (works council) and the *overlegsvergadering* (follow up meeting), their dealings with coalition governments and provincial assemblies, with three trade union confederations, two employers' federations, and complicated processes of negotiation leading to the CAO (collective works agreement).

Furthermore the Dutch have been masters in the operation of matrix organizations, ones with two organizational axes – usually product and territory – crossing each other and giving organizational members double reporting lines. This has been expressed in the perfect tense since matrix organizations are not 'the flavour of the decade' in the 1990s, when the trend has been towards dedicated manufacturing plants supplying regions (groups of countries) with a diminished managerial input from individual countries. But even if a little dated, the cross-cultural comparison is interesting: the Americans don't like matrix organizations but the Dutch have managed them well.

It is only a small point but Dutch managers also make something of a cult of punctuality (just like the Germans they so love to criticize). It is always interesting to see what words or expressions from their mother tongue people will employ when speaking English as a foreign language. In the Dutch case a word they are inclined to use in the middle of English speech is *agenda*. It means diary: not the kind in which you record thoughts and events, but the kind in which engagements and appointments are listed. This small point has a wider meaning: the Dutch respect for appointments is a recognition of time as an externality and man as subject to it. Dutch people will often remark that man is puny in the face of nature by pointing to the ever present risk of flooding in the Netherlands: 'If we get it wrong' they say, 'we get our feet wet.' A very Calvinist trait is the anti-corruption ethic. Not only is Dutch management splendidly uncorrupt itself, Dutch managers often mention lack of corruption as something that distinguishes management in the Netherlands from that of (some) other countries.

In his inaugural lecture at Rijksuniversiteit Limburg, Geert Hofstede suggested that one role that the Dutch like to play is that of preacher. They like, that is to say, to exhort others, tell them what to do, and if necessary condemn what they do do. So that Dutch managers like to censure others for display and flamboyance; they censure the Germans for presumptions of authoritarian hierarchicalism, the French for offering tied aid to Third World countries (aid that can only be spent on French goods and services: the charge does not seem to be supported by the facts, but it is the Dutch belief that counts), and even the British for wallowing in class-consciousness and the mire of inequality.

Dutch management is pragmatic. It is not driven by theory or by doctrine. It sets itself straightforward objectives, and pursues them in readily comprehensible ways. Dutch enthusiasm for business strategy is subdued when judged by Anglo-Saxon standards. While Dutch managers 'can see the point' of strategy their appreciation is suffused by a feeling that it is also 'a bit highfalutin', that it is somehow or other immodest to erect such a grandiose structure around money-making.

Motivation

Dutch managers are also restrained in the matter of executive remuneration. While they are not badly paid, what international salary data that has come my way suggests that net pay for managers in the Netherlands would be a little modest compared with say France, Switzerland and Germany, though these countries are not significantly richer in GDP per capita terms, nor does one typically encounter in the Netherlands the 'sky is the limit' salaries for chief executives that are common in Britain and the USA. Again comparative salary data for the Netherlands tend to suggest a modest salary differentiation among and between the management ranks, where the gap between the most highly paid manager and his or her deputy, or between the heads of different functions/departments – finance, manufacturing, sales, R&D, personnel, and so on – are more modest than in some other European countries. There is also an element in the Dutch character that is offended by the idea of purely financial incentives: in this connection I recall a management consultant in the Netherlands testifying that Dutch managers sometimes react negatively to stock option schemes, saying in effect, 'as though I would work harder just for money!' As a little test of the salience of management remuneration I checked every management job advert in a current issue of *Intermediair* and only three actually named a salary or indicated a salary range, as opposed to vague references to 'an appropriate remuneration' (even these vague references were not that frequent.) The three companies concerned were made up of one British, one American, and Shell (Anglo-Dutch).

There tends to be more emphasis in the Netherlands on working climate, environment, friendly colleagues, cooperative atmosphere, freedom and challenge. This has been very clear in job advertisements across two decades, as well as being a recurrent theme in my own interviews at Dutch companies (Lawrence, 1991). A nice illustration of Dutch tendencies in this matter, for employees generally rather than just for managers, is offered by Henk Mulder (1989) who quotes the results of an in-house survey at Heineken where people were asked what aspects of the job they saw as most desirable, and the following proportions emerged:

Pleasure in the work	60%
Decent remuneration	47%
Interesting work	46%
Ability to take decisions	41%
Likeable colleagues	40%
Feeling valued as a person	37%

Informality and networks

The informal system is important in Dutch organizations, in a way that it is not in Germany. That is to say the relations between people, as whole human beings not just role incumbents, are important. So there are norms, channels of communication, common evaluations which are independent of the formal organization with its structure and systems.

Dutch companies are marked by their networks. This is readily conceded by research interviewees and is a recurrent theme in Henk Mulder's portraits of 49 companies in the Netherlands. With regard to larger companies it is often asserted that as the individual progresses he or she will have three sets of networks:

- Those who joined the company at the same time, the recruits of the year 2000 or whatever.
- Those in the same management function – production, personnel, finance, design or whatever – even though they may be spread around a variety of plants and sites, sometimes over several countries.
- One gets to know those on in-house training courses; the more exclusive and senior the episode of training, the more significant the interpersonal network created.

A nice example of this phenomenon offered by Henk Mulder, quoting from a Unilever director:

There exists inside Unilever an awful lot of informal networks. And you really must not shut yourself off from these. In the ten years I have been with the company I have made masses of good friends during the courses and seminars that take place. That means colleagues with whom you maintain enduring contact during your career. If sometimes you have a problem, then you phone someone. Such personal contact can also play a role when you are looking for someone to fill a vacancy in your own organization (Mulder, 1989:262, translated by Peter Lawrence).

Or again Mulder quotes from the personnel director at the MNB bank (now Ing Bank) as saying:

The office doors of most of the managers stand open all the time, including mine. If you want to see a member of the *raad* (executive board) you can be sure of getting him on the telephone (Mulder, 1989:217, translated by Peter Lawrence).

This NMB director ends by saying that two members of the *raad* were among the team of eleven that played football against the OR (works council).

At the national level there is an elite network, and there are some serious attempts by Dutch writers to map it, for instance, Jos van Hezewijk, (1988) and in a more historic sense Ernst Zahn, (1984). This is so despite the genuine Dutch attachment to egalitarianism, though the latter often makes them reluctant to admit the former. This networking at the top is facilitated by the relative smallness of the Netherlands, although it has the sixth largest economy in Western Europe (the pecking order is Germany, France, Italy, Britain, Spain and the Netherlands). Networking is also facilitated by regionalism with a concentration of political, administrative, and corporate power in the *Randstad*. There is even in Dutch an expression '*ons soort mensen*'(our kind of people) to denote fellow elite-network members.

It is easy to miss this given the pragmatic, informal, down to earth approach of the Dutch. Neither of course do the Dutch have the battery of elite institutions dear to the British. So there is no equivalent in the Netherlands of our Harrow or Eton, of our Oxford and Cambridge, our Guards Regiments, County families, or London clubs. They do have a monarchy but it is more democratic in demeanour. The monarchy received a big boost in affection and esteem relating to the person of Queen Wilhelmina during the Second World War: she symbolized national pride and the spirit of resistance, lived frugally in England and devoted her considerable energy to the Dutch cause. Winston Churchill once said of her 'All my life I have been afraid of no man, but Queen Wilhelmina, . . .'. It was said of her granddaughter Queen Beatrix that when her children were small she used to drive to the primary school herself to collect them at the end of the day, in a Mini. Whether or not it is true, the story is indicative. Homely conformity not aloof magnificence brings credit in Dutch society.

So elite networks are milder and gentler in the Netherlands, less clearly based on visible institutions or collectivities. There are little networks based for example on:

- graduation from a particular university or technical university,
- women in business, who all know each other,
- Mars and Mercurias, an organization for army officers who have gone into business (Prince Bernhard was an honorary member),
- people with Indonesian colonial connections,
- membership of Lions and Rotary, some sailing clubs, and golf – an expensive and exclusive club sport,
- networks within particular professions, for instance the law and consultancy.

Regarding the first of these, university background, the one most cited as an elite springboard is the law school at Leiden University, and to a lesser extent the law school at Utrecht University. Graduates of these institutions are over-represented in top corporate positions. For the generation in mid career now, a favoured university starting point is the department of economics at Erasmus University in Rotterdam. There is also the Nijenrode management college outside Utrecht, originally specializing in post experience courses, but achieving university status in the 1980s. In addition to the quality of its education Nijenrode also prides itself on the facilitation of sporting recreations and on its contacts, including international contacts.

One also finds in Dutch business circles overlapping *Raad van Commissarissen* (supervisory board) memberships, close relationships between particular banks and particular companies, and a tendency to 'promote' the head of the *Raad van Bestuur* (executive board) to the *Raad van Commissarissen* towards the end of his or her career. And in view of our previous remarks about qualified attitudes in the Netherlands towards ambition and mobility it will come as no surprise that Dutch companies tend to 'grow their own timber', that is to say, to promote from within. There is no American style presumption that the head of Chrysler should be recruited from Ford.

Education

It might be appropriate to note at this point that Dutch management is consistently and decently educated. The Netherlands, like Germany, has a tier of further education below the university level, and this tier, invariably known by its initials HBO is strongly vocational. Now just about anyone in a managerial or professional role in a Dutch company will be either HBO or university educated. Advertisements in the famous *Intermediair* invariably ask for 'HBO or university' or 'at least HBO education'. On the other hand there is no tier above the universities corresponding to the *grandes écoles* of France, nor is the doctors degree common among Dutch managers as it is among their German counterparts: both would be at odds with Dutch modesty.

To this should be added Dutch linguistic ability. English speaking is near universal, and there are all sorts of tell-tale signs that English is 'domiciled' in Dutch everyday life. Advertising copy, for example, is sometimes in English, so sometimes are company organization charts, wholly or partly. Dutch TV programmes imported from America and Britain are broadcast in English with rather skimpy Dutch subtitles. And perhaps rather more telling, news and political discussion programmes in Dutch will switch to interviews in English without any voice-over (the same applies to interviews with British and American pop groups in the numerous Dutch pop music and top twenty countdown shows.) Two of my children briefly attended Dutch secondary schools: they did English and French in the first year, and added German in the second (German is regarded as a bit of a pushover).

Decision making

In Dutch companies decision making is not radically different in style from that in other European countries, but there are three points of relative emphasis that might be mentioned. First of all it is pragmatic, judging the issue on its merits rather than in terms of a grand strategy. Second the Dutch are strong on attention to detail: in the Dutch mind detail is not something trivial to be delegated to someone else lower down. Third, at least some decisions involve a variety of constituencies that will have to be consulted and account taken of their views. The extreme case would be instituting redundancies or plant closure. Such a development will involve both boards, the trade union and the OR, and probably national and provincial government as well as the media. This all takes time. The impact of this was brought home to me when I visited a shipyard in Canada that had downsized, just after having worked in the Netherlands. I asked my Canadian interlocutor how they handled their large scale redundancies and received the laconic reply: 'We just say goodbye!' In the Netherlands you never just say goodbye.

Judging others

It has been argued by Geert Hofstede (1987) in his inaugural lecture that the Dutch like to preach and tell others what is good for them – and what they ought not to do! We have introduced this idea of Hofstede's and given examples, but it ought to be qualified. Dutch condemning tends to be at the level of the general – condemning some Third World countries for corruption, or Britain for old-fashioned class consciousness. But the Dutch are less ready, less inclined to judge individuals close to them or known to them. This point is argued strongly by American sociologist Derek Phillips working expatriately in the Netherlands in the 1980s. His view is that Dutch conformity inclines them not to welcome outstanding performance and not to censure poor performance: it is a syllogism in the form of conformity leads to mediocrity leads to acceptance of that which falls short of proper standards (Phillips, 1985). I have been aware of the phenomenon, particularly in conversations with personnel managers talking about recruitment and management development. They don't like the idea of 'high-flyer' programmes, or judging people too soon on their work and career or making an irrevocable judgement. They will set a standard of attainment, say an entry requirement, and then point out in some cases there may a good reason why the individual does not meet it, which one has to take into account. But perhaps a more characteristic explanation than that expressed by Derek Phillips would be to say this reluctance to judge others close to you is rooted in humility. If you judge others, you set yourself above them, and that is the role of God. Also it is noticeable that where individuals fail, the Dutch tend to prefer impersonal solutions of the re-organizing, restructuring kind. The Dutch do not have a hire and fire mentality.

Calvinism meets managerialism

This account has stressed some elements of Dutch management behaviour loosely deriving from a set of Calvinist values – modesty, restraint, quiet decency, and so on. It is probably necessary to qualify their interpretation in the context of late twentieth century managerialism. The 1990s have seen something of a convergence on an Anglo-Saxon model of business, with its accompanying rhetoric of go-getting individualism. This ethic has certainly found its way into the wording of management advertisements. Perusing that invaluable source, *Intermediair*, the adverts are littered with words and phrases I had scarcely encountered in the 1980s including:

Klantgericht instelling – customer focused
Resultaatgericht – results oriented   (now a near mandatory requirement)
Gesluitvaardig – decisive

There are new elements in the way the companies are described too, with phrases such as:

Starke nadrup op ondernemerschap
(strong emphasis on entrepreneurialism)

and:

ambitieuze groeiplannen
(ambitious plans for growth)

Among the qualities sought in the successful applicant perhaps the most telling is *stressbestandig*, or capable of handling stress. Ten years ago in the Netherlands the view would have been that if organizations inflicted stress on their members they should jolly well change themselves so as to end such a deplorable state of affairs, not treat stress as a given and find people who can cope with it.

But the commonest element in the new rhetoric is about the post requiring a strong personality. Consider as a representative example of this genre:

U bent een sterke persoonlijkheid die zich overtuigend presenteert
(You are a strong personality, who presents himself with conviction)

Doesn't sound very Calvinistic, does it?

So it is likely that there is change, in the same way as there is change in the traditional attitude to inter-company mobility discussed earlier – but there is also a world of caution. This is that it is difficult to know how deep all this goes. Discussing these developments with a management professor at a Dutch university while writing this chapter, the view was expressed that job adverts are not conclusive evidence. They may be seen as an opportunity to engage in a new managerial correctness without actually committing anyone to anything, and this is particularly possible where a consultant acting as head-hunter is interposed between the applicants and the ultimate employer. That is to say, we cannot tell if the employer will actually like these strong, convincing, decisive, stress coping personalities when they turn up.

Internationalism

Finally we should pull together some of the strands to make the case for Dutch internationalism. Notwithstanding the regionalism and some more parochial elements noted earlier, internationalism is a distinguishing feature of Dutch society and Dutch business. Consider in this connection:

- the role and achievements of the Dutch MNCs,
- the export orientation of Dutch managers, and the export achievement of the country,
- a colonial and commercial tradition,
- strong trading instincts, adept at trade manoeuvres,
- cooperation with Britain in particular,
- pre-eminent in supra-national organizations; Benelux 1953, founder members of what is now the EU 1957–58,
- widespread English speaking ability,
- strong banking system,
- pre-eminent in international transport and freight; has the world's oldest airline and the world's biggest port and Europe's most dense railway network.

One might add to this the fact that the Dutch, in manners and in other ways, are adaptable abroad. Neither they nor their companies proclaim Dutchness (cf. the Americans). As one well-travelled Dutch manager put it to me: 'there is nothing Dutch in Indonesia, but everything is British in India'. Finally, the Netherlands is also an over-contributor in relation to its size to international charitable organizations and to Third World Aid.

It is a record to be proud of.

References

Hezewijk, Jos van (1988) *De Netwerkern van de Top-Elite*, Amsterdam: Uitgeverij Balans.

Hofstede, Geert (1987) 'Dutch Culture's Consequences: Health, Law, Economy', inaugural lecture, Rijksuniversiteit Limburg.

Lawrence, Peter (1984) *Management in Action*, London: Routledge & Kegan Paul.

Lawrence, Peter (1986) 'Management in the Netherlands: a study in Internationalism?' report to Technische Hogeschool Twente, Enschede, the Netherlands.

Lawrence, Peter (1991) *Management in the Netherlands*, Oxford: Clarendon Press.

Mulder, Henk (1989) *De 49 beste bedrijven om voor te werken in Nederland*, Utrecht: Veen.

Phillips, Derek (1985) *De Naakte Nederlander: Kritische overpeinzingen*, Amsterdam: Uitgeverij Bert Bakken.

Shetter, William Z. (1987) *The Netherlands in Perspective*, Leiden: Martinus Nijhoff.

Zahn, Ernst (1984) *Das Unbekannte Holland*, Berlin: Stedler Verlag.

CHAPTER 12

Britain

American President Theodore Roosevelt, the one after whom Teddy Bears are named and who was in office before the First World War, once observed:

> My rule is a simple one.
> Do the best you can,
> with what you have,
> and do it now! (Brands, 1997:453)

The appeal of this dictum lies of course in its directness and simplicity: how nice to have a simple rule to know what you have and what to do with it. Indeed the fascination of Teddy Roosevelt is his enjoyment of certainties: he knew America was destined to be great, that it was right to kick Spain out of Cuba, stamp out corruption in the New York City Police force, and curb the powers of the Corporations that weighed on ordinary people – a moral absolutist, if ever there was one.

Beginning a chapter on the country of my birth makes me envy other people their certainties. It is more difficult for most of us to know what is different and interesting and important about our homeland than it is to make these judgements for other countries. This is because of a mix of over-familiarity and subjectivity, of not being able to see the wood for the trees, of the excess of experience precluding any clean cut generalization.

But Britain is also a special case of this dilemma. For a thousand years Britain has been at the centre of European development, and in the twentieth century which has seen its eclipse, it has endlessly pondered the reasons for that eclipse. The result is that it is difficult to come to questions about Britain with an open mind, or still less with an empty mind. One is confronted with the weight of evidence, an established literature, and with received wisdom – on what British society is like, on the place of wealth creation within it, and on the standing of industry and management.

The legacy of national character

I once told a German production manager whom I had just watched chair a lively meeting on new machinery acquisition that I had found the whole discussion jolly interesting and 'typically German'. The manager reacted like one electrocuted to this unthinking remark, and demanded to know what was 'typically German'.

No British person ever has this difficulty. We all know what is 'typically British'. It is a nice mix of traditional and sense of humour, class consciousness and style, conservatism and character, privacy and privilege, suffused with intimations of effortless superiority. There is even a Ph.D. thesis which says so!

The thesis in question is the work of an Irishman whose focus was the cultural determinants of organization behaviour in Britain (Terry, 1979). That is to say, he Terry sought to set up a model of the British national character and link behaviour in organizations to it. Using a variety of constituencies – other people's surveys, his own survey, the testimony of foreign nationals working in Britain, a set of British managers, and so on – he generated a short list of values or features most often confirmed across these constituencies. The top values, in descending order, were:

Conservatism
Class
Compromise
Liberty and individualism
Fair play
Reserve
Tenacity
(Terry, 1979:260)

The thesis is cleverly argued and engagingly illustrated. These values are almost what we British have been brought up to think. They are now, as in Terry's research, often articulated by foreigners seeking to define the British national character.

Yet even at the time of the research in the late 1970s, did not these values 'feed off' Britain's past rather than its present? Consider for a moment the first and the last items in Terry's list. It is rather nice to be a citizen of a country credited with tenacity (the implication being that it is character-displaying tenacity deployed in a good cause). But if one asks for a good example of this tenacity, that professed is invariably the early stages of the Second World War, the 1940–41 period when all other countries opposed to Nazi Germany had been beaten but Britain alone chose to fight on, without the slightest hope of being able to win the War unaided. Now whether one ascribes this epic decision to quiet decency or to Winston Churchill's fear that since the Conservative Party did not really want him as prime minister, if peace came he would be chucked out, perhaps we really did 'save Europe by our example' and may feel proud of 'our finest hour'. But it is still something that happened in 1940. When in the subsequent 60 years is Britain supposed to have given the world a demonstration of its tenacity?

Or consider conservatism. At the time of Terry's research, to cite just two things, Britain had recently transformed its system of secondary education with the creation of comprehensive schools (something that France and Germany have never done) and granted self-government to most of the former British Empire. Since then Britain has conspicuously led Europe in privatization and deregulation; and incidentally Britain is one of the still quite small number of countries to have had a woman prime minister, and not just as a stop gap but as a forceful and popular premier who won three general elections in a row. Nor have our most traditional institutions been immune from change. It is generally recognized that the monarchy is being transformed (the Queen has been made to pay income tax and the heir to the throne has been interviewed on television about his sex life), while Tony Blair's government is doing its best to heave the hereditary peers out of the House of Lords.

What, one might ask, would Britain have to do *not* to be viewed as a conservative society.

The legacy of economic critique

In the thirty years or so after the Second World War two things happened. First of all the western countries including Britain became much richer. Second, Britain's economic performance was not, however, as good as that of most competitor countries especially with regard to the manufacturing industry. The first (everyone got richer) tended to obscure the second (relative under-performance by Britain), so it was some time before the second became a matter of public debate. Since it has, however, and it certainly had by the early 1970s, with the First Oil Shock (1973–74) and the ensuing period of high inflation, there has been an endless witch-hunt to find the causes.

The first and broadest of these follows from the previous section on presumptive national character. Here the essential idea is that a mix of national pride (at having shown such tenacity in 1940), conservatism, class consciousness, the famous sense of humour inviting us not to take serious things such as economic performance seriously, produced an environment hostile to economic achievement in general and to successful manufacturing in particular.

The most elaborate and forceful formulation of this thesis is in Correlli Barnett's intellectual blockbuster *The Collapse of British Power* (1972). Barnett's remarkable contribution is to bring together a whole range of themes and issues – the impact of Empire, the anti-industrial values of the (fee-paying) public schools, the failure of British foreign policy between the First and Second

World Wars, and so on – to produce the mega-thesis of national decline. This thesis is echoed by the American historian Martin Wiener in a later book piquantly entitled *English Culture and the Decline of the Industrial Spirit* (Wiener, 1981), a briefer work than that of Correlli Barnett in which the author is concerned to play up the idea that various strands in English culture and society in the nineteenth and twentieth centuries, especially the cultural dominance of rural landowner and aristocratic values, were inimical to industry and a national commitment to manufacture.

And a variation on this theme is the idea that Britain's success in surviving and winning the Second World War was in a sense counter-productive, that it led to intimations of moral superiority, and a 'rest on our laurels' attitude causing us not to try hard enough as a nation thereby allowing other European countries to get ahead of us in the economic race. A tighter formulation on this argument is again offered by Correlli Barnett in a later work *The Lost Victory: British Dreams, British Realities* in which he argues that the Labour government after the war were wrong to pursue the establishment of a welfare state and the over-regulation of economic life that went with it, when we should have put our effort and resources into rebuilding the material infrastructure after the war, and in measures to promote industry and export (Barnett, 1995).

A second strand in the literature on Britain's relative economic underperformance emphasizes the allegedly low status of industry and management, and the relatively poor formal qualifications of British management in the past. The 'case for the prosecution' at that time is made ably and in detail by Ian Glover in a substantial report *The Backgrounds of British Managers: A Review of the Evidence* to the British Department of Industry (Glover, 1974). Foreign comparisons, showing that managers in other countries were better or more relevantly qualified were germane to this line of attack. Evidence on German management qualifications was assembled by Brigitte May in another substantial report to the Department of Industry (May, 1974), and some of the survey data, together with new evidence from researches in Germany were offered in an earlier book about German management (Lawrence, 1980). Again Ian Glover recast the case with additional cross-country comparisons in a chapter in a book *Manufacturing and Management* edited by himself and a Senior Economic Adviser at the Department of Industry, Michael Fores, in which the education and qualifications of British management were compared with those of France, Germany and Sweden (Fores and Glover, 1978).

What emerges from these studies is that:

- A smaller proportion of British managers had a university education at that time.
- There were more managers who were without formal qualifications entirely, having either worked their way up from shop floor related positions or having been appointed and then advanced on the basis of the right social credentials, such as a public school education and contacts.

- Some managers had qualifications whose relevance might be questioned, such as arts degrees, or that might be thought to be disfunctionally one-sided, such as accountancy qualifications supposedly inclining those who have them to a short-termist view.

Another strand in this literature is the idea of the low status of industry leading to the low remuneration of managers. Michael Fores again 'weighed into' this debate with data showing that a qualified engineer/manager in Britain was less well paid than a senior civil servant or a university professor while in Germany these relativities were reversed (Fores, 1972).

Fuel is added to these flames in a longitudinal study tracing patterns of managerial recruitment and qualification over the period 1890–1990 (Keeble, 1992). A key element in Keeble's discussion of the issue is the reluctance of British industry until the 1980s to take formal qualifications seriously, to prefer to promote from a pool of 16-year-old school leavers who were immediately subject to first hand experience, rather than to try to work out what to do with 21- or 22-year-old university graduates, who might have been educated beyond their usefulness. This (former) British penchant for the practical man 'unspoiled' by formal education has not been shared by the countries of continental Europe.

The 'bottom line' in this debate is that manufacturing indirectly attracted neither the social nor the educational elite in Britain.

A third strand in the explanatory research literature is to posit the low status of engineers in Britain, compared with their counterparts in other countries, and the enervating effect this may have on manufacturing. Again comparisons with other countries, especially Germany, were central to this debate. Although there was a gap in time between the studies, a survey of British engineers in the 1960s (Gerstl and Hutton, 1966) and of German engineers in the 1970s (Hutton and Lawrence, 1981) came out strongly in favour of the Germans in the sense that:

- They had stronger qualifications all the way from apprenticeship to engineering doctorates.
- They seemed more professionally secure, had less status grievances, more access to senior management posts, and were less inclined to 'job hop'.
- They were more professionally active in the sense of keeping up with technical developments and producing papers on technical subjects for presentation at conferences or for publication in technical journals.
- They had a much higher rate of technical invention and of the patenting of such inventions.

Interestingly, while in the British survey engineers in the public sector earned more than their colleagues in industry, in the German survey not only did the engineers in industry earn more than their public sector colleagues, but they also had more of everything else – greater job satisfaction, higher degree grades, more subordinates, wider responsibilities, more technical publications and more patented inventions (Hutton and Lawrence, 1981). In this way the various notions of the low status of management, inferior qualifications, and low status of engineering come together.

A fourth exploration of British under-performance centered around industrial relations, and especially the matter of days lost through strikes. While Britain did not have the worst record internationally in the 1960s and 1970s, Britain did have a bad record (Lawrence, 1980). This was variously attributed to:

- British class divisions engendering more envy and less respect by blue-collar workers for their managers.
- Correspondingly poor communication between 'the two sides of industry' compared with more egalitarian countries, several of which have been discussed in the present book including Denmark, Sweden, Holland, and (West) Germany in the post-war period.
- The stubborn refusal of British industrialists to countenance any form of codetermination or industrial democracy, again already documented in this book with regard to Germany, Sweden and Holland.
- The uncooperativeness of trade unions or their members, reaching a high-point in what came to be known as 'The Winter of Discontent' (1978–79).

On the basis of some observational case studies where I spent two or three days as an observer with samples of production managers in companies in Britain and West Germany, I was able to add a dimension to the industrial relations critique. The essence of this is that below the level of the strike, whether official or wildcat, there was a much higher level of 'small change' industrial relations aggro in Britain than in Germany. This was in the form of worker complaints about work allocations, supervision, working conditions, demarcation, sub-contracting, and so on, together with a general employee disinclination to assist management. These were, as such, small issues but taken collectively they tended to slow things down, pose contingencies for management – as well as 'burn-up' management time. I have offered a range of examples and highlighted the impact of all this on delivery performance in an earlier book (Lawrence, 1984).

Things seemed to be changing in the 1980s with Margaret Thatcher's enterprise culture, a reduction in the power of the trade unions, and some engagement of the general public in the world of business via the wave of privatizations under the Conservative government. Yet the 'what's wrong with British industry' movement had one more salvo to fire. This was in the form of some influential reports drawing attention to weaknesses in the area of management training and in particular to the neglect of many companies of post experience training for people the company has already hired (Mangham and Silver, 1986; Handy, 1987; and Constable and McCormick, 1987). Again several of these studies made use of foreign comparisons to punch home their message.

The effect of this consequential and multi-dimensional critique that has run for a quarter of a century is that it is rather more difficult to come in with an open mind at the end of the century and say what British management is like, as we have done for other countries discussed in this book. There is a 'weight of evidence' lurking in the background, a legacy of cultural presumption and critique, and it is difficult to try to characterize British management without taking cognizance of this critique and engaging with it: but we will try, dipping into the critique occasionally, and coming back to it at the end.

Management in Britain

Having talked to managers in a variety of European and other countries, it is only fair to say that British managers do make good interviewees.

The authors once gave a joint paper on some current research at a conference in San Francisco, where most of the presenters were of course American. In the afternoon session of the first day we spoke first, in turn; the next presenter by chance was also one of the few British delegates; the next person to present his paper was an American who began by bemoaning his fate in following English speakers with the remark:

> The English can make reading from a telephone directory sound more interesting than a book by Herbert Simon.*

British managers are communicators. They are self-aware without being self-conscious; they typically enjoy an ability to articulate their perceptions, an ability that cuts across class and educational lines; they are at their best responding to open-ended questions – of the kind that terrify Germans. Thinking about this British proclivity after I had lived successively in Germany, Switzerland, and Sweden, my feeling was that the British can talk about their jobs, organizations, industries, and company culture without worrying about whether what they are saying is objectively verifiable, they will blur the line between reality and one's experience of it – and it does make for interesting listening.

Generalism

In the discussion of several of the countries considered in this book we have broached the idea of a continuum running from specialist to a generalist view of management, where the former, the specialist view, emphasizes the distinct nature of particular jobs and industries and seeks to fill management and other positions on the basis of specialist qualifications, particular competence, and

---

* The reference is to the justly famous American administrative theorist and Nobel Prize Winner, H. A. Simon

relevant experience. Germany is a strong example of this specialist approach, and so on the whole, is Switzerland. This may be contrasted with the energy and system-driven generalism of the Americans, or with the intellectual generalism of the French *cadres*.

The British are also at the generalist end of this continuum. In the Loughborough study the proposition:

> Above all the manager needs specialist knowledge and relevant experience

elicited a weaker response from the British and the French than from the other national groups in the study, with statistically significant differences. Or again the British response to the proposition:

> To be effective in any given company the manager needs knowledge and experience of that company's branch of industry

was weaker than that of any of the national groups except that of the French. In everyday experience it is noticeable that the term 'a good all-rounder' has a positive ring in English, and is implicitly contrasted with boffinism and tunnel vision.

Yet this British generalism has a character of its own; that is to say it is probably based on different beliefs and presumptions from the generalism of either the French or the Americans. In the British case fitness for management is based on personal qualities, particularly on social and political skills. One fortunate enough to be endowed with these should be able to deploy them in a variety of *milieux*. The British are disposed to reach up to the big picture, rather than reach down to the operational detail. British management recruitment has traditionally been in terms of character and social skills, a conclusion reached by Theo Nichols in an early study of British management recruitment (Nichols, 1977).

In deference to the Terry-Barnett-Wiener characterization of British culture canvassed earlier in this chapter it is probably fair to add that this generalism may also have been influenced by a one-time amateur tradition. The argument would run along the lines of the amateur wishing to eschew the detail-driven involvement of the specialist, have a lightness of touch in command, and get it right without trying too hard. There is indeed a mild deprecation of specialism in British culture; consider that Winston Churchill's wartime quip that 'scientists should be on tap but not on top' usually generates smiling acquiescence among fellow citizens.

Mobility

Generally there is a positive relationship between mobility, in the sense of job moves between companies, and a generalist view of management, and this holds in the British case (Lawrence, 1996). A good reverse example, as we have seen in an earlier chapter, is Germany, where a specialist, somewhat expertise-based view of management work tends to keep managers within their function or department longer, and any moves between companies will typically be between the same sorts of jobs in different companies in the same industry.

In this discussion the reference is primarily towards the way high or low inter-company mobility is viewed in the different countries, hard international comparative data being rather difficult to come by, but it is what people believe that matters. As we have seen, in the Netherlands too much movement between employing organizations is seen as flighty, in Germany it seems to violate the notion of specialist competence fundamental to the execution of any job, while in the USA inter-company mobility is seen as evidence of drive and ambition, and in Britain it is viewed positively on the whole, seen as serving to develop generalist capability and the ability to 'take an overall view!'

Leadership

British culture tends to valorize leadership, something which is probably determined by our history. A country that was among the first in Europe to achieve national unity, that has not been successfully invaded since 1066, that ended up on the winning side in most of the wars it fought in the eighteenth, nineteenth and twentieth centuries, that once had the largest empire the world has ever seen, is bound to develop a belief in the importance of heroic individuals. Nor is it simply a matter of war and rugged nationalism, given Britain's pioneering role in industrialization and the development of parliamentary democracy. Or again to take a simple measure of intellectual creativity, in the award of Nobel Prizes since the inception of this institution in 1901, Britain is top relative to population, and with regard to the Nobel awards for science comes second only to the USA in absolute terms. All this is conducive to the conviction that the talents and qualities of individuals will be critical in a range of achievements. This view certainly permeates British management with its diffuse emphasis on picking people for personal qualities – from foreman to Chief Executive.

In the Loughborough study the proposition:

Management and leadership are coterminous

was fully accepted by the British managers in the sample (interestingly this proposition was rejected by the French and the Germans, presumably putting their faith in brains and specialized competence respectively.) Or again in the Nene study the proposition:

Senior managers must 'lead from the front' to ensure organizational success received its strongest support from the British, though it was accepted by all the national groups represented in the sample except the Dutch, who probably found it a bit too assertive to be compatible with those norms of modesty explored in the previous chapter. In terms of the mean scores for the proposition it was the American managers who came a close second to the British in this matter of 'leading from the front', yet it is possible that there is a difference of emphasis in the minds of the two national groups.

The Americans, that is to say, would tend to see the leader as the embodiment of organizational achievement, as the 'mover and shaker' who made it all happen. The British are more inclined to view the leader in inspirational terms, as the embodiment of the right values and purpose. In the language of leadership studies it is the difference between transactional and transformational leadership, with a British inclination to the latter. The two are not mutually exclusive of course, and we are simply positing a difference in relative emphasis.

Formal or informal?

On a visit to an iron foundry in Germany I recall being taken to lunch by two production superintendents, neither of whom had visited England but were keen to discuss their image of 'the sceptred isle'. One of the superintendents said that when he thought of England he pictured lords in top hats walking along Piccadilly in the middle of the morning (the last bit, mid morning, no doubt signifies an aristocratic disdain for anything resembling work).

Given this strong traditional-conservative-formal image that Britain seems to enjoy in the wider world it is worth asking: How formal is British management – in manner, appearance and patterns of interaction? Well whatever it may have been, in several common-sense ways it is not at all formal in the 1990s, viz:

- positional job titles of the *Herr Direktor* kind are not used much,
- nor are academic titles, though to be realistic, few managers in Britain have a doctor's degree,
- Christian names are widely used, among equals and across ranks,
- dress is not especially formal, apart from banks, and a 'dress-down Friday' is common (though this does pose a social challenge to those of humble background),
- it is quite common for even senior managers to have an open-door policy, that is, make themselves accessible to others (unthinkable in, for example, France),
- a lot of British companies are Americanized in the sense of having done away with territorial status space and instituted open plan offices, public working areas, and hot-desks, having meetings in dedicated rooms avail-

able to all by need rather than in the office of the most important person; in this connection it is worth noting that American influence is probably stronger in Britain than in Continental Europe, and certainly the coming of American companies was a feature of the inter-war period rather than of the post-war period in the British case.

Another consideration that might be raised in this discussion of British informality is the role of humour. The British are the only people who like to claim a sense of humour as a nationally defining characteristic. Much interaction in British society is suffused with humour, and this applies to management and company meetings. Indeed it has been argued by Jean-Louis Barsoux that in a management setting humour is not just the sport of the British but serves several identifiable functions (Barsoux, 1993) viz:

- It serves to reduce tension.
- It helps to build rapport at an initial meeting for business purposes.
- It builds sub-group solidarity (via in-jokes or a particular humour style).
- Humour can be a way of ameliorating failure or coping with distress.
- Humour facilitates criticism upwards; fashioned as a pretend joke criticism is more acceptable.
- Humour is also a vehicle for trying out *outré* ideas in meetings (if it backfires it can be treated as 'just a joke').

Indeed British people get to take the role of humour for granted and are unaware of the effect it may have on people who are not British. Christine Communal, a French academic working in Britain tells a story in her doctoral thesis which compares management behaviour in four countries in which the same French multi-national company operates (Communal, 1999). Communal relates that she became so used to humour in the time she spent in the British subsidiary, that on her first visit to the German office when the German general manager told her, with a smile that can only have betokened polite welcome, that the German operation had downsized and made people redundant, she was convinced this must be a joke and burst into uproarious laughter (it was not a joke).

Management realism

There is an element of unpretentious realism in British management. It is not doctrinaire but rather pragmatic, tending to emphasize what needs to be done to get the desired result. This view is not easy to define, but it comes out in various small ways in the Loughborough and Nene studies which have been cited at various points in this book.

The Nene study, for example, includes the proposition:

Decision-making is the essence of managerial work, that is what managers are there for

which is rejected by the British but accepted by the other national groups. What does this tell us? That the British find the emphasis on decision-making a bit Olympian; it is too rational and formal, and they can see that implementation and control will be the real issues. This view is born out by a proposition in the Loughborough study:

Higher education and intelligence are important in enabling managers to see things clearly and to make rational decisions

Here again the British managers reject the proposition but all the other national groups accept it. It is not that the British are opposed to education and intelligence, but they see that rationality is not a force sufficient to itself, management is politics rather than science and the manager has to be concerned with what is doable rather than with what is perfectly rational. Another proposition in the Lougborough study is:

In practice the work of the manager is more about managing situations than taking decisions

The British managers accepted this proposition more enthusiastically than the other national groups: it constitutes another appeal to a political interpretation of management work as being about ways and means and getting round the road blocks, not about Olympian detachment. Interestingly the contrast between the British response on this item and that of the French and German managers is statistically significant. There is a similar item in the Nene study:

Taking decisions is easy; implementation is the difficult part

and again the British come out top, that is they have a higher mean score registering stronger agreement with the proposition than the other European managers.

Discretion versus systems

Traditionally British management has identified with discretion rather than systems. The manager would be identified by the exercise of discretion – using judgement in critical situations not covered by rules or procedures, acting in short as a leader, rather than as a designer and upholder of systems. That is to say, this exercise of discretion was what the managers were there for, it made demands on leadership qualities, it was the capability for which managers were hopefully picked and advanced, and the exercise of discretion both reflected and reinforced their status. And at any time, up until the 1990s, one would have advanced this view with confidence.

The managerialist movement of the 1990s, has however, has impacted on the notion of discretion and shifted the emphasis in the direction of systems and controls. More specifically 1990s managerialism has:

- emphasized performance measurement wherever possible starting from a definition of standards (bench-marking),
- included the codification of service levels,
- instituted codes of practice and appeals systems for 'customers' in a rather broad sense.

At the same time the recession of the early 1990s led to more downsizing and to tighter operations. All this has been supported by greater power of information technology, so that managers are increasingly likely to 'know the facts', have the relevant information to hand, which in turn renders decisions and behaviours more programmed, and marginalizes the exercise of discretion.

Again this shift from discretion to systems is not a black-and-white contrast, but a shift in relative emphasis over time and in an increasingly competitive and internationalized business context. It is also complicated by the fact that there are still at the end of the century different groups of managers 'in play', different by generation and by legitimization. To bipolarize the issue, there is a hard core of managers (critics would say a 'soft core') recruited on the basis of personal qualities and advanced well before the advent of manageralism. This *corps* are often in influential positions, beyond the reach of performance appraisals, IT-driven decision-making, and BS 5750! Behind them is a 'hungry generation' of younger managers, grown up in the 1980s and 1990s, computer-literate, focused, careerist, and playing by the new rules.

That uncertain feeling

In Geert Hofstede's famous study of IBM employees in a variety of countries, one of the four dimensions was the tendency to avoid uncertainty (Hofstede, 1980). While on the dimensions of power distance and individualism the Anglo-Saxon countries and more loosely the western countries, tend to hold together, this is not the case with regard to the relative strength of uncertainty avoidance. To put this more positively Britain demonstrates a high tolerance for ambiguity (or a weak uncertainty avoidance): this tolerance for ambiguity is somewhat higher than that demonstrated by the USA, is much higher than that shown by the Germans, and massively higher than that of the French.

We would like to offer three comments on this fascinating finding. First of all, it is entirely consistent with many of the other findings canvassed in the last few pages. In contrast to some of their counterparts in Continental European countries the British do not put their faith primarily in the authority of specialist knowledge, educated cleverness, or the supremacy of the rational decision. Instead they recognize the messiness of the management process, the presence of political and non-rational issues, the challenge of implementation, and the need to 'manage situations' (rather than issue directions to be peerlessly executed by dispassionate subordinates). All this is consistent with a high tolerance for ambiguity, as is the traditional inclination of senior management to exercise discretion and judgement rather than to depend on systems of operation and control.

Second, one might note that this tolerance for ambiguity is well served by the English language, as used by the British rather than by others of Anglo-Saxon origin. Consider that in this native usage:

- precision is not a virtue as in French,
- explicitness is not a virtue as in German, a language that lends itself marvellously to heavy exegesis,
- directness is not a virtue as in American.

English is the language of irony and understatement, of allusion and metaphor, of the rendering of pastel shades of meaning, the language of 'fudging'. One can fudge a lot better in English than in French.

Third, one might ask whether this weak uncertainty avoidance is a strength or a weakness. In the past the tendency has been to view it as a weakness, or at least as the reflection of a weakness. Detractors would argue that there was a chaotic element in manufacturing at operational level, a *melange* of shortages, breakdowns, stock-outs, power cuts, conflicting orders and industrial relations disruption – an ethos zealously portrayed in an earlier book (Lawrence, 1984). In these conditions a high tolerance for ambiguity is a must – the conditions of order being regrettably absent. One might add to this the fact that the further one goes back in time the greater the predominance in British management of people without formal education beyond secondary school level (Keeble, 1992). Crossing these two issues tended to breed a race of robust crisis-handlers and energetic copers, who depended on their wits and drive to solve problems on the hoof, rather than a race of system builders and planners preferring prevention to cure. Speaking personally on the basis of a lot of first-hand contact with manufacturing industry in Britain and in West Germany in the late 1970s to the early 1980s, this order versus improvization difference was the sharpest contrast (Lawrence, 1984). The German companies were very well-organized and well-run at an operational level – but a bit dull, whereas life in the British firm was stimulatingly chaotic with 'never a dull moment.'

At the same time there is a defence, even a gain in this British tolerance for ambiguity. Management is as much an art as a science, there is much in life that is unpredictable, human beings often act in idiosyncratic and indeed in ingenious ways rather than engaging in law-like behaviour, and there is arguably a gain in sense and realism in recognizing this, in an awareness that desirable outcomes cannot be guaranteed by IT or control systems, by experts in command or by the reign of the cleverest.

Management and status

Given Britain's image in the wider world as a deferential society – lords walking down Piccadilly in top hats and all that – it may be worth raising the question: How status conscious are British managers? Whatever the weight of tradition and the persistence of the 'top hat' image the late 1990s evidence from the Nene and Loughborough studies does not suggest a strong status-consciousness.

In the Nene study the proposition:

Managers and subordinates should be able to work on equal terms

was accepted by the British managers, who had a higher mean score (indicating stronger agreement) than any of the other national groups in the study. In the same study most of the national groups disagreed with the proposition:

Managers because of their status are entitled to respect from their subordinates

and the British managers disagreed more strongly than anyone else, and indeed the contrast between the British and American managers on this proposition is statistically significant at the 0.001 level. Again from the Nene study the proposition:

Most employees like to be told what to do

was rejected by the British, more strongly than by the Continental Europeans.

Ironically in the 1970s doubts were commonly expressed about the standing of management as a career in Britain, with evidence drawn from salary data, surveys of relative occupational status, even choices of subject at university by British students having high 'A' level grades (Bayer and Lawrence, 1977). But all this seems to have changed.

From the late seventies onwards British universities inaugurated undergraduate courses in business administration and management science, enrolments grew throughout the 1980s and 1990s, MBAs were founded in abundance and the business schools at both the old and new universities soon emerged as the largest departments in their establishments measured by staff and by student members.

At the same time the rather anti-business ideology of the 1970s was put on the defensive from 1979 when the Conservatives came to power under Margaret Thatcher's leadership, and somehow or other this anti-business ideology seemed to evaporate during the recession of the early 1980s. The Conservatives changed the level of income tax to the advantage of the better paid, including managers of course, and Conservative legislation emasculated the trade union movement. The enterprise culture flowered, while privatization and deregulation roared.

In short the status of management in Britain rose, and the attractiveness of management careers became widely accepted. But as already noted so far as our survey evidence is representative this rise in status does not seem to have led to status consciousness among British managers of the kind normally espoused by, for example, *les cadres* in France.

Professionalism

If one raises the question of how professional is British management, perhaps the most telling reply is to note that the non-stop critiques of earlier decades have evaporated, the last blast probably being the batch of reports in the mid 1980s drawing attention to deficits in the *formation* of British management and corporate neglect of training, noted earlier in the chapter. Ten years later, it is claimed in an Institute of Management report by Andrew Thomson and his fellow researchers at the Open University, that much of this has changed (Thomson *et al.*, 1997). The executive summary states boldly:

> The priority given by organizations to management development has increased significantly compared to ten years ago, and is expected to increase further in the foreseeable future (Thomson, 1997:1).

What more could one ask!

But there is more. Not only is more training being offered by more companies, but it is being done for what the researchers clearly see as the right reason:

> The main underlying drivers of management development appear to be strategic rather than operational or external (Thomson, 1997:1).

Yet perhaps the most telling point in this generally up-beat Institute of Management sponsored report is the view of the authors that the enhanced commitment to management development reflects a real change in corporate consciousness:

> ... there has been a great move forward in the language and definition of management competencies, something that was badly missing a decade ago, when Mangham and Silver (1986) pointed to a picture of conceptual poverty as to what sort of training was needed (Thomson, 1997:76).

There is some support for this idea of a strong commitment to management development. One thing that emerges from the study is that some of the Continental countries, led by Germany and Switzerland, take the view that whatever the importance of management development it can, indeed should, be safely left to personnel/HRM specialists. The British response, however, suggested a diffuse responsibility for management development with line managers playing a key role. On the proposition:

Managers should set an example by committing time and resources to the development of their staff

the British mean score comes between 'agree' and 'strongly disagree' and the contrast with the less enthusiastic response of the German managers is significant at the 0.001 level.

There is also survey evidence suggesting a clear commitment by the British to targets and results. In the Loughborough study the proposition:

Management is primarily about the setting of objectives and the monitoring of plans for their achievement

is accepted by all the national groups, with the mean score for the British being among the highest. Similarly the proposition:

The key change in the last 10 years is the greater emphasis on results, performance and accountability

drew the highest mean score (strongest agreement) from the British, with statistically significant contrasts with the French and Germans.

Regarding another aspect of professional responsibility the Nene study probed management attitudes on environmental questions. The propositions:

Businesses should be made to pay for environmental damage resulting from their production processes and the use of their products

and:

Government legislation should aim to control products and processes which are damaging to the health of the public

both drew the highest mean scores (strongest agreement) from the British.

The views and data cited in this section are of course limited. But they are positive, which in itself represents a break with the fairly recent past.

Strategy

Now that we are able to see these things in the rear view mirror it would appear that 'in the good old days' of world economic growth after the Second World War, nobody bothered much about strategy, except the Americans. Now, sharper competition, slower growth, and greater internationalization inclines everyone to greater strategic awareness. It is only fair to note that this generalization includes the British, indeed British management might make some claim to be in the European vanguard. This is certainly my conclusion on the basis of a series of interviews with senior executives drawn from a range of companies and industries, conducted in 1998–99.* These executives were able to give coherent, forceful and discriminating accounts of:

- developments in their industries, particularly in the course of the 1990s,
- defining the position of their company in the industry,
- detailing competitive advantage, both achieved and aspired to.

One theme running across these interviews, was an inclination to reconfigure the business, shifting the company's activities or making changes in their relative importance as a way of enhancing competitive advantage. In some cases these were little things that would yield cost-efficiency gains. A logistics/distribution company, for example, referred to computer chips embedded in the tyres of its trucks which would monitor tyre pressure (correct tyre pressure = fuel savings) and having installed a computer in the cab which monitored the fuel-efficiency of gear changes. Another company in the same industry spoke of a planned move from trucks devoted to serving a single customer to trucks carrying 'mixed loads' (cargo for a variety of customers) thus yielding better truck space utilization.

At the other end of the scale, some companies were 'thinking the unthinkable'. One motor manufacturer was reported as saying that its strengths were designing and marketing vehicles, rather than their construction, and could envisage a situation in which the company would host rather than perform vehicle manufacture, in the sense that it would provide and maintain manufacturing premises to which contractors would deliver *and fit* sub-assemblies and components.

Another thread in these executive testimonies concerned the role of product quality. The presumption was that quality would be treated as a given by the market so that competitive advantage would shift to some ancillary or support service – organizing purchasing finance for customers, after sales service, life cycle costing, range of product made available, additional in-store services in the case of retailers (cash back facilities, post boxes inside shops), manufacturers helping customers with their supply chain management, and so on.

Interestingly this British inclination to reconfigure the business and to re-think competitive advantage is also reflected in the Nene study. The proposition:

> Today well-made products for which there is a known demand are likely to ensure a company's profitability

is accepted by the Continental European managers but rejected by the British and Americans (most strongly rejected by the British). This can be seen as a vote for a richer understanding of the ways in which companies compete (inter-

---

* At time of writing, early 1999, there is as yet no published output from this ongoing study, conducted jointly with David Smith of Nene University College, Northampton.

estingly it is the German managers who most enthusiastically accept this proposition in favour of quality goods selling themselves). There is a hint of the same sentiment in the response to the proposition:

> The engineering function should be an obvious path to senior positions in the manufacturing industry

which is rejected by all the national groups, including the Germans, but with the British 'leading the charge'. This is not a reflection of the under-representation of engineers in senior management positions in Britain; in a recent study Richard Barry and his colleagues have shown that graduate engineers are well represented in top positions in manufacturing and outnumber accountants three to one (Barry, *et al.*, 1997). We would rather like to suggest that it reflects a recognition of the complex nature of competitive advantage, as comprehending considerations going beyond technical excellence. The Loughborough study included a general proposition concerning strategy:

> Strategy is the first concern of the senior manager

All the national groups responded positively to this proposition, with mean scores coming well on to the 'agree' side of the mid-point: but the British mean score was higher than that for France, Germany and the USA.

Proactivity

It is reasonable to view the positive attitudes to strategy and competitive advantage, briefly reviewed in the last section, as evidence of proactivity: after all, strategy is about how to organize for profitability in the future – rather than hoping that it will 'just happen'. The Loughborough study offers in a small way some further confirmation of this proactivity. For instance, the proposition:

> A manager should constantly challenge how things are done rather than deferring to hierarchy and precedent

was affirmed by all the national groups, with the British managers having the highest mean score (most positive response). Or again on the proposition, deliberately cast as a negative:

> Line managers are not encouraged to innovate and take risks

the British managers were the only national group whose mean score expressed disagreement. In the Nene study the proposition:

> At the end of the day, most managers want subordinates who are loyal rather than critical or challenging

was rejected by nearly all the national groups, but the British rejection of this view was the most resounding. This small finding is particularly interesting in that deference-leading-to-uncritical-conformity is part of the traditional view of Britain, and was expressly formulated as a criticism of British management by Robert Dubin, albeit not in the 1990s (Dubin, 1970).

Pressure and change

In this chapter on Britain we have used the results of the Loughborough and Nene studies more heavily than elsewhere in the book, in part in the hope of putting some control on the subjectivity of writing about one's own country; the two studies have also been used as a check on each other. If we take these studies as a primary source and raise the question, what is the strongest impression that may be derived from them, it is that above all, British managers have a sense of all pervading change and a feeling of being under pressure. Let us review a little of the evidence.

The Loughborough study tried to probe the essence of management work in the late 1990s with the proposition:

In today's climate management means above all the management of change

The British mean score is the highest (the American managers came second) and most of the differences between Britain and the other national groups are statistically significant. In response to the proposition:

Downsizing and de-layering have put increasing pressure on middle management

the British came second only to the Americans in their affirmation and ahead of all the Continental European groups. Likewise the proposition:

The key change in the last 10 years is the greater emphasis on results, performance and accountability

elicits from the British a mean score of 4.29 on a 1–5 scale, ahead of the Americans as well as the Continental Europeans. Indeed there are points in the Loughborough study when the British emerge as more hard-bitten (or is it hard-driven) than the Americans. All the national groups reject the proposition:

Negotiations with third parties should focus on getting the 'best deal' for one's company, not on building long-term relationships

in the sense that their mean scores are on the disagree side of the mid-point of the scale. But in the British case it is very close: the British are more sympathetic to the statement than any of the other national groups, all the contrasts are statistically significant, and the contrast with the Americans is the most striking!

Turning for a moment to the Nene study the simple proposition:

Change is normal in business life and management work

is accepted by all the national groups, with the British and German managers having the highest mean score (strongest agreement).

Similarly all groups accept the proposition:

Change affects all people in all organizations: managers therefore need to consult widely to facilitate the implementation of change

is also accepted by all groups with the British top. The response to the proposition, deliberately couched in the negative, that:

Management jobs are no more pressured today than they were 10 years ago

is rejected by most of the national groups, with the Americans in first place and the British in second. The same result, that is to say one registering anxiety, greets the proposition:

Concern over job security affects more managers than 20 years ago

that is, the Americans are most concerned followed by the British. Finally, in this section, the proposition:

No market is secure, no business segment is discrete, no company is safe from takeover: this is the essence of today's business world

is again affirmed most vehemently by the Americans with the British in second place.

The critique revisited

We began the chapter with an overview of the omnibus socio-cultural economic critique of Britain, purporting to explain under-performance throughout much of the post war period. We are far from having 'all the answers' but it probably makes sense to offer a few comments in the light of material and ideas introduced in this chapter.

First of all, insofar as the critique posited a lack of quality and ability in British management, we find no evidence. There is nothing in the results of the Loughborough and Nene studies, cited frequently in this chapter, to suggest lack of ability, motivation, or understanding on the part of British managers. The only word of caution from these studies is that they give abundant evidence of the embracing of managerialism to the point that pressures and controls may be counter productive.

Second, the same positive testimony would have to be recorded regarding the 1998–99 series of interviews with senior executives, discussed in the previous section on strategy. These interviews gave abundant evidence of strategic awareness and an understanding of the dynamics of competitive advantage.

Third, one would have to admit that some of the elements in the critique, for instance the idea that:

- management as a career had low status,
- and was poorly remunerated relative to other professional level jobs,
- that British culture was somehow hostile to business activity,
- that the country lacked an entrepreneurial culture,
- that the economy suffered from over-regulation or from too many organizations being in the public sector,
- that the efficiency of industry was undermined by an industrial relations malaise,

simply seemed to evaporate in the course of the 1980s. Even the idea that our engineers were the victims of low status and poor remuneration seems to have receded somewhat. It is a few years since one has heard complaints from the engineers' professional associations on the subject of poor remuneration. Richard Barry and his co-researchers, tell us that the engineering graduate is three times more likely to become a top executive than is the accountant – though the odds are changing in the accountant's favour (Barry *et al.*, 1997). Barry also disposes of another myth, popular with foreigners, that British companies are run by people with posh degrees in inappropriate subjects: the study in question shows that while there are some arts and social science graduates among the ranks of British top executives, there are far fewer of them than there are graduates in science and engineering, and the performance of these arts graduate led companies is in any case, in no way inferior (*ibid.*, 1997).

Fourth, when it comes to the question of managers' formal educational qualifications, it all seems a bit fuzzy at the end of the century. The Institute of Management surveyed 3000 of its own members in 1996 and analysed the responses from the 724 who replied (Institute of Management, 1996). 32 per cent of these had a first degree, and 23 per cent a masters degree, these two categories overlapping of course. These proportions are rather less than I would have expected by the mid 1990s, but one has no way of knowing whether Institute of Management membership appeals to managers with any particular educational profile. Again, Richard Barry and his colleagues refer to half of their 43 000 top executives being unqualified, where qualified is defined in terms of having a first degree or a full accountancy qualification (Barry *et al.*, 1997).

But as suggested earlier we are probably in a transitional stage, where many of those at the top now were recruited at a time that predated the expansion of educational opportunity and the greater emphasis placed on formal educational attainment for recruitment or advancement to management posts. After all with 33 per cent of the age group entering higher education in the late 1990s and 30 per cent of the age group graduating, how much longer can it be before management is a graduate profession. Or as Barry and his colleagues put it:

> We seem to be witnessing a sharp decline in the proportion of unqualified top executives (Barry *et al.*, 1997, vii)

Fifth, again as noted before, the critical literature reviewed at the start of the chapter seems to have petered out in the course of the 1990s. Not only that, the 1990s have seen the emergence of what might be termed a counter-literature, tending to suggest that it never was as bad as all that.

William Rubinstein for instance argues that Britain's pre-eminence in banking and international finance is more indicative of economic health than any under-performance in manufacturing. An economic historian he also 'back-tracks' to the 1930s depression and argues that economic failure and unemployment in the traditional industries of the north co-existed with a boom in new industries in the south and the Midlands (Rubinstein, 1993).

Or again David Edgerton in a fascinating book on the British aircraft industry, focusing on the first half of the twentieth century, argues that this industry:

- owed its origins to powerful entrepreneurs,
- who were wealthy men from good families,
- and the companies they founded did attain a viable size (that is, did not freeze at SME level),
- and it attracted skilled and committed workers, who were proud to work in the industry,

and above all the whole industry was driven by strong commitment to a new technology, to the point that its protagonists came to believe the Second World War could be won by the force of this technology, thus escaping the trench warfare casualties of the First World War (Edgerton, 1991).

Edgerton's account reaches a climax when he demonstrates that in one hour on 23rd May 1943 the Royal Air Force dropped two-times the tonnage of bombs on Dortmund as the *Luftwaffe* had dropped on Britain in 170 days and nights in 1940–41.

This is heady stuff. A challenge to the Correlli Barnett – Martin Wiener view outlined earlier, albeit on the basis of a single industry. Edgerton makes the case with such conviction I was moved to go to the Imperial War Museum and look at some of these bombers, and discovered there were enormous differences in their disposable loads (disposable load = bombs plus fuel), when one compared the British and American planes, viz:

B17 Flying Fortress	4–5 000 lb	American
B24 Liberator	8 000 lb	American
AVRO Lancaster	14 000 lb	British

Whatever else, the British seem to have bought the idea of the heavy bomber.

A more upbeat tone is also observable in some of this literature. A good example would be Ian Glover writing about British manufacturing in 1998 and asserting:

> Contemporary discussion on UK economic 'decline' must be tempered by reference to the country's economic performance of the mid 1990s. Growth of GNP and unemployment trends compare well with those of major competitors. Real after tax incomes in the UK are now on a par with those in Germany and Sweden . . . (Glover *et al.*, 1998)

This is an indicative testimony since Glover's scholarship in the 1970s and later contributed to the original critique. Or to take another example Charles Leadbeater in his 1997 DEMOS report argues the case for Britain becoming the California of Europe by prioritizing high tech, high growth industries (Leadbeater, 1997). Just think if California was an independent state it would have the eighth largest GDP in the world! Whether or not Leadbeater's vision is viable, one could not imagine such a scenario being explored in say the 1970s.

Caution

This is not to say that everything is perfect. There is an acknowledged problem of under-investment in British industry. Again Richard Barry and his colleagues give this argument a new twist by suggesting that British top executives have difficulty identifying and exploiting *profitable* investment opportunities (Barry *et al.*, 1997). They make the contrast with physical investment in services which have profitability rates above average for the G7 countries, but are not really able to explain the problem in manufacturing.

Again if one asks consultants they will often be able to indicate underperformance in particular companies, or structural problems adversely affecting whole industries. To put it another way, because of the critique outlined at the start of this chapter there is a tendency for developments in Britain to be measured against the past: the assessment of progress made on post experience management training mentioned earlier is a good example (Thomson *et al.*, 1997). Yet of course it invariably makes better sense to compare the performance of a company with others in the same industry or to compare industries across countries. So if one wanted to get a sense of the achievement of say Rolls Royce (aircraft engines not motor cars), it would be interesting to trace what the company had achieved over the last 20 years, but the acid test would be a comparison with GE and Pratt & Whitney in the USA now.

In 1998, 228 people in Britain became millionaires as a result of wins on the National Lottery. A key question would be how many other people achieved this status for themselves or their companies by judicious investment in British manufacturing.

Two countries divided by a common language

A *leitmotiv* of this book, indeed its *raison d'être*, is the differences between countries, with the partial exception of the three Scandinavian states – Norway, Sweden and Denmark – and to a lesser extent of Germany and Switzerland. So one might well ask, is there any other country that Britain resembles? We would like to suggest that Britain has more in common in matters of business systems and management practice with the USA than with any of the countries of Western Europe, notwithstanding British admiration for Germany, affection for Holland, and such enduring commercial links as a trade treaty with Sweden that dates from the time of Oliver Cromwell and has never been abrogated.

Most of the past research literature by both British and American writers has tended to draw attention to the differences between Britain and the USA. In a way this is very easy to understand given the differences in style and deportment between British and American people. Our survey evidence, however, tells a different story.

If we take the Nene study this contains 72 propositions to which managers were invited to respond on the classic five-point scale from 'strongly agree' to 'strongly disagree'. The results of this exercise yielded:

- 32 statistically significant differences as between the British and Dutch managers (so much for the mutual admiration society).
- 42 statistically significant differences between the British and the Italians.
- 43 statistically significant differences between the British and the Germans.

In other words the British managers in the sample differed from their counterparts in Italy and Germany on more than half the items on the questionnaire.

The corresponding figure for differences between the British and American managers is 13. The Anglo-American closeness is probably more marked than this bald statement of 13 out of 72 points of difference would suggest. Of these 13 statistically significant differences only 1 is significant at the 0.001 per cent level, and the item in question, already mentioned in the attempt to qualify the traditional stereotype of the British is:

Managers, because of their status, are entitled to respect from their subordinates

where the British managers disagreed much more strongly than their American counterparts.

To restate briefly some of the points already made in the substantive discussion of British management, the two groups – British and American – are broadly agreed that:

- conflict over scarce resources is inevitable; and that conflict in a company is not evidence of management's inability to manage,
- change is normal in business and management; the rate of change is greater than ever before; there is greater pressure now in management work,
- business is changing in the sense of separate industries being collapsed into each other; product-market segments are being defined in new ways; competitive advantage is being construed anew (the re-configuration of business referred to in the section on strategy),
- there is broad agreement on environmental issues.

But it is in the area of propositions concerning corporate strategy that agreement is most extensive. Here the two groups agree, as we have seen, that well-made products are not a guarantee of business success (the German view). Again the British and American managers both agreed that companies have a need to exploit *a variety* of competitive advantages. They also agree about the desirability of a five-year planning horizon, and of taking account of the actions/responses of competitors in framing strategy. And as we have seen, the proposition:

> No market is secure, no business segment is discrete, no company is safe from takeover: this is the essence of today's business world

evoked a groan of agonized conviction both in Britain and the USA.

Friends and neighbours

There is a view to the effect that if one wants a 'true and fair picture' of another country, to use the auditing accountants' favourite phrase, one should canvass opinion in neighbouring countries. So that if one wants to know 'the truth' about Americans, one should ask Canadians; if one wants to know about the Belgians, try the Dutch; in Colombia they have strong views on Venezuela, and so on. So whom should one consult on the character of the British: naturally, the French!

Working on this principle we thought it might be fun to end a discussion of British management by looking at the section on Britain in Christine Communal's Ph.D thesis (Communal, 1999). What she has done is to look at the operation of the same (French owned) IT company in Britain, France, Sweden and Germany, and the interest here is that she looks at Britain from a French viewpoint. The first characteristic she explores, for instance, is the role of humour in management in Britain, noting *en passant*:

> Humour can also be used as a powerful weapon against annoying situations or individuals. In this sense, humour is to the British what shouting is to the French*

Communal also emphasizes the importance of verbal skills in British management culture, quoting one of the British managers as saying:

> My strength is that I communicate with people very well

Communal herself observes:

> Verbal skills are very important and considered an asset in the British context

And as a foreigner speaking English well, but still as a foreign language, she is aware of the 'shaded' quality of English among native speakers:

> For a non-native speaker it can be difficult to differentiate between a neutral statement, an understatement and an exaggeration. The British constantly pick and mix.

She also takes the view that British management is marked by informality:

> Christian names are used at all levels in the organization. British managers are informal particularly by French standards. One illustration of this is the relative ease with which interviews were arranged. The top managers made themselves available and appeared to be equally available to their staff.

Communal goes on to speak of senior managers answering the phone themselves, using e-mail, and not having or depending on secretaries.

To boldly go

Both Communal herself and some of the other (non-British) nationals in the study were struck by the bold optimism of the British (though this should perhaps be tempered by Communal's remark about the British enthusiasm for any business that does not involve manufacturing.) She quotes one British manager as saying:

> It is the idea that you can shape it if you want

and one of the Swedes to the effect that:

---

* All the remaining excerpts in this chapter are taken from Chapter 9 of Christine Communal's thesis (Communal 1999).

The UK person said the problem was all solved (in a group discussion with a potential customer). We (Swedes) would have expressed it as 'we don't know what it is all about yet. It is not solved . . .'. So the British have a way of expressing optimism which we don't have.

and again:

The British are more like the American people, if I may say so, with a more positive way of handling things

The essence of this optimism is that those concerned can do anything necessary to give a (new) customer satisfaction, even if the assignment involves all sorts of contingencies and challenges that have not been handled before. Not only will the British sound confident, they will actually be confident. This in turn Communal links to the high tolerance for ambiguity revealed in Hofstede's classic study (Hofstede, 1980); she notes that:

British people are relatively comfortable not knowing exactly what the future holds

and explains this in part to 'an enduring British attachment to appearances and notions of leadership'. Again this bold confidence was especially marked in sales situations, in the sense of attempts to win new organizational customers for IT services. She quotes a British manager as saying:

Well, I guess we have always put a lot of emphasis on salesmanship, so we went out and won contracts in that area and developed a way of delivering those contracts as we were winning them

and again referring to the Swedish operation:

They would be confident before they went out to speak to a client. We didn't, perhaps we're more like pirates.

The audacity and salesmanship riding on confidence and resourcefulness is of course profit-directed. Communal reports an early conversation with a company employee in which she asked about company priorities, and received the answer:

Profit, profit, profit, it is a quote from management!

Another company member commented:

I think delivering on the numbers, so that we meet the expectations, is the overriding thing.

All of which was made clear by one of the British managers:

The Chief Executive is setting company targets with the share price in mind. The share price and the shareholder value, that does direct his thinking.

Ways and means

Firstly, when it comes to motivation there is something that struck Communal as distinctively British and this is the very explicit emphasis on financial rewards. Discovering that the company recruited via the internet she looked up the entries for the four countries, only to discover that the British alone listed a plethora of material inducements, viz:

- competitive salary,
- life and health insurance,
- corporate pension scheme,
- relocation allowance,
- company cars,
- profit related pay,

and even discounted holiday packages. Moved by the insight Christine Communal checked the company salary hierarchy in each of the countries, where the salary hierarchy denotes the gap between the highest and lowest paid person in each company operation: this is a variation on the salary contrasts offered in the earlier discussion of Denmark. Using 1997 salary and exchange rates the hierarchy for the countries comes out like this:

British subsidiary	£162 780
(that is, British CEO earned £162 780	
more than the least well-paid employee)	
Swedish subsidiary	£94 870
German subsidiary	£84 889

Any British reader experiencing at this point a sense of shame at the country's inequality and materialism may take comfort from the fact that the French head office declined to provide salary data for the French operation, giving rise to the presumption that their salary hierarchy is even longer.

Secondly, British decision making in this IT company is described by Communal as authoritarian. That is to say, as one of her interviewees put it:

Democracy does not rate here

The British managers would consult at their discretion, but decide themselves. Not only Christine Communal but some of the German interviewees commented on this. She quotes one as saying:

In England . . . was der Chef sagt gilt und wird gemacht, hier wird diskutiert (In England what the boss says goes and will be done, here it will be discussed)

However, this British proclivity for hierarchy-driven decision taking is counterbalanced in Communal's view by a strong sense of accountability for results.

Finally, there is a little surprise to come. We all know what an unequal society Britain is. The 1996 World Competitiveness Report issued by an independent body based in Geneva (World Economic Forum, 1995), surveyed 48 countries and ranked Britain 38th for career opportunities for women. Well guess which national subsidiary had the highest proportion of women employees – the British one (Sweden came second, Germany was bottom.) And these were not women in low grade jobs either: it is an IT company, there are no menials.

Having written as a foreigner about a range of Continental European countries, it has seemed only fair to give 'the last word' on Britain to a French person. The intriguing fact is that Christine Communal's account of British management is rather consistent with the view expressed in the previous section, that in matters of business and management Britain is more like the USA than any other country discussed in this book.

References

Barnett, Correlli (1972) *The Collapse of British Power*, London: Methuen.

Barnett, Correlli (1995) *The Lost Victory: British Dreams, British Realities, 1945–1950*, London: Pan Books.

Barry, Richard; Derek Bosworth and Rob Wilson (1997) *Engineers in Top Management*, Warwick: Warwick University Institute for Employment Research.

Barsoux, Jean-Louis (1993) *Funny Business: Humour, Management and Business Culture*, London: Cassell.

Bayer, Hermann and Peter Lawrence (1977) 'Engineering, Education and the Status of Industry' *European Journal of Engineering Education*, No. 2.

Brands, H. W. (1997) *TR The Last Romantic*, New York: Basic Books.

Communal Christine (1999) 'A Cultural Kaleidoscope: Managing the European Company', University of Leicester unpublished Ph.D. thesis, Leicester, England.

Constable, J. and R. McCormick (1987) *The Making of British Managers*, London: BIM/CBI.

Dubin, Robert (1970) 'Management in Britain – Impressions of a visiting professor', *Journal of Management Studies*, Vol 7, No. 2, pp. 183–98.

Edgerton, D. (1991) *England and the Aeroplane*, London: Macmillan.

Fores, Michael (1972) 'Engineering and the British Economic Problem' *Quest*, No 22.

Gerstl, J. E. and S. P. Hutton (1966) *Engineers: the Anatomy of a Profession*, London: Tavistock Press.

Glover, Ian; Paul Tracey and Wendy Currie (1998) 'Engineering Our Future Again: towards a long term strategy for manufacturing and management in the United Kingdom' in R. Delbridge and J. Lowe (eds), *Manufacturing in Transition*, London: Routledge.

Glover, Ian (1974) *The Backgrounds of British Managers: A Review of the Evidence*, London: Department of Industry.

Glover, Ian (1978) 'Executive career patterns: Britain, France, Germany and Sweden' in Ian Glover and Michael Fores (eds), *Manufacturing and Management*, London: HMSO.

Handy, Charles (1987) *The Making of Managers*, London: MSC/NEDC/BIM.

Hofstede, Geert (1980) *Culture's Consequences*, Beverley Hills: Sage.

Hutton, S. P. and P. A. Lawrence (1981) *German Engineers: the Anatomy of a Profession*, Oxford: Clarendon Press.

Institute of Management (1996) *The Qualified Manager: a survey of managers' attitudes to business and management qualifications*, London.

Keeble, S. P. (1992) *The Ability to Manage: A Study of British Management 1890–1990*, Manchester: Manchester University Press.

Lawrence, Peter (1980) *Managers and Management in West Germany*, London: Croom Helm.

Lawrence, Peter (1984) *Management in Action*, London: Routledge & Kegan Paul.

Lawrence, Peter (1996) 'Through a Glass Darkly: towards a characterisation of British management' in Ian Glover and Michael Hughes (eds), *The Professional Managerial Classes*, Aldershot: Avebury.

Leadbeater, Charles (1997) *Britain: the California of Europe?*, London: DEMOS.

Mangham, I and M. Silver (1986) *Management Training: Context and Practice*, London: Economic and Social Research Council.

May, Brigitte (1974) *Social Educational and Professional Background of German Management*, London: Department of Industry.

Nichols, Theo (1977) *Living With Capitalism*, London: Routledge and Kegan Paul.

Rubinstein, W. D. (1993) *Capitalism, Culture and Decline in Britain, 1750–1990*, London: Routledge.

Terry, P. T. (1979) 'An Investigation of Some Cultural Determinants of English Organisation Behaviour', University of Bath unpublished Ph.D. thesis, Bath, England.

Thomson, Andrew *et al.* (1997) *A Portrait of Management Development*, London: Institute of Management.

Wiener, Martin (1981) *English Culture and the Decline of the Industrial Spirit 1950–1980*, Cambridge: Cambridge University Press.

World Economic Forum (1995) *World Competitiveness Report*, Geneva: posted on Internet @ http.www/issues/edfi/worldrep.html.*l*

CHAPTER 13

Will *the* vertical mosaic survive?

This book has explored differences between Western European countries. The focus has been on management, industry, and economy, though the discussions of the various countries have often been wider than this, seeking to relate an economic and managerial present to:

- a national past,
- wider social values and cultural disposition,
- particular national institutions.

This endeavour has been sustained in that a range of differences has been established and illustrated, while taking some of the commonalities of business and management as read. Whilst we have noted some regional similarities among the Scandinavian countries, some overlap between Germany and Switzerland, and a convergence in management attitudes as between the British and American managers, difference predominates as between the countries reviewed in the previous chapters. What is more this difference is most prevalent in the soft areas of values, perceptions, priorities, style, deportment and the reflection in management behaviours of the wider cultural values of the national society concerned.

It would also be fair to say that this difference between countries, certainly up to the late 1990s, has proved to be durable. The empirical work for the Weinshall (1977) and Hofstede (1980) studies dates from the 1970s and documents substantial differences. My own research in a series of European countries dates from the 1970s to the late 1990s, with some country repeats and updates. As we have seen in earlier chapters both the Loughborough and Nene surveys, begun in 1996 and still (1999) in progress in the sense of enlarging national samples and adding samples from new countries, continue to show a range of differences in the views and values of managers from different countries.

In short we have depicted Western Europe as a vertical mosaic, where the different coloured pieces of the mosaic are different countries, with national institutions and cultures rising from them, in turn shaping business and management. And we have shown this mosaic to have persisted over a quarter of a century, with a few qualifications. But will it survive?

Threats to the heterogeneity of Europe

We have already flagged up some of these ideas in the first chapter, but there is a need at this point for a more forceful exegesis. There are three threats to the heterogeneity of Western Europe. The first of these is the end of, to use the French expression, *les trentes glorieuses*, the thirty years or so of seemingly effortless growth of the Western economies from the end of the Second World War until the 1970s. This rising prosperity was not only good for ordinary people, who saw their disposable income rising through this period, it was also good for governments, and particularly for government revenue, with low unemployment, booming economies, and a high tax take. What is more, with continual economic growth (and at the time no-one had any reason to suppose it would not be permanent, that the world had not somehow turned an economic corner since the Great Depression of the 1930s), government felt able to spend – on welfare, on improving the lives of their citizens, on reducing some of that social inequality which, like the poor, had always been with us. Indeed government, during *les trentes glorieuses* (and for some time after), felt relaxed about borrowing money to achieve these goals of human betterment – after all, continued economic growth together with a bit of help from inflation would mean that these debts would not be such an awful burden.

Then it all collapsed in the 1970s, though it was some time before it was recognized that the golden age was over; a golden age is always in the past.

So now governments want to limit their borrowing, reduce the debts from the past, and to downsize themselves as providers of services to their citizens. This in turn has driven government moves to privatize and deregulate, even if this has happened at different times and to different degrees in the various Western European countries, led by Britain in the 1980s. If, for example, one asks why the British government decided to privatize the water authorities, the answer is that it could not afford/did not want to pay for the environmental upgrading commanded by the EU. Or to take a non-European example, in the early 1990s the Canadian government decided to privatize the country's airports, previously a Crown Corporation (Canadian for nationalized industry), because many of them had been opened in the early 1960s and only had a 30-year 'life expectancy'.

In this debate one should also factor in the ageing population in the West crossed with the availability of expensive medical treatment. Consider, for instance that once upon a time there were no heart bypass operations: but in 1997 there were 1.1 million bypass ops world wide.

The second threat to European heterogeneity is the dynamic internationalization of business. This is not a new phenomenon, in some of its manifestations it is as old as the century, but it has grown in scale and scope in the 1980s and 1990s. In part it derives from the end of the *trentes glorieuses*, but it is a complex phenomenon and there are a number of manifestations. These are some of the strands:

- As the easy gains of *les trentes glorieuses* evaporate a growing consciousness on the part of business leaders that they will have to think through what they are doing, make choices, set objectives, and devise ways of achieving them: in short, the birth of business strategy, world-wide, not just as an American specialism.
- A move to exploit new markets as western markets become saturated with regard to some goods and services.
- Ditto, to spread the increased costs of R&D (research and development) and of marketing, sometimes in the face of enhanced customer expectations and shorter product life cycles.
- The emergence of a kind of 'war games' mentality among MNCs about where they want to be, and to confront their rivals in all key markets of the Triad (North America, Japan, Western Europe); that is, they seek to have market share in all three regions both for its own sake and to stop their rivals having it.
- Improvements in transportation and IT that allow the exploitation of wage and other cost differentials between countries: off-shore manufacture on an unprecedented scale, sometimes facilitated by multi-country trade alliances, for example, NAFTA that encouraged American companies to site routine manufacturing operations in the now famous five mile strip south of the US-Mexican border.
- With the end of the golden age an increased concern with cost reduction and efficiency, in turn leading to a variety of moves – mergers and acquisitions, downsizing, de-layering, control and employee replacement through IT, outsourcing, off-shore operations, and BPR (business process re-engineering).
- Ditto an unwillingness by companies to tolerate labour disputes and other industrial relations disruption; a move from personnel (passive administration) to HRM (human resource management) seen as strategic, pro-active, and individualist.

The third force is managerialism, and its twin 'shareholderism', though this is rather more difficult to unpack. The 1980s saw a new interest in management, wealth creation, and entrepreneurialism, which intensified in the 1990s. The status (and remuneration) of managers rose, business schools were founded or expanded, enrolments increased massively, and business administration became a strong choice for good students (ones with good pre-university exam grades). These developments have occurred in varying degrees across Western Europe, including some countries in which management had previously been regarded as a weak and uncertain career choice, countries such as Britain and Holland. This managerial movement has tended to make the countries of Europe somewhat more like the USA in their management thinking, training and institutions.

This managerial movement, conjoined with government concerns over spending and debt in a changed world economic environment, has inclined governments generally to see the private sector as a possible saviour (privatization and deregulation) and to see non-profit making entities in terms of a business paradigm emphasizing the specification of objectives, performance measurement and the targeted allocation of resources. This, as noted in the first chapter, tends to reduce the difference between private sector and public sector organizations, and at the same time to increase cross country similarities in the sense that all the countries have bought into managerialism to some extent and are thus all 'headed in the same direction'.

The fact that managerialism has been espoused by governments has a further effect, that these governments have become more sympathetic than in the past to the imperatives of internationalizing business. The result is a general acceptance of cross-border mergers and acquisitions, even where these lead to redundancies in particular countries and thus to costs (unemployment benefits, retraining, premature pensioning) for the governments of affected countries. And this is happening side by side with inter-state deregulation that facilitates cross-border mergers, raising cross-border finance, and cross-border share purchase.

Thus the three broad themes indicated here – the response of governments to the end of easy economic growth, internationalization in its various forms, and managerialism – are all interacting with each other, and tending to reduce national differences at least in terms of business culture. Whether this will translate into homogeneity of management style and behaviour across the countries of Western Europe is at this stage an open question.

Patterns of change

So far we have suggested that there are forces for homogeneity, and tried to show what they are and to hint at some of their inter-relations. But it is also fair to ask in this connection: Are there any signs of these forces for homogeneity at work in the particular countries reviewed in this book? We would like to respond to the question selectively, picking out various manifestations in one or two countries. Let us begin with France.

France

France has always been rather distinctive with regard to the form that capitalism assumed in that country. Sometimes wittily dubbed *capitalisme sans capital* the French economy in the past has been marked by:

- a high level of Government ownership, albeit fluctuating during the post-war period,
- a high level of state involvement, with the state acting in a *dirigiste* mode, setting objectives and using state influence to shape outcomes,
- a lack of Anglo-Saxon style shareholding in the form of unit trusts and pension funds, tending to shield French companies from market forces,
- this relative protectedness of (some) French companies, reinforced by cross-shareholdings and cross-directorships, the whole show being kept on the road by state sponsorship and government contracts,
- stability of employment both for *les cadres* and for ordinary people, with high indirect costs of employment, and pensions seen as sacrosanct,
- companies enjoying some of the *droit administratit* of the state, being in practice somewhat above the law.

That was then! From the late 1980s all this began to change. First, there was a wave of privatization in 1986–87 when Jacques Chirac came to power as right-wing prime minister albeit 'serving' under socialist president Mitterand. This privatization has carried on in fits and starts in the 1990s. Second, there has been a freeing up of the interface between the French economy and the rest of the world, an interface that was traditionally policed by the French state. So that for the first time French companies were 'allowed' to fall into foreign ownership, FDI (foreign direct investment) in France was 'permitted', in some cases in the form of high profile enterprises such as the Daewoo car plant in Lorraine. Corporate de-merger ceased to attract government opposition and control as in the past. Third, internationalization assumed a new vigour in the 1990s. While France had been a founder member in 1957–58 of what is popularly known as the Common Market, and has been in the *avant garde* of this movement ever since, for example being in the first wave of EMU (European Monetary Union), the focus of France in the past has been European in particular rather than international in general. Yet against this background in the 1981–92 period FDI in France increased nearly five fold, and French investment abroad nearly ten fold. While there were similar increases for other western countries, for instance Britain and Japan, the break with the past was more marked for France. And a lot of this outward investment has been outside of Europe and has focused particularly on the USA.

The 1990s in France have also seen the introduction of more flexible forms of employment (rightly or wrongly taken for granted in Britain) with a growth in part-time and short-term (contract-based) employees. The decade has also witnessed 'the end of immunity' for corporate chiefs and senior public-sector figures, with investigations and suspensions from office of such figures for suspected wrongdoing. The most famous case was the trial and actual imprisonment of the former mayor of Grenoble for taking bribes to award the Grenoble water contract to Lyonnaise des Eaux (and that company's local partner).

All this represents a significant change for France, diminishing that country's rather self-contained economic exclusiveness.

Holland

In the earlier chapter on the Netherlands we coat-trailed the fact that there were signs in the 1990s of the manageralist ideology making some progress in that country, reflected in the wording of job advertisements. It might be helpful to start a little further back.

In 1985 I had my first research sojourn in the Netherlands, and in an early conversation with a business school professor put a general question about the status of management. After a gravely thoughtful pause the professor replied that at least a lad would not be ashamed to admit at school that his father was a manager – as had been the case in the 1970s! (Lawrence, 1986). In fact things had probably moved further than this by the time of the conversation. Business administration as a university subject (*bedrijfskunde* or *bedrijfseconomic*) was rising in relative status (traditionally it had been considered a poor relation to *bestuurskunde* or public administration), enrolments burgeoned, public interest in management matters was awaked, and government reports on industrial policy and business magazine surveys of management salaries cascaded down.

But the development that particularly caught our eye was the change in the tenor of management job advertisements. In the mid 1980s advertisements for management posts were very restrained. There was no reference to pay or fringe benefits (the latter expression is actually quite difficult to translate into Dutch). The companies seeking to hire were depicted in terms of quiet decency – having a good work climate, a nice set of colleagues, a long history, and so on. There was no sabre rattling talk of 'big league players', or 'industry leaders'. The work role for which applicants were sought would be described in low key terms, shimmering with Calvinist modesty.

Yet as we have noted in Chapter 11 a lot of this has now changed. Companies are depicted in go-getting terms of their market dominance and growth targets. And the managers sought for employment in these corporate go-getters are described in terms that sound more American than Dutch. Indeed in scanning these advertisements in the 1990s I came across words and expressions in Dutch that were quite new for someone who had only lived in Holland in the 1980s, words such as *besluitwaardig* (decisive) and *stressbestandig* (able to cope with stress).

Now it is conceivable that this is an exercise in managerialist rhetoric rather than in management reality, that the companies concerned would not actually like the thrusting, larger than life recruits they were asking for if they materialized, would opt in practice for decent, sober Dutch recruits attracted to the prospect of a good pension forty years down the road. But even if the wording of these advertisements is no more than rhetoric, it is still new, a phenomenon of the 1990s, and represents a break with the traditional formula. In a sober and traditional society such as the Netherlands even such rhetoric must be seen as significant.

Germany

While the West German tax payer was shouldering the burden of re-integrating the former GDR into a unified Germany, West German companies were in many cases making acquisitions in what had been the GDR and frequently extending their operations into other Central and Eastern European countries after the fall of European Communism in the 1989–91 period: in what had been Czechoslovakia alone two-thirds of the joint ventures between Czech and foreign firms were in fact with German companies. These were the business activities that were in the spotlight, but other developments were taking place, notably a two-way process of internationalization involving the Anglo-Saxon business community.

The outgoing part has been quite high profile. The 1990s saw both Mercedes Benz and BMW establish manufacturing facilities in the USA, in Alabama and South Carolina respectively. Indeed in 1993 Daimler Benz become the first Germany company to be listed on the New York stock exchange, a process stage-managed by the US bank Goldman Sachs, newly established in Frankfurt.

The same decade also saw some high profile acquisitions by German companies: VAG bought Rolls Royce, BMW bought Rover, Deutsche Bank bought Morgan Grenfell and Dresdner Bank bought Kleinwort Benson, and early in 1999 Mercedes announced a merger with Chrysler of the USA. These moves are quite uncharacteristic for Germany, whose companies have traditionally put their faith in organic growth, and expected to penetrate foreign markets by virtue of the superiority of German products, rather than achieving both these objectives by means of cross-border merger and acquisition.

But there is another side to this internationalization, which is about what the Anglo-Saxon business community is doing to Germany! The story goes like this. When German companies need to engage in capital expenditure, for a variety of reasons from escalating R&D costs to internationalization initiatives, and the capital they need exceeds their cash flow (that is to say they cannot meet the cost out of retained earnings), then they need investment capital in the form of buyers for their shares. And guess who are the worlds' largest providers of investment capital: pension funds in Britain and in the USA. But what are the costs for the seller?

The problematic has been explored on a case study basis by the German academic Christian Berndt. What Berndt has done is to track the experiences of three German companies – Veba, RWE , and Thyssen – during the late 1990s (Berndt, 1998). All three companies are big, but not as big as the 'global elite' companies such as Siemens or Daimler Benz; they are all diversified conglomerates, and all based in the Rhine-Ruhr area, the industrial heartland of (West) Germany. These three companies also found themselves in the position of needing additional capital, and turned to international financial markets to get it. Christian Berndt is able to detail all sorts of consequences, some of them at odds with traditional German business practice:

- The companies found themselves under pressure to adopt American rather than German GAAP (generally accepted accounting principles); among Berndt's three companies Veba was the first to adopt US GAAP as part of its ambition to tap US financial markets.
- The three companies did indeed achieve a measure of internationalization measured by the conventional criterion of proportion of turnover generated abroad – albeit a modest share.
- The companies came to have an increasing proportion of their employees outside Germany.
- The three companies came to appoint CEOs who were not in the traditional German mould: two promoted finance directors to the CEO position (very un-German) and the third, Thyssen, appointed a CEO that was not from Thyssen Stahl, the core steel business part of the Thyssen empire (this again is rather un-German).
- The companies began to offer more extensive financial performance information; this again is a little un-German, where German companies, rather like those of Switzerland, have tended to be rather sparing when it comes to publishing financial performance data.

But perhaps more striking than any of this is the fact that these companies became exposed to an Anglo-Saxon business critique, that said in effect, we don't care about your making the best marine diesel engines in the world, how good are your margins and are you making your assets sweat? Particular points included:

- Criticizing the high gearing of these German companies, the fact that their bank borrowings were higher in relation to the value of their share issue than is normal in the Anglo-Saxon world.
- Criticizing the fact that the companies were diversified conglomerates, where some product divisions were more profitable than others, but this did not lead to divestment of the less profitable and concentration on the more profitable.

- Pushing them generally away from high skill, *Technik* and long term (as suggested in Chapter 7) towards low skill and short term.
- Wanting financial performance criteria to be applied rigorously to the various product divisions of these conglomerates.

There was even one famous case where a pension fund, CALPERS (California Pacific Employees' Retirement System) objected at the AGM of RWE, one of the three case study firms, to the multiple voting rights exercised by various local authorities in the Ruhr, an historical anomaly dating from 1924 when these local authorities were compensated for the devaluation of their shares.

In short, the need of these German companies to tap in to international financial markets led them to adapt their activities and behaviour in a variety of ways to Anglo-Saxon rather than to Continental European business norms.

But this is not as the lawyers say an 'open and shut case' as was demonstrated by a *cause célébre* from 1997. Something quite shocking to Germans occurred at the time when Krupp-Hoesch tried to take over its larger and healthier competitor Thyssen. Since Krupp-Hoesch could not itself fund such a takeover it got the (London) City offshoots of German banks, namely Morgan Grenfell and Kleinwort Benson, together with Goldman Sachs, to pledge the 15 million DM with which to buy Thyssen. But the CEO of Thyssen mobilized employees, trade union, and *Land* government influence to fight off the hostile takeover bid, and won.

Yet the story is instructive. German companies are increasingly being driven into international finance markets which will confront them with Anglo-American style demands for financial performance rather than product excellence. At the same time, the German companies are locked into national systems of industrial democracy, trade union power, and responsibility to *Land* and federal governments – and in any conflict these latter, as in the case of the attempted takeover of Thyssen, may prevail.

We are mapping here the emergence of forces that are new for Germany, and the tension created between international financial demands and German national expectations – it is not clear in which direction this tension will be resolved.

Britain and America

In the preceding chapter on Britain we tried to make the case that similarities exist between business and management in these two countries, that Britain arguably has more in common with the USA than with the countries of Continental Europe in these matters. And we constructed this case partly in terms of a simple analysis of business systems, and then more originally by drawing on the findings of the Nene study.

While this exercise does allow us to posit some similarity or overlap at the time of writing, it is rather more difficult to say whether change has taken place, whether Britain started off different but has moved towards American management and business norms. In short it would have been nice if someone had administered the Nene questionnaire to comparable samples in the two countries in say 1976 (and would do it again in 2016): this kind of longitudinal study might have established a case for change.

In default of such longitudinal evidence, however, one can at least look at the literature. Writing on both sides of the Atlantic in the 1960s and 1970s does in fact emphasize the differences between the two countries, broadly apostrophizing American management as professional, as emphasizing the importance of the management prerogative *vis-à-vis* ordinary employees, and as generally hard-driving and efficiently organized around management systems. This same literature tended to see British management in terms of the opposite qualities: amateurist, old-fashioned and class conscious, lacking killer instinct, and endlessly at the mercy of clamouring trade unionists (Lawrence, Senior and Smith, 1998). So we may cautiously posit some degree of Americanization of British management in the last quarter of the century.

What has been suggested in this section, where we have back-tracked to look at various manifestations of change in four of the countries discussed in previous chapters, is a mild, uneven, and as yet inconclusive convergence on an American model. Whether or not this is feeding through to identifiable management behaviours and styles, the changes noted here do suggest a limited convergence at the level of the structure of the economy, the fate of the nation state in the world economy, and the growing prevalence of international business norms.

We might express this idea a little differently by arguing that the three forces examined at the start of the chapter:

- the end of *les trentes glorieuses*, and the effect on governments,
- internationalization,
- managerialism,

and their inter-related effects make it more difficult for a western country to be different. And before ending this chapter we would like to try to develop this idea, the limitations on distinctiveness, with reference to one more country.

Sweden

At the end of the chapter on Spain we suggested that Spain had changed more than any country discussed in this book. Certainly if one had looked forward from the mid-point of the twentieth century one would not have predicted that by the end of the century Spain's isolation would be long over, that the country would have had twenty-five years as a stable parliamentary democracy, and nearly fifteen years as a member of the EU.

The change that Sweden has experienced in say, the last twenty years of the twentieth century, is much less dramatic than this, and has not been driven by a change in the type of political regime. But Sweden is a more interesting test case for trying to unpick the forces working against the national differences explored in this book, in the sense that it was most difficult to start with.

Consider what Sweden had and stood for a mere twenty years ago. In 1980:

- Sweden had the second highest GDP per capita in the world after Switzerland (excepting a few Arab oil states),
- a very high welfare provision,
- a narrow salary and income distribution,
- high income tax, steeply graduated,
- central wage bargaining at the highest level (LO and SAF as described in Chapter 9),
- the 1976 Codetermination Act was in full force; it was the high point of Sweden's industrial democracy,
- the *Löntagerfonder* (wage earner funds) described in Chapter 9 were about to be introduced; a radical pro-labour move,
- unemployment rates were low,
- absenteeism rates were high (at 20 per cent including people released from work for educational purposes); it was a national joke that on a Monday morning 25 per cent of the workforce of Saab and Volvo were absent,
- trade union membership rates were high.

By 1999 all this has changed, or is under pressure to change, except the high trade union membership. Welfare expenditure is being squeezed, income tax is not as high (though still high by western European standards), there has been some salary expansion at the top with some executives grabbing big salaries and organizing golden handshakes and parachutes, central wage bargaining has gone, the 1970s codetermination system has been modified, the *Löntagerfonder* have been abolished, unemployment is up, and absenteeism is down. Sweden has sunk to around fifteenth place in the world GDP stakes, and is behind Norway, Denmark and Finland.

There is another change central to all of the above. In 1980 Sweden enjoyed an international status, had genuinely international major companies as indicated in Chapter 9, and exported a high proportion of GDP. But it was not in the Anglo-American sense an *open* economy. There were also no foreign banks operating in Sweden: foreign banks could only do things in Sweden via indigenous Swedish banks. And the Stockholm stock exchange was a rather low-profile affair, and Swedish companies were largely protected from hostile takeover by cross-shareholdings, cross-directorships, and cosy membership of three loose blocks centering on the three principal banks of the day. The big

Swedish companies were 100 per cent Swedish, registered in Sweden, head-quartered in Sweden, and run from Sweden no matter how extensive their international operation.

So whatever happened to Sweden?

The beleagured state

First of all the State got caught by the end of *les trentes glorieuses*. The welfare state depended on steady economic growth, of the kind Sweden enjoyed to a high degree after the Second World War, as we showed in Chapter 9. But Sweden does not have steady economic growth any more. The Government's debt is 80 per cent of GDP (compared with 50–60 per cent in Britain) and a third of this debt is owed abroad. There are countries with a worse debt ratio, Belgium for instance where debt is 100 per cent of GDP, but in the Belgian case the debt is all owed to Belgian citizens.

As suggested at the start of this chapter, all western governments are being caught in this way, but it is worse for Sweden than for most because of the scale of its welfare expenditure and corresponding debt. It is also adversely affected by two secondary factors. One of these is the cost of an ageing population, already mentioned in general terms, where the life expectancy rates in Sweden are among the highest in the world. The other is that Sweden has at various times encouraged immigration from developing countries (and Finland) to increase the labour force in good times, and had a generous asylum policy. The result is that:

5% of the population are foreign (non-Swedish).
5% were born foreign.
5% are the children of immigrants.

This represents one-sixth of the population. Some of these non-Swedes are difficult to integrate into the economy. Islam has become the second religion in Sweden after Lutheran Protestantism.

All this has put the government into a difficult position where it feels constrained to do non-sustainable things to fund welfare. For example there is a tax on wealth. In Sweden if you own property, have other assets, or simply a lot of money in the bank, you pay tax on it (compared with Britain where only the interest or capital gain is taxed). But wealth tax drives out rich people, as we will show in the next section. And Swedish managers paying high income tax are tempted by offers from other countries (they all speak English anyway).

Not only is income tax high in Sweden by the standards of most western countries, but the threshold is low as well. In Sweden people start paying tax at around SKr. 9000 per annum (about £700) so that children with Saturday jobs become tax payers! And this high direct and indirect cost of employment in Sweden tends to limit growth in the service sector. That is to say, in manufacturing, productivity can be raised by substituting automation for employees, but many service operations are people intensive.

Or consider a little example. The Swedish government decided on a substantial increase in the taxation on cigarettes, pushing the purchase price from around £2.50 a packet to £4.00. But this led to cigarette smuggling. People who had previously been drug dealers turned to cigarette smuggling; after all it was a much bigger market, and the penalities were much less – just a fine in fact, hardly 'a real crime' at all. So the government lost revenue and had to back down. Just a small example, but it shows what a government may be up against trying to increase its revenues.

Another consideration is ideological. The normal government in Sweden is the Social Democratic Party, usually in coalition with other parties. Because of its commitment to equality it is reluctant to prioritize *selective* education for an intellectual elite. Sweden's strength is at the lower vocational educational level, but it is the last country in the world that would think to set up French style *grandes écoles*. But it is the selectively educated intellectual elite who are likely to drive what the French call *industries de point*, that is to say, industries built around innovative technology or scientific advance.

As the mayor of Shanghai said; 'I like Europe, I like Sweden, but you are just a bit too socialist over there.'

At a more down to earth level this disinclination to prioritize high level education for the few is bad for the national R&D (research and development) capability. It reinforces in a gentle way a trend that has been all too clear in the 1980s and 1990s for Swedish MNCs to site the R&D facilities anywhere but Sweden. MNCs typically recruit their R&D scientists from a variety of (mostly western) countries; for the most part such staff will not be attracted to Sweden given its combination of long, dark winters, and high personal taxation.

What is more the options open to the Swedish government are reduced by its membership of the EU. In the 1980s its debt to GDP ratio was its own business, but when it joined the EU in 1995 the debt ratio became everybody's business. With its present debt ratio Sweden does not meet the Maastricht criteria, and could not join first wave EMU even if it wanted to (and unlike Italy will not know how to fudge it).

Indeed there is a point of view that says that it is jolly lucky for Sweden that Britain did not join EMU at the start of 1999 – that this gives Sweden a breathing space. The two countries have strong trade links, indeed Britain is the second (from top) destination for Swedish exports, and Sweden is the ninth export market for Britain. In fact Britain sells more visible goods to Sweden than to Japan, Saudi Arabia, or Canada, and per head of population sells more to Sweden than to anyone except the Dutch and the Irish! But Britain may join EMU in the second wave, and Sweden will have the EU presidency in 2001, and then . . .

Business and the crisis of Swedishness

In the 1990s and even before, Swedish companies have been getting much less 'blue and yellow' (the colours of the Swedish flag) as the Swedes themselves like to put it. There are so many examples of this that it is difficult to know where to start. But perhaps that rather old-fashioned, low-profile institution, the Stockholm stock exchange would be a useful *point de départ.*

In fact the Swedish stock market has grown massively. Stock market capitalization for Sweden is now more than 100 per cent of GDP, which is (a little) more than in Britain, which in turn is much higher than in the USA. In fact this ratio of stock exchange capitalization to GDP in Sweden is only exceeded by that of Switzerland and Luxembourg!

There is in Sweden what appears to be a constant demand for equities. Much of this demand comes from outside Sweden. While there is not much FDI (foreign direct investment) in Sweden in the sense of foreign companies wanting to set up manufacturing facilities in Sweden, there is a lot of foreign interest in buying the shares of Swedish companies. Some 20–40 per cent of the shares of L. M. Ericsson, for example, are said to be owned by (guess who?), the British and American pension funds. These trends are expected to continue. Indeed the Stockholm stock exchange became the first listed stock exchange in the world. So you can not only buy shares *on* the Stockholm stock exchange, but buy shares *in* the Stockholm stock exchange. Stockholm was also a leader in opening up its customer base by inviting, not just allowing, people with no fiscal presence in the jurisdiction of Sweden to participate.

So if low FDI and high foreign ownership in Swedish companies is the first strand in the crisis of Swedishness, the second is Swedish companies that somehow or other just seem to float out of Sweden. Consider L. M. Ericsson again. For some time Ericsson have had an R&D centre at Crawley, Sussex. This establishment is sufficiently sizeable for there to be a Swedish language school for the children of employees. Then in October 1998 Ericsson announced it was introducing performance-related pay, and was slammed by the trade unions for so doing, and not long after this it was said that the head office would move to London, though the company would continue to be incorporated in Sweden.

Ericsson is not an isolated case. Electrolux is moving its headquarters to the Netherlands, to somewhere in the *Randstad*. Pharmacia of Sweden merged with Upjohn of the USA, and put the head office in London as a compromise. Then operating problems emerged, and the American CEO took the head office to the USA. A more subtle version of this scenario may occur with another Swedish pharmaceuticals company, Gambro, which specializes in treatment for renal failure. Gambro has 97 per cent of its employees outside Sweden, and 99 per cent of its turnover abroad as well. In fact 60 per cent of both are in the USA, and it is anticipated that the next CEO will be American (the present incumbent is Swedish) which gives rise to the speculation, will he want to move from Denver to Stockholm? Or again Norbanken, one of the big three Swedish banks, headquartered of course in Stockholm, merged with a Finnish bank and is now headquartered in Finland.

Entwined with this trend is the tendency for entrepreneurs, company owners, to exit Sweden. So for example the founder of Ikeå, Ingmar Kamprad now lives in Denmark and Ikeå is incorporated in the Netherlands. And, it is rumoured, the owner of Hennes and Mauritz, the fashion retail chain, was contemplating the same manoeuvre to avoid the 1.5 per cent Swedish wealth tax, so the Swedish government fiddled it for him so that he could 'stay home'.

Then again Swedish MNCs have always had a significant proportion of their workforce and turnover outside Sweden, which is after all only a small market. But a more recent trend has been systematic cross-border outsourcing. Ikeå again is an example, switching suppliers from Scandinavia to Central and Eastern Europe. And the Swiss-Swedish MNC, ABB, headed by the legendary Swedish CEO Percy Barnevik, has during the 1990s run-down the ABB's labour force in Western Europe and increased it in Eastern Europe. And it goes without saying that Swedish ships sail under the flag of the Philippines.

Finally, there is of course merger and acquisition. The 1990s began with Saab being bought by General Motors. Swedbus was bought by Stagecoach, the quality daily newspaper *Svenska Dagblat* was bought by a Norwegian media group (for Swedes this is rather like the *Wall Street Journal* being bought by Mexicans) and the start of 1999 saw the Ford bid for Volvo, as well as a proposed merger between Astra of Sweden and Seneca of the UK (and guess where the headquarters will be).

Sweden in fact has a variety of strengths and it is surprising that it has not done better in conventional FDI. After all in addition to political stability it has a well-educated work force, strong vocational education, universal English-speaking ability, low inflation, and relatively modest corporation tax at 28 per cent. But from a business viewpoint its disadvantages are:

- It is a small market.
- The country has an indebted and over-regulating government.
- Personal taxation is too high, and there is a tax on wealth.

We have explored the case of contemporary Sweden in some detail because as we have tried to show, twenty years ago it was probably the most distinctive society-economy in Western Europe. As such, if extra-national forces for convergence are at large, it is likely to show more in Sweden than elsewhere – we believe that it does.

Or to put it another way, Sweden is a testimony to the fact that no state can escape its indebtedness or withstand the forces of the internationalization of business.

At a general level two questions remain. The first is whether and to what extent the partial convergence on Anglo-Saxon capitalism argued here will lead to a homogeneous management style, standardardized management behaviour, to the progressive dissolution of the differences between countries portrayed in the previous chapters. This has to be an open question at this stage.

The second question is even more unanswerable. It is not too difficult to envisage future change if one does so in terms of a continuation of present trends. So that in 1941 no-one doubted Germany would win the Second World War; in 1951 no-one doubted that the USA would always dominate the world economy; in 1961 no-one doubted that the growth in western prosperity would continue for ever.

But these trends we have identified, trends concerning:

- government retrenchment,
- internationalization,
- managerialism,
- the convergence on Anglo-Saxon capitalism,

may to a future generation seem as much a chimera as German victory in the Second World War. Or as they say in existential psychiatry, you don't know what you don't know.

References

Berndt, C. (1998) *Corporate Germany at the Crossroads? Americanisation, Competitiveness and Place Dependence*, Cambridge: ESRC Centre for Business Research, WP98, University of Cambridge.

Hofstede, Geert (1980) *Cultures Consequences*, Beverley Hills, Los Angeles: Sage.

Lawrence, Peter (1986) *Management in the Netherlands: a study in Internationalism?*, Enschde, The Netherlands: Technische Hogeschool Twente.

Lawrence, P. A.; B. Senior and D. Smith (1998) 'The Anglo-American Contrast: A New Look', International Academy of Management Conference, City University, London, April 1998.

Weinshall, Theodore (1977) *Culture and Management*, Harmondsworth: Penguin.

Index